Boston University Papers in African History

Volume One

Boston University Papers in African History

VOLUME ONE

Edited by

Jeffrey Butler

Research Associate, African Studies Program
Boston University

Boston University Press
Boston, Mass.
1964

Boston University Papers in African History, I

Library of Congress Catalog Card Number: 64-15197

TABLE OF CONTENTS

PREFACE

These papers are the products of a faculty history seminar, a student African History Club, and of work by graduate students at the African Studies Program of Boston University. As the Roman numeral on the title page hopefully implies, there is to be a series of volumes like this one, which will make available some of the work being done both by historians in the New England area, and scholars overseas. The papers deal with a wide range of subjects: we remain interested in the problems of colonial policy and we hope also, of course, to contribute to African history as it has developed since World War II.

The faculty seminar and the publication of these papers would not have been possible without the generous support of the Director of the African Studies Program, Professor William O. Brown. Furthermore, though an editor suffers some exasperation in the often tedious work of editing, he also receives unexpected kindnesses, even from his colleagues! I thank, therefore, Dan McCall and Norman Bennett, both of the African Studies Program. Mrs. Alyce Havey made the arrangements for typing and publication; Janice Hall Dyer was an excellent secretary; and Jacoba van Schaik gave essential help with the wearisome task of proofreading.

There is, however, one acknowledgement which must stand on its own. Dr. Robert E. Moody, Chairman of the Boston University Press and Chairman of the Department of History, gave much of his time to show me what an editor ought to do. Of course, I am responsible for such editorial blemishes as remain.

Boston University
October, 1963

JEFFREY BUTLER

I.

Historical Inferences from Linguistic Research in Sub-Saharan Africa

by

JOSEPH GREENBERG

Professor of Anthropology, Stanford University, Stanford, California

THE PURPOSE OF THIS PAPER is to describe the principal methods by which inferences of interest to the historian can be derived from linguistic data, and to illustrate these methods by using examples from African languages. Close study of language and careful interpretation of the results can yield a rich harvest. There are great possibilities in African studies in this field, but it is fair to say, almost everything remains to be done. However, it is important neither to overestimate nor to underestimate those possibilities.

I

Historical interpretations drawn from languages in Africa have, on the whole, been done poorly, in many instances so poorly that the intelligent non-linguist can easily perceive the weaknesses of the methods being used. The methods criticized here are exemplified in the works of C. K. Meek, H. R. Palmer, and more recently E. Meyerowitz.[1] Their procedures consist, in part, of isolated guesses regarding the historical connection between words in different languages, usually without any clear distinction between resemblances based on borrowing and those based on common origin. The hypotheses may be called isolated since they are not advanced within a framework of classification of the languages involved, the well-established methods of comparative historical reconstruction ("comparative philology") or systematic consideration of the factors involved in borrowing. The other main class of inferences concerns the etymology of specific words within a language, largely place names and tribal names. Particularly in the case of proper names, the fact that the words are often not transparent etymologically in the

---

[1] Representative examples of the procedures of these authors are contained in such works as C. K. Meek, *Tribal Studies in Northern Nigeria* (2 vols., London, 1931) and *A Sudanese Kingdom* (London, 1931), R. H. Palmer, *Sudanese Memoirs* (3 vols., Lagos, 1928), and E. Meyerowitz, *The Sacred State of the Akan* (London, 1951).

language concerned, opens the door to abundant but unverifiable results.

These methods can be illustrated by an example from the work of C. K. Meek. It is to be understood that this is but one of many instances of similar methods that could be drawn from a variety of writers. I do not wish to imply that Meek, the value of whose contributions to African studies are not in question, sinned more grievously in this respect than a number of other investigators.

In his work on the Jukun of Nigeria, Meek seeks to etymologize the name of their chief god Chidô.[2] The following quotation will indicate the starting point of Meek's speculations.

> The meaning of the expression Chidô is not clear. Mr. Lowry Maxwell, who is a competent Jukun scholar, asserts that Chidô = "The one who is above," from the root chi or ki = to be and dô = above. This is the explanation given by most intelligent Jukun. But as the root *chi* in the sense of sky-god, earth deity, sun, moon, it would seem probable that the above explanation is a late rationalization.

There then follows a long list of words from many parts of Africa. Further, a connection is asserted with the Egyptian Osiris, which is interpreted as *usi* (one of the numerous variants of the *chi* root followed by *ra*). The latter is identified with Ra, the Egyptian god of the sun so that *Usira* means "Lord Ra." No attempt is made here to explore fully the numerous other ramifications of this complex of conjectures. Rather, a few considerations are advanced for their methodological interest in the present context.

Thus, in regard to Meek's explanation of Osiris as consisting of the widespread *usi, uchi* + *ra,* the name of the sun god, it may be pointed out that such an etymology would surely be rejected by any respectable scholar of Egyptian. The name of Osiris in Egyptian is *wśr* while the name of the sun god is *rʿ*.[3] The word *rʿ* contains as its second consonant the pharyngeal ʿ which is quite stable in Egyptian and cannot be disregarded. We have no right therefore to analyze *wśr* into *wś,* which does not occur by itself in Egyptian

[2] Meek, *Sudanese Kingdom,* especially 179-83. The quotation which follows occurs on 180.

[3] Ancient Egyptian forms are cited without vowels since these were not expressed in writing.

+ *r*‘. This leaves Meek's root *uchi* without any foundation in Egyptian.

Of the forms of this root which Meek cites from numerous Bantu languages, two quite different roots are involved, one reconstructed as **se*, meaning "earth" and the other as **ɛdi*, meaning "moon."[4] Here Meek quotes examples from present-day Bantu languages without paying any attention to the elaborate body of work on reconstructed Bantu roots initiated by Meinhof and based on systematic comparison of the correspondences of sounds.

It would be understandable if a negative reaction against this type of methodology were to lead to a general rejection of linguistic methods. It would, however, be unjustifiable. Once the historian realizes that reliable methods of interpreting linguistic materials exist, he will be wary of assuming that the linguistic key will magically unlock all the boxes of historical secrets. Linguistic methods are capable of giving answers to certain questions but not to others. Moreover, these results range from very nearly certain conclusions in some instances to suggestive but highly uncertain results in others.

In what follows, the basic methodology for historical conclusions based on language will be outlined and illustrated, as far as possible, by African material.[5] Because this type of investigation has not yet been undertaken on a wide scale in Africa, and because of the relatively undeveloped state of comparative linguistics in that continent, the examples given are, for the most part, not to be taken as definitive conclusions. Such conclusions cannot yet be asserted with the assurance which may eventually accrue to them and to many others when research of this kind will have progressed beyond its present fledgeling state.

---

[4] The transcription of Proto-Bantu forms is modified here in accordance with present practice. In Meinhof's system they would be *-*ki* and *-*γeli* respectively. The most extensive collection of proto-Bantu etymologies is W. Bourquin, *Neue Ur-Bantu-Wortstämme* (Berlin, 1923).

[5] The arrangement follows in basic outline the analysis contained in the classic and still usable essay of Edward Sapir, "Time Perspective in Aboriginal American Culture," reprinted in *Selected Writings by Edward Sapir in Language, Culture and Personality*, ed. D. G. Mandelbaum (Berkeley and Los Angeles, 1949), 389-462.

II

In one way or another, classification is the basis for practically all historical inference drawn from language. From the purely linguistic point of view, the importance of classification is that by this means languages are classed together as showing unmistakable evidence of common origin, that is, as ultimately deriving from divisions in an original speech community followed by divergent developments. Historical comparative linguistics has a highly sophisticated body of method through which such languages may be compared and many of the features of the extinct ancestral language can be reconstructed. Classification has not only this fundamental significance for comparative linguistics as such; in itself it leads to certain inferences of significance based solely on the classification together with the geographical distribution of the people who speak the languages. The key principle governing such conclusions has been named the center of gravity principle or the principle of least moves.[6] It can easily be understood from an illustration. The present example is that of the origin of the Bantu, obviously a key problem in African culture history.

Bantu languages cover an enormous area, almost all of Central, South and East Africa. They are so similar to each other that their relationship was recognized at an early date. Since it takes time for linguistic differences to develop, the relative uniformity of Bantu over a large area suggests a fairly recent and rapid spread of the Bantu-speaking peoples. In spite, then, of the large area and numerous population, the Bantu group can be treated almost as a single language and its place can be discovered within a much larger group of languages. This larger group is the Niger-Congo family, the most extensive family of languages spoken by people of the Negroid physical type.

The Niger-Congo family consists of six branches, each presumed to consist of languages descended from a distinct dialect of the ancestral Niger-Congo language. These six branches are West Atlantic (e.g., Fulani, Wolof, Temne) in the extreme west of Africa,

[6] For a brief exposition of these principles, see J. H. Greenberg, "Historical Linguistics and Unwritten Languages," in *Anthropology Today*, ed. A. L. Kroeber (Chicago, 1953), 265-86.

the Mande, spoken chiefly in the central basin of the Niger River, the Gur or Voltaic spoken in the same general area but on the whole farther to the east, e.g., in northern Ghana and Upper Volta, the Kwa group occupying a coastal strip from Liberia to the Eastern Regions of Nigeria, the Benue-Congo group except for Bantu concentrated in Nigeria and the part of Cameroun bordering Nigeria. Only the sixth branch, Adamawa-Eastern, is spoken in regions not usually included in West Africa. Even here the extensive Eastern subbranch spoken as far east as Zande in the Sudanese Republic bears the same evidence of recent rapid expansions as Bantu.[7]

This predominance of branches in West Africa strongly suggests West Africa as the original homeland of Proto-Niger-Congo and is the first illustration of the center of gravity principle, namely, that each genetic subfamily gives equal and independent evidence regardless of the number of speakers or areal extension. As was mentioned in passing, Bantu is affiliated with the Benue-Congo subfamily of Niger-Congo and all of the non-Bantu languages of this subfamily are found in Nigeria and the Cameroun. There are scores of Benue-Congo languages and this branch in turn may be tentatively subdivided into five major groups, one of which contains Bantu along with Tiv, Batu, Ndoro and Mambila. Since these latter languages are all spoken in the same general area of the central Benue valley in Nigeria, we reach the conclusion that Bantu originated in the general Nigeria-western-Cameroun area and, more specifically, though somewhat less certainly, arose somewhere in the central Benue region.

The assumption that Bantu developed as a separate group in, for example, East Africa would force us to assume numerous separate and independent migrations by the other languages of the Benue-Congo group, all providentially arriving in approximately the same general area of Nigeria and neighboring portions of Cameroun.

Another example of the operation of this principle in Africa concerns the Fulani, who are found in separate areas from Senegal to the Lake Chad region in the east. The Fulani language belongs

[7] For a more detailed account of the membership and distribution of Niger-Congo and other African language families, mentioned in this article, see J. H. Greenberg, *Languages of Africa* (Bloomington, 1962).

to the West Atlantic branch of Niger-Congo. All of the other languages of this subfamily are found in the western part of this area. Again, the consideration of more detailed relationships leads to a more specific hypothesis. Within West Atlantic, Fulani is most closely related to Serer-Sin and somewhat more remotely to Wolof, both spoken in Senegal. This suggests that the Fulani-speaking population of the Fouta Sénégalais is the nuclear population from which the others split. The western origin of the Fulani is, indeed, attested from the historical record, much of the eastward movement having taken place in recent times.

III

In addition to the place of origin, we should like to have an absolute rather than a relative chronology. Here the only objective method thus far devised is glottochronology.[8] It is based on the common-sense notion that when dialects have developed into languages, the more recent the date of separation the greater the resemblance. The percentage of common retention of original words in a standard vocabulary list is used as the measure of this resemblance. This is translated into an absolute chronology on the basis of the rate of change in this same list observed in areas such as the Near East and Europe where there are written records. The assumption is being made, of course, that this rate of change is reasonably constant everywhere.[9]

It must be realized, of course, that determination of dates by this method is subject to a number of sources of unreliability. At the very least, the confidence limits based on pure sampling error must be taken into account. In the case of Africa, very little use has been made of this method as yet. Olmsted arrived at a date of approximately 1000 B.C. for Proto-Bantu.[10] Another example is that of the separation between Malagasy, the language of Madagas-

---

[8] A survey of glottochronology theory with a full bibliography is to be found in D. H. Hymes, "Lexicostatistics so Far," *Current Anthropology*, I (1960), 3-44.

[9] This assumption has been brought into serious question by K. Bergsland and H. Vogt, "On the Validity of Glottochronology," *Current Anthropology*, III (1962), 115-58.

[10] D. L. Olmsted, "Three Tests of Glottochronological Theory," *American Anthropology*, LIX (1957), 839-42.

car, and Maanyan of Borneo, apparently the most closely related language within Malayo-Polynesian. The date given by Dyen is 1900 years before the present, in other words, the very beginning of the Christian era.[11]

IV

The type of inferences discussed so far only tells us about the movement of peoples with, hopefully, a time dimension based on glottochronology. We would, of course, also like to know basic cultural facts, for example, those relating to technology, subsistence economy, social organization and religion. At this point, valuable information can be derived by application of comparative linguistic method. As was mentioned earlier, the systematic comparison of related languages allows at least a partial reconstruction of sound system, grammar, and vocabulary of the ancestral language. This method has been worked out in great detail in the course of its application to Indo-European and a number of other language families.

Many of these results are, obviously, of no intrinsic interest to any one but the linguist. Thus, to know that the Proto-Indo-European word "three" was in all probability **tréyes* (in the nominative masculine and feminine) reveals nothing of interest to the general historian. However, that we can reconstruct original numbers up to one hundred does suggest certain conclusions. There must have been something worth counting. This seems to have been cattle, for which there is indeed an ancestral Indo-European vocabulary. From these and other elements of the Proto-Indo-European vocabulary there emerges the picture of the ancestral Indo-Europeans as a typical Neolithic village people.

Much more tentative conclusions of this kind can be drawn from African materials at the present state of our knowledge. In the two largest language families of Africa, Niger-Congo and Afroasiatic (Hamito-Semitic), there appear to be striking differences in the reconstructible vocabulary for wild animals. Thus, there is definitely a Proto-Afroasiatic word for "lion" but none for "leopard". In Proto-

---

11 I. Dyen, Review of O. C. Dahl, *Malgache et Maanyan*, *Language*, XXIX (1953), 577-90.

Niger-Congo, on the other hand, there is an ancestral word for "leopard" but none for "lion". This, of course, suggests a forest habitat for the original speakers of Niger-Congo and a more open country for the speakers of Afroasiatic.

Turning to domestic animals, the evidence here is very challenging. For Proto-Niger-Congo there are undoubted words for "cow" and "goat". The former could conceivably refer to the West African dwarf cattle (Muturuwa) before domestication, but the latter is difficult to explain away. We have no glottochronological estimate for Niger-Congo as a whole, but the differences among Niger-Congo languages are such that at least 8,000 years is indicated; probably more. Until recently, dates of approximately 7,000 years have been current for the age of the first plant and animal domestication. In view of these and other considerations from African linguistic data, recent evidence assigning greater age to the Neolithic are welcome (e.g., the radiocarbon date of 10,000 B.P. for Jericho). There may also be a Proto-Niger-Congo word for "to cultivate" if the root of Proto-Bantu **lim-* and Fulani *rim-* is more widespread than appears on present evidence.

The Afroasiatic data definitely point in the same direction. There is an inherited word for "cattle". Further, there is a verb and associated noun "to hoe the ground, cultivate" and "hoe". It seems not to have been pointed out previously that Akkadian *marru*, "hoe", and *marāru* "to hoe", Arabic *marr* "a hoe" and Egyptian *mr* (vowels not known) "a hoe" find their counterpart in the western subgroup of the Chad branch of Afroasiatic spoken in the northern region of Nigeria. Here we find Ngamo *marra*, Bolewa *mara*, Kanakuru *mira*, Angas *mar*, Ankwe *maar*, all meaning "to hoe, to do farm work" and Sura *mar* "a farm". This is a highly probable etymology from the viewpoint of sound correspondence and meaning. Borrowing among Egyptian, Akkadian, and Arabic is possible, but unlikely, even for Arabic, with the predominantly non-Moslem Chad groups just cited. If anything, the time-depth of Proto-Afroasiatic is even greater than that of Proto-Niger-Congo. The earliest written Egyptian of about 3,000 B.C. is already very different from Akkadian, the earliest recorded Semitic language. A guess of 7,000 B.P. would be a conservative one.

V

Another major source of historical inferences is the study of loan words. In many but not all cases it is possible to show on purely linguistic grounds that borrowings have taken place. In a certain fairly high proportion of such cases it is feasible, again from purely linguistic considerations, to discover which is the source language and which the borrowing language. A comparison of the sound systems of the languages will sometimes show that one language which does not have a particular sound will regularly substitute another similar sound in borrowings. Or, again, the word will be analyzable grammatically in one language but not in the other. These points can be illustrated from a study of the linguistic contacts between the Hausa of the northern region of Nigeria and their eastern neighbors, the Kanuri-speaking people of Bornu near Lake Chad.[12]

The Hausa word for "reading" and "writing" would be expected to come from Arabic in view of the undoubted fact that writing first came to the Hausa with the coming of Islam. In fact, the Hausa word for "reading" *karātū* obviously resembles the Arabic *qaraʔa* "to read". The word for "writing", however, *rubūtū,* is nothing like Arabic. However, it is always possible that an indigenous word with a related meaning has been transferred to a new meaning. Thus, English "to write" is not borrowed from Latin but is a Germanic word meaning "to scratch", cf. German *ritzen, reissen.* It will be noted that both of these words in Hausa contain a suffix *-tū.* This suffix is not fund otherwise in Hausa.

A comparison with Kanuri soon makes it clear that the words are both borrowed from Kanuri, which has a suffix *-t* to form verbal nouns and indeed has precisely these two formations, *karatə* "reading" and *rəbotə* "writing". Hausa, which has no such vowel, substitutes *i* or *u* in such cases, an example of the phonetic criterion mentioned earlier. The Kanuri word for "read" has been borrowed from Arabic, so that the word in Hausa is an indirect loan from

---

12 For a detailed discussion of Hausa-Kanuri borrowings, see J. H. Greenberg, "Linguistic Evidence for the Influence of the Kanuri on the Hausa," *Journal of African History,* I (1960), 205-12.

Arabic, via Kanuri. The root for "write", however, *rəbo-*, is indigenous, as is shown by the cognate form in Teda, *arbu-*, which means in this language "to draw designs, incise".

The words for "market", "town-wall", and "walled town" are also well attested borrowings from Kanuri into Hausa. The historian immediately sees the significance of all this. It suggests that Islam came to the Hausa via the Kanuri. But, and this is what makes the matter of further interest, Hausa tradition assigns conversion to a delegation in the fourteenth century from the Mandingo kingdom of Mali considerably to the west, evidently a connection of greater prestige. I do not doubt that this connection with the west also exists and that a delegation, whose descendants are still in Kano, did in fact come. However, when we consider the attested historical fact of the early existence of the Kanuri-speaking kingdom of Kanem as a powerful state and the relatively weak and unorganized Hausa city states at the same early period (approximately eleventh and twelfth century A.D.), this suggests a reinterpretation of the history of the Islamicization of the Hausa.

There are occasions when not only the establishment of the source language of borrowings and the cultural implications derived from their contact are important, but also the mere fact of borrowing having taken place at all. This is the case when the peoples involved are no longer in direct geographical proximity. In such cases, it often happens that since the contact was at an earlier period, the source of the resemblances is not the languages in their present form, but is the resultant of former cultural intercourse involving ancestral languages. Thus we have a combination of the two factors already discussed, the ancestral word method and borrowing. For example, it is well established that certain words of Germanic origin in Finnish derive from the ancestral Proto-Germanic rather than from any specific present-day Germanic language and it is even agreed that the number for "100" was borrowed by Proto-Finno-Ugric speakers from Proto-Indo-European.

A case in point in Africa, which cannot be discussed here in more than cursory terms and still requires much further investigation, concerns the evidence for early borrowing between certain speakers of Nilotic languages in East Africa and speakers of Cushitic, a large subfamily of Afroasiatic (Hamito-Semitic) found chiefly in

Ethiopia and Somalia. The Nilotes chiefly concerned are the Southern Nilotes (Nandi-Suk, Tatoga) and the Eastern Nilotes (Masai, Lotuko, Teso, Turkana, Bari and others). I will only consider the former case here. It is part of the intricacies of such problems that one of the questions which has not yet been resolved is the extent to which these borrowings in the two Nilotic groups were independent of each other, and possibly from different Cushitic groups, and the extent to which words of Cushitic origin may have passed secondarily from one Nilotic group to the other.

The Southern Nilotes are at present divided into two groups linguistically and geographically, the Nandi-Suk of western Kenya and the Tatoga, a small group farther south in Tanganyika. The fact that most of the suspected Cushitic words are found both in Nandi-Suk and Tatoga and that one of them, the number "nine", shows the regular working of a striking sound shift by which earlier *l* was changed to *sh* in Tatoga (Nandi *sokol* "nine" = Tatoga *sagesh*) indicates that the borrowings occurred at a time when the linguistic separation between Nandi-Suk and Tatoga had not yet taken place.[13]

The Cushitic languages are also divided into a number of distinct groups. Here the evidence points to the Eastern Cushitic languages consisting of the following subgroups: 1) Afar-Saho, 2) Sidamo group, 3) Galla-Conso, 4) Somali, Baiso, Rendille.[14] In fact, further investigation may confirm the present very tentative hypothesis that it was the ancestral language of the fourth of these subgroups that was the immediate source.

Sometimes our interest in regard to borrowing may concern the terminology of a particular cultural sphere, e.g., iron-working or cattle duration, rather than the period, and type of contact between individual peoples. This parallels the cultural anthropological distinction between diffusion and acculturation studies. Thus, a study of the word for "horse" and the terminology for saddles and other

---

[13] The importance of this sound shift for the problem of the age of Cushitic borrowings in Southern Nilotic was first noted by Harold Fleming in an unpublished work.

[14] Baiso, a hitherto unreported language, is spoken on Hano Island in Lake Margherita, Ethiopia. I am indebted to Herbert Lewis and Harold Fleming for material on this language.

riding accoutrements in Africa sheds some light on the manner of spread of this complex; e.g., the probable existence of a term of ancient Egyptian origin for "horse" in Beja, a large area chiefly in the Sudan, in which the Arabic word has diffused and, the spread of another term for horse of apparent Mande origin southward into the forest area of West Africa and certain coastal regions in which the Portuguese term has taken root.

VI

A further type of linguistic evidence can also make contribution, i.e., etymological data from a single language. This is notoriously dangerous but can, in certain instances, give reasonable results, particularly where compounds or fixed phrases are involved. This can be illustrated from Hausa. Here the word *k'arfe* means both "metal" and "iron". The term for "copper" is a phrase *jar k'arfe,* literally "red iron" or "red metal". This suggests the chronological priority of iron and is supported on non-linguistic grounds. Another example is the Hausa term for "maize" which is *dawar Masar,* "sorghum of Egypt". This again suggests the priority of sorghum which was certainly domesticated in Africa and is at present the staple crop of the Hausa. It also seems to indicate that maize came from Egypt, or at least that the Hausa thought it did. Possibly Egypt here is to be taken as a general term for the Arab north. It is indeed very suggestive of the cultural contacts of the Hausa that maize, brought by the Portuguese from the New World to Africa, should have come via the Arabs, from the north, rather than from the relatively close forset zone to the south.

VII

All the methods considered here have been based on contemporary linguistic analyses without reference to earlier written sources which give linguistic information. In Africa such documentary evidence is frequently important and can be combined with methods of the kind described above to lead to new hypotheses or to corroborate or to correct conclusions not based on other evidence. For example, the apparent survival of the Meroitic term *qereny,* an important subordinate official in certain languages of the Nuba hills of Kordofan, most strikingly in Koalib *kweleny* "chief", suggests Meroitic political influence in an area where it had only been vaguely suspected.[15]

Evidence of a quite different sort is furnished by the very few vocabularies of African languages spoken by slaves in the New World. Thus a vocabulary of Hausa in Brazil in the late nineteenth century showed that the Hausa spoken there had not undergone a sound shift already recorded in the early nineteenth century in Africa itself, thus indicating the establishment of a Hausa community in Brazil with linguistic patterns sufficiently well established to resist changes from later migrants at a period at least as early as the eighteenth century.[16]

The principles described do not exhaust the methodological possibilities, but they are the most important ones. There is no doubt that when the vast detailed work necessary has been carried out, contributions of real significance will be made by linguistic methods to the history of Africa.

---

[15] In fact, *kw-* is the singular prefix of the personal class in Koalib but it may have been folk-etymologized in this manner. Compare Swahili *ki-tabu* "book" with Arabic *kitāb* where *ki-* has been interpreted as a class prefix.

[16] For more detailed evidence see J. H. Greenberg, "The Application of New World Evidence to an African Linguistic Problem," *Mémoirs de l'Institut Français d'Afrique Noire,* XXVII (1953), 129-31.

II.

Some Thoughts on State-Formation in the Western Sudan Before the Seventeenth Century

by

JOHN D. FAGE

Director of the Centre of West African Studies,
University of Birmingham, Birmingham, England

THE HISTORY OF THE WESTERN SUDAN from at least the tenth century up to the time of the Moroccan invasion of 1591 is largely the story of three successive great empires: ancient Ghana, ancient Mali, and the Songhai empire of Gao. These were not the only states of the region during this time, of course. In the far west, in the middle Senegal valley, before the thirteenth century, there were the significant little kingdoms of Takrūr and Silla. A thirteenth century interlude when Ghana was in decline and Mali was only just emerging was marked by a brief predominance of the Sosso kings of Kaniaga. South of the Niger bend, in the upper Volta basin, the Mossi-Dagomba kingdoms, such as Wagadugu, Yatenga and Dagomba, began to emerge about the fifteenth century[1] among a people who had previously been noteworthy mainly for their raids against Mali and Songhai, and these states were to display remarkable stability for the next four centuries. Over in the east were the small Hausa states, founded perhaps about the tenth or eleventh centuries, and behind them lay the more powerful kingdom of the Sefawa, who began to flourish in Kanem about the eleventh century and who later established themselves in Bornu. However until the seventeenth century, Hausaland was subject to influences and pressures from Mali and Songhai, pressures and influences, incidentally, which doubtless served to check expansion from Bornu/Kanem.

Although from time to time reference will be made in this paper to features of these other states, this is done essentially for purposes of comparison, to illuminate the nature of the imperial character and history of Ghana, Mali and Songhai. For there can be no doubt that throughout the period under discussion the dominating politi-

[1] This is not, perhaps, the generally accepted date (cf. M. Delafosse, *Haut-Sénégal-Niger;* L. Tauxier, *Le Noir de Yatenga* etc.), but is that reached by the present author as the result of independent research on Dagomba and Mamprussi—see the forthcoming proceedings of the International Seminar on Ethno-History held at Dakar in December 1961.

cal, economic and cultural initiatives and influences stemmed from these three great empires. There seems no question in fact that the empires of Ghana, Mali, and Songhai rank among the highest achievements of Negro Africans in history. The intention of this paper, then, is to try and assess what were the formative principles at work in these states.

Information about Ghana, Mali and Songhai comes from a variety of sources.[2] There is some relevant archaeological evidence, though as yet nothing like as much as one would like to have. A fair amount of their own historical tradition has survived. In the case of Mali and Songhai, this was successfully maintained by oral means into modern times when it could be rendered in writing by European observers, initially by explorers like Barth[3] and later mainly by colonial administrators like Maurice Delafosse,[4] or by European-educated Africans.[5] Some of the tradition of ancient Ghana has also survived, not directly, but as prolegomena to the tradition of Mali. As such it began to be written down in Arabic, together with some of the tradition of Mali, from the sixteenth and seventeenth centuries onwards, by Sudanese scholars, especially those of Timbuctu, whose primary purpose was to provide more or less contemporary chronicles (*Ta'rīkhs*) of the Songhai empire and of the Moroccan conquest of 1591-92 which brought this to an end.[6] This leads us to a third source, namely the writings of geographers, historians and travellers of the medieval Islamic world. Some of these authors had themselves visited the western Sudan,

---

[2] There is an extensive treatment of the history of ancient Mali in Ch. Monteil, "Les Empires de Mali", *Bull. Com. Et. Hist. Sc. A.O.F.*, XII (1929), 291-447, and of Songhai in J. Rouch, *Contribution à l'Histoire des Songhay*, Mém. d'I.F.A.N., No. 29, 1953. For ancient Ghana, see R. Mauny, "The Question of Ghana", *Africa*, XXIV, 1954, and J. D. Fage, "Ancient Ghana; a Review of the Evidence", *Trans. Hist. Soc. Ghana*, III, 2 (1957), 77-98.

[3] H. Barth, *Travels and Discoveries in North and Central Africa* (5 Vols., London, 1857-1858); see especially IV, 406-36, 579-630.

[4] M. Delafosse, *Haut-Sénégal-Niger*, (3 vols., Paris, 1912).

[5] For example, in recent years, especially Dj. Tamsir Niane, e.g. his "Recherches sur l'Empire du Mali au Moyen Age", *Recherches Africaines*, 1959.

[6] Abderrahman es-Sadi, *Tarīkh es-Soudan*, ed. and trans. by O. Houdas (Paris, 1900; and Mahmoud Kati, *Tarīkh el-Fettach*, ed. and trans. by O. Houdas and M. Delafosse (Paris, 1913).

for example Ibn Hawqal in the tenth century[7] and Ibn Battūta in the fourteenth; others based their accounts on what was known in North Africa from its continual and growing trans-Saharan contacts with the Sudan. In the latter category, al-Bakrī (1067), al-Idrīsī (1154), al-'Umarī (c. 1345), Ibn Khaldūn (c. 1400) and al-Maqrīzī (c. 1420) are particularly significant.[8]

In many respects this Arabic literature, both domestic and external, is the best source for this enquiry into the nature of Sudanic empire-building. It is specific as to time (i.e. the date of composition is usually known, and events mentioned in the texts are often dateable from this if they are not already explicitly dated) and often also as to geographical orientation. Secondly what these authors have to say about the western Sudan is written and commented upon (sometimes also, and notably in the case of Ibn Khaldūn, analysed) from a fixed point of reference, namely that of the Muslim civilisation of the time.

It would be impossible here to relate the known history of Ghana, Mali and Songhai in any detail. A very cursory outline will have to suffice.[9] Ghana was already in existence when it came within the sphere of Muslim North African observation in the eighth century. Indeed, it may well have come into being some centuries earlier than this. The centre of the state lay some 200 miles north of modern Bamako. The exact boundaries of its empire are not

---

[7] It is the general opinion that Ibn Hawqal visited the western Sudan in person; whether this was actually so may perhaps be another matter.

[8] Relevant extracts from the texts of all these authors, with a parallel French translations may be consulted: Ibn Hawal, *Description de l'Afrique*, trans. *et Aegypti,* 13 facsimiles, Cairo, 1926-1938. More specifically, the following translations may be consulted: Ibn Hawgal, *Description de l'Afrique*, trans. M. G. de Slane, *Journal Asiatique* (Paris, 1842); El Bekri, *Description de l'Afrique Septentrionale*, trans. M. G. de Slane (Algiers, 1913); Edrisi, *Description de l'Afrique et de l'Espagne*, trans. R. Dozy and M. J. de Goeje (Leyden, 1866); Ibn Battoutah, *Voyages*, trans. C. Defrémery and B. R. Sanguinetti (4 vols., Paris, 1853-1859) (see also new translation by H. A. R. Gibb in progress for the Hakluyt Society, London); Al-Omari, *L'Afrique moins l'Egypte*, trans. M. Gaudefroy-Demombynes (Paris, 1927); Ibn Khaldoun, *Histoire des Berbères*, trans. M. G. de Slane (new ed., 4 vols., Paris, 1925-1956). A translation of the relevant part of Maqrīzī is to be found in Demombynes' translation of 'Umarī.

[9] This is based on the literature noted in note 2.

known, and were probably in fact ill-defined, but at the peak of its power, which was almost certainly in the tenth century, it seems to have been effective within a radius of some 200 miles. Thus its southern limits lay close to the upper Senegal and the upper Niger, while northwards it reached into the desert to a considerable extent. The dominant people in the empire were the Soninke, a northern branch of the great bloc of peoples speaking Mande languages. In 1076, Ghana was overrun by the Almoravids, and thereafter began to decline. It finally disappeared as an independent state early in the thirteenth century, when the power of Mali was beginning to rise.

Mali was the creation of a clan or group of clans of the southern Mande who lived in the upper Niger valley. It reached its peak of power and size in the mid-fourteenth century. At that time, Takrūr in the west was at least nominally vassal to Mali, while in the east Malian influence was felt as far as Hausaland. To the south-west its boundaries were close to the northern limits of the thick forest; in the south-east it was bounded by the Mossi kingdoms. Its empire extended northwards into the desert to Walata and north-eastwards towards Air. This sizeable empire began to decline during the fifteenth century, when the reins of power began to be taken over by the Songhai, a people from the middle Niger upstream of Gao, whose kings had earlier been numbered among the vassals of Mali. From 1464 onwards, a new Songhai empire was being erected on the ruins of the old Malian one. Its capital was Gao, some 700 miles east of Niani, the capital of Mali. Songhai's power was accordingly less extensive in the west, where indeed an independent remnant Mali state remained in the upper Niger valley, but it was more effective in the east, where at least the western Hausa states were tributary. It was also more extensive in the north, where it included Air and also the valuable rock-salt deposits at Taghaza. The Songhai empire fell to pieces following the capture of its three principal towns—Gao, Timbuctu and Jenne—in 1591 by an expeditionary force from Morocco.

Although a large part of the available information about Ghana, Mali and Songhai comes from Muslim writers (including, be it remembered, Muslim Sudanese); although it would seem that, from the time of the Almoravids onwards, the Muslim world in North

Africa was willing to accept these empires as part of the Muslim comity of nations; and although their history has recently been learnedly and at length related and analysed by a modern Arabist, J. Spencer Trimingham, in a book entitled *A History of Islam in the Sudan,*[10] it would seem to be a mistake to think of these empires as Muslim states.

It is in the first place quite obvious that the first of the three states, Ghana, had an independent pagan existence before the Arabs and Islam began to reach across the Sahara from the Maghrib. The famous description of it written by al-Bakrī[11] (from what would appear to be excellent first-hand sources) on the very eve of the Almoravid invasion, clearly pictures a pagan monarchy in which the role of the Muslims—who would seem likely to have been Maghribians for the most part—was limited to trade with North Africa and to the provision of some technical administrative assistance.

However al-Idrīsī, writing of Ghana a century after al-Bakrī and the conquest by the Muslim Almoravids, gives a picture of what appears to be a thoroughly Islamised monarchy (which even claimed to be sherifan) ruling in an Islamic manner over a thoroughly Islamised people, at least in the capital.[12] There are difficulties in Idrīsī's account which cast some doubts on its authenticity, but there is nothing inherently improbable in it. There is evidence that nearby Takrūr had begun to undergo a thorough Islamisation even earlier. Al-Bakrī reports the conversion of its king something like a generation before the Almoravids even.[13] Moreover, by the fourteenth century, at least, its people, the Tukulur, had begun to produce the class of Muslim clerics, the *tōrodbē,* for which they were later to be famous, and who were to play an important role in the large-scale Islamisation of the whole western Sudan that began some 400 years later.[14] (However it may not be irrelevant to this enquiry to note that after about the fourteenth century, Takrūr seems to have been *politically* of no account. It disappears as an independent state, and until the

[10] London, 1962.

[11] El Bekri, *Description,* 327-31.

[12] Edrisi, *Description,* 6-7.

[13] El Bekri, *Description,* 378.

[14] See Trimingham, *History,* 47, 160-62.

eighteenth century, indeed, its people were commonly subject to alien and pagan dynasties.) Al-Bakrī also reports the conversion of the king of 'Malel', further into the interior beyond Ghana, and this is doubtless to be identified with one of the petty riverain Mande chieftaincies from which the great empire of Mali was to spring.[15]

It must be admitted that the evidence relating to Ghana and its neighbours in the eleventh and twelfth centuries is slight. The contemporary sources really amount to no more than a few pages of al-Bakrī and of Idrīsī, and to these may be added little more than the very late and brief remarks of the Timbuctu *Ta'rīkhs* and of Ibn Khaldūn. Nevertheless the picture that results is a consistent one of a thorough islamization of the whole region, beginning just before the Almoravid invasion but greatly accentuated after it. This picture would seem to be confirmed by such archaeological evidence as is available. The French archaeologists, Thomassey and Mauny, see no reason to doubt the identification of the site that they excavated at Koumbi Saleh with one at least of the capitals of ancient Ghana, and what their excavations revealed was to all intents and purposes a medieval North African city.[16]

The evidence available for an assessment of the Mali and Songhai empires is much fuller. Much more of their own indigenous tradition has survived and has been recorded; Mali was well known to contemporary North African writers; and some at least of Songhai's own Arabic chronicles remain available for analysis. These last, incidentally, show that local tradition regarded Mali as the natural, lineal successor to Ghana.[17] As will be seen later, this would appear to be good history. Therefore it would seem reasonable to infer that much of what is known of Mali once applied also to Ghana.

There is a fair amount in the evidence for Mali and Songhai to suggest that the islamization which seems to have characterised post-eleventh century Ghana was carried over into the later empires. For example, all the Songhai kings from 1464 to 1591 are known to have had Muslim names, and this appears to have been the

---

15 El Bekri, *Description*, 331.

16 P. Thomassey and R. Mauny, "Campagnes de Fouilles à Koumbi Saleh", *Bull. I.F.A.N.*, 1951, 438-62; B, 1956, 117-140.

17 Es Sadi *Ta'rīkh es-Soudan*, 18-19; Kati, *Ta'rīkh el-Fettach*, 75-76.

case for at least half of the kings of Mali from c. 1240 to c. 1400. A fair number of these kings apparently made the pilgrimage to Mecca. Ibn Khaldūn suggests that this custom may have developed at a very early stage, namely in the twelfth century—but he is a very late authority.[18] The first reasonably certain pilgrimage would seem to be that of the *Mansa* Wali (Ule; Ali?) of Mali in the 1260's.

These points are perhaps not very significant. The wealth, pomp and splendour displayed in some of these pilgrimages, notably the very well attested ones of the *Mansa* Muṣa of Mali in 1324-5 and of the *Askia* Muhammad of Songhai in 1495-7,[19] might suggest that their purpose was primarily to further political and economic relations with North Africa. They certainly had this effect. They led, for instance, to the transmission of regular embassies across the Sahara; to the establishment of hostels for Sudanese students in Cairo; to the coming to the Sudanic courts of men like as-Sahili (who is said to have built mosques and palaces at Timbuctu and Gao) and of other less well remembered advisers, technicians, clerics, jurists, and simple adventurers; and they certainly led to an increase in trans-Saharan trade, particularly with Egypt.

If the purpose of the pilgrimages was essentially political and economic, then there would have been no need for the Sudanese kings who went on them to have been very devout or deep Muslims. Indeed the superficiality of their Islam might seem to be suggested by an anecdote of al-'Umarī's about *Mansa Musa*, whose pilgrimage is usually accounted the most splendid of all. Al-'Umarī says that until Musa arrived in Cairo, he did not know that it was unlawful for him to have more than four wives.[20] But probably the moral of the story is rather the reverse, namely that if in 1324, Musa was not as yet very well instructed in Islam, his intentions were devout and sincere, for it is said that when his error had been pointed out to him he at once announced that he would mend his ways.

However, we need not rely simply on evidence of royal names and pilgrimages to suggest the extent of Islam in Mali and Songhai.

---

[18] Ibn Khaldoun, *Histoire*, II, 111.

[19] See for Mansa Musa: Al-Omari, *L'Afrique*, 70 et seq.; Maqrīzī (in *Ibid.*, 89-93); Ibn Khaldoun, *Histoire*, II, 112-14; for Askia Muhammad: Kati, *Ta'rīkh el-Fettach*, 25-27, 124-32.

[20] Al-Omari, *L'Afrique*, 53.

For Mali, there is the first hand evidence of Ibn Battūta, who toured the empire during 1352-3, and also the account written from first-hand sources by al-'Umarī about the same time.[21] Both authors seem concerned to stress the strength of Islam in the state. It is true that al-'Umarī mentions the wide spread of what he calls magic and sorcery, but he is at pains to point out that murders by sorcery are punished by the king. It is possible to read Ibn Battūta's account and almost to conclude that Mali was a Muslim state. He was obviously greatly impressed both by the general justice and public security that were maintained throughout the state, and by the particular care taken to protect the persons and property of visiting North Africans. Both he and al-'Umarī agree that the king of the time, Sulaiman, was a devout Muslim. The latter wrote:

> He built mosques of worship and convocation and minarets, and instituted weekly prayers, gatherings and the call to prayer. He attracted jurists of the Mālikī rite to his country, and was himself a student of *figh*.[22]

At the Mali capital Nyani, Ibn Battūta noted the people's

> punctiliousness in observing the prayer sequence, their assiduousness in attending congregational prayers and in bringing up their children to observe them. On Fridays the crowd is so great that unless one goes early to the mosque it is impossible to find a place.[23]

He also comments on the popular observance of the great Muslim festivals.

A comparable picture is given in the Timbuctu *Ta'rīkhs* of the situation in the Songhai empire in the time of the *Askia* Muhammad, who liberally supported the *'ulamā* of Timbuctu and Jenne, 'performed both the obligatory and the superogatory duties' of Islam, and 'established Islam on sure foundations'.[24]

But there is really no evidence in these Muslim authorities to show that Islam was at all relevant outside the larger towns, such as Nyani, Jenne, Timbuctu and Gao. There is nothing to suggest, for example, that the system of *qādīs*, noted by Ibn Battūta and

---

21 See note 8.

22 Al-Omari, *L'Afrique*, 53.

23 Ibn Battoutah, *Voyages*, IV, 421.

24 Kati, *Ta'rīkh el-Fettach*, 114-15.

others, extended beyond the limits of these towns. It seems quite possible that even within them their jurisdiction was limited to Muslims, conceivably even to immigrants from North Africa, a class to which some at least of the *qādīs* themselves probably belonged, at least initially. Elsewhere, it must be supposed, justice was administered according to pagan custom.

More than this, the Muslim authorities contain a good deal to suggest that the fundamental organization of government was still pagan, even if the literate Muslims were employed as scribes and technical advisers. Thus Ibn Khaldūn thought that the royal succession at Mali sometimes, at least, went through the female line.[25] This al-Bakrī had said was the normal mode of succession in pre-Muslim Ghana.[26] The exact significance of these observations is not clear (matrilinealism is certainly not characteristic of the modern Mande).[27] Nevertheless, here there was something about the monarchy which struck Muslims as very queer and outlandish. Furthermore, although the Mali court had acquired some oriental trappings, Ibn Battūta's first-hand description of its ceremonial suggests close resemblances to the pagan practices at the Ghana court of al-Bakrī's time. Thus subjects coming into the presence of the king had to bare themselves to the waist, prostrate themselves, and cover themselves with dust. The king did not speak directly with the people, but only through a linguist or herald, and he was surrounded by his court drummers and *griots*.[28]

The offices of government would seem essentially indigenous. The Mali king was *mansa*, the head of a Mande clan (whose residence is Mali (or Mande), namely 'where the master is'). His local representatives were *fariba* (cf. *fa*, 'family head'). His military officers were *fararis*.[29] For Songhai, we have *fari* or *farma* for a minister or local governor; *hi-koy* and *dyini-koy* for the commanders of the riverain navy and of the army respectively; *hari-farma* for

---

[25] Ibn Khaldoun, *Histoire,* II, 111.

[26] El-Bekri, *Description,* 328.

[27] The subject is fully discussed by N. Levtzion in "The Kings of Mali," *Journal of African History,* IV, 3 (1963), 341-54.

[28] Ibn Battoutah, *Voyages,* IV, 403-08.

[29] For a full description and terminology, see Monteil, "Les Empires", 309-17.

the official in charge of navigation and fishing; *korey-farma* for the minister in charge of relations with North Africans—and so on.[30] (Incidentally this last example suggests once again that North African Muslims had an extrajudicial status. It is also worth noting that this list of Songhai titles would appear to be a mixture of Songhai and Mande terms.)

It would seem reasonable to suppose that the Muslim traits in Mali and Songhai were essentially glosses on a type of monarchy that was fundamentally pagan. Exactly what this type of monarchy was is not now easy to discern. But there would seem to be enough clues in what is known of pre-Muslim Ghana and of Islamised Mali and Songhai to suggest that it originally may not have been unlike that of ancient Kanem further to the east. The evidence here is for a divine kingship of a typical Nilotic (or perhaps Negro) pattern. This seemed very strange to early Arab commentators. Thus al-Muhallabi (late tenth century) wrote

> they exalt and worship [the king] instead of the most high God. They falsely imagine that he does not eat, for his food is taken into his palace secretly, and if anyone should meet the camels carrying it, he is instantly killed. . . . The religion [of the people] is the worship of their kings, for they believe that it is they who bring life and death, sickness and health. . . .[31]

Nearly 400 years later Ibn Battūta reported that the king of Kanem 'never shows himself to his people and never speaks to them except from behind a curtain',[32] a custom that persisted into the nineteenth century.

It is generally presumed that this tradition of divine kingship originated east of Kanem, in the Nile valley. How strong it ever was west of Kanem is perhaps an open question. It certainly seems to have travelled up the Niger to the Songhai, whose first dynasty, the *Zas*, seem to have been of this type (together with the kings of Bornu, Yoruba, etc.). Its existence among the Mande can really

---

30 For a full list of Songhai ministerial titles, see Rouch, *Contribution*, 192-93, n.2.

31 No original text of al-Muhallabi is known; this passage is quoted by Yaqut. See F. Wustenfeld, *Jacut's Geographisches Wörterbuch* (6 vols., Leipzig, 1866-1873), II, 932-33.

32 Ibn Battoutah, *Voyages*, IV, 442.

only be inferred, from al-Bakrī's description of Ghana and from what might seem to be residual traits in Mali, for example that of giving audience through an intermediary. This question is of some importance because of the undoubted extent of Mande influence in the formation of the great historic empire of the Songhai. The small Songhai kingdom of the *Zas* became tributary to Mali, and first regained its independence under what its tradition represents as a second dynasty, the *Sis* or *Sonnis*. The founders of this second dynasty (probably about 1275), Ali Kolon and his brother, may have been Mande. If not, they would certainly appear to have been men who had held high appointments in the Mali service.[33] It was the last of this line, *Sonni* Ali (1464-92), who was the effective founder of the great empire which superseded that of Mali. It was the founder of the next dynasty, the *Askia* Muhammad, who did most to consolidate it, and he seems certainly to have been of Mande origin.[34]

But if the line which led to *Sonni* Ali had originally been Mande or Mande-influenced, by his time it had become thoroughly naturalized. *Sonni* Ali's success in founding a new empire to replace that of Mali as ascribed by the Timbuctu *Ta'rīkhs* to his success in mobilizing the pagan spirit of the Songhai against the Islamising tendencies of the Mali regime. Though it would seem that he himself owed some nominal allegiance to Islam, the Timbuctu chroniclers regarded him with hatred as a pagan who was implacably hostile to the Muslim (and doubtless Mande-inspired) tradition of civilization and scholarship in the towns.[35] Ali's militant paganism was so strong, indeed, that it bred a Muslim reaction under one of his generals, Muhammad, who became the first of the new *Askia* line. The subsequent history of Songhai has been interpreted by Jean Rouch almost in terms of a continual competition for power

---

[33] Es-Sadi, *Ta'rīkh es-Soudan*, 9-12; Kati, *Ta'rīkh el-Fettach*, 93-94, 334.

[34] *Ta'rīkh el-Fettach*, 114, where it is stated that Muhammad came from a Soninke clan, and 113 where his surname is given as "Toule" = Touré, cf. Sekou Touré. Note also, 106, that initially Muhammad was supported by only one of the great chiefs of the realm, and this, significantly was a descendant of Mansa Musa.

[35] Es-Sadi, *Ta'rīkh es-Soudan*, 103-04; Kati, *Ta'rīkh el-Fettach*, 81-83. See also Rouch, *Contribution*, 181-86.

between two parties in the state, the one pagan and national (tribal?), the other Muslim and universalizing.[36] This competition was so sharp that it weakened the state and was a factor in explaining the easy success of the Moroccans in occupying the main centres of the empire. Ultimately, however, the invasion of the Muslim Moors resolved the internal conflict of Songhai. The kings and their kingdom could maintain their independence and individuality only by going over whole-heartedly to the pagan cause, and by fighting back from the ancient pagan centres of the Songhai stock further down the Niger in Dendi.

It seems plausible to paint the end of Mali in similar colours. For, with the rise of Songhai, the once great empire was reduced to the status of a petty state in the upper Niger valley, its original homeland. When a Mande kingdom once again becomes noteworthy, it is sailing under manifestly pagan colours—hence the style *Bambara* for the kingdom of Segu developed by Biton-Kululabi towards the end of the seventeenth century. But the character of the Mali empire at its birth is less clear. Local traditions would appear to confirm al-Bakrī's story of the advent of Islam to the Mande of the upper Niger just before the time of the Almoravids.[37] Their coming, and the later dispersion of Islamised Soninke following the fall of Ghana,[38] must have tended to increase the islamization of the area. But before the thirteenth century, what became the nucleus from which the Mali empire was to be developed seems to have been divided between a number of petty states and competing dynasties.[39] The dynasty that founded the empire, that of the Keita, would seem to have been immigrant Mande from further down the Niger. It is possible that the Keita had already been in contact with Islam.[40] But the great folk-heroes of this dynasty, its founding-father, Nare Fa Maghan (c. 1200-18), and the real originator of the empire, Sundiata (c. 1230-55), are

36 Rouch, *Contribution*, 192-209.

37 Monteil, "Les Empires", 344-45.

38 See Trimingham, *History*, 31, 60.

39 See Monteil, "Les Empires", 305, 344-53.

40 Monteil, "Les Empires", 349-51. Note that if the Keita came from downstream, they came from the direction of Jenne, which according to Es-Sadi, *Ta'rīkh es-Soudan*, 23, was a Muslim city by c. 1200 A.D.

recalled in indigenous tradition by these pagan Mande names. There is, of course, a Muslim name for Sundiata, namely Mari-Diata. But, against this, tradition ascribes Sundiata's success in relieving Mali of the pressure of the Sosso and building up his empire essentially to his command of pagan magic.[41] Sundiata, in fact, seems just as much as *Sonni* Ali, to have been a harnesser of pagan forces.

The conclusion then, whether we look at Ghana, Mali or Songhai, seems to be that these empires were in origin pagan creations which, once they had become established, found a degree of islamization convenient for reasons of state. In the cases of Mali and Songhai, there is reason to believe that this islamization was somewhat superficial. In Ghana, because of the Almoravids, it may have been more fundamental. (But here it is worth pointing out that Muslim Ghana was a steadily declining power.) What were these reasons of state that led to a degree of islamization in these pagan empires?

Fundamentally they would seem to be connected with trade. From the economic point of view, the function of these empires was the control and exploitation, by ambitious West African peoples or clans, of the Western Sudan's trade with North Africa, a trade in which the exchange of West African gold for Sharan salt was perhaps of particular importance. This control and exploitation could be achieved in two complementary ways. One was by expanding laterally across the internal West African trade routes running north towards the Sahara, and so channelling these through centres which the empire-builders controlled and which became the markets for North African traders. The early prominence of Ghana is clearly due to its position north of the gold-producing region of Wangara (equivalent to the modern Bambuk). Later, after the upsets caused to the westernmost trans-Saharan routes by the Almoravid outburst and by the disruption of Ghana, first the Mande and then the Songhai sought to control a new diagonal by-pass running along the natural route of the Niger north-eastwards to Timbuctu, the West African export centre nearest to North Africa. This route also cut across the supply line running northwards from the Gold Coast, whose mines were opened up as a result of Mande initiative about

---

[41] See e.g., Monteil, "Les Empires", 359-65.

the middle of the fourteenth century.[42] In this connection it would appear that the issue of whether or not the Keita were Muslims is less significant than the tradition that they were *traders* reaching the Mande centres in the upper Niger valley from further downstream. Equally, the domination by Songhai boatmen of riverain traffic, at least as far upstream as Macina, was doubtless an important factor in Songhai's victory over Mali later on. Doubtless too it helps to explain why it was so important to Sonni Ali to appeal to the pagan sensibilities of his people.

The second way in which western Sudanese empire-builders sought to gain wealth was by levying tribute on other clan groups and their villages. This undoubtedly helped to create at their capitals exportable surpluses of marketable commodities, since initially much trade was probably state or royal trade. In this connection it is worth noting that Charles Monteil once remarked that 'a Sudanese empire is essentially an association of individuals aiming to dominate others for profit.'[43]

Once an empire of this type had been established, then there were obvious advantages in its royal and mercantile classes adopting an Islamic front so as to establish surer relations with the Muslim states and traders of North Africa who were their customers and suppliers. But in its origins, the empire-building process would seem to have been fundamentally a pagan reaction to the development of North African trade. Furthermore, following the initial success of Ghana, it seems to have been essentially a Mande or Mande-inspired process.

However there is a difficulty in this interpretation. From the time of the Almoravid conquest onwards, it would appear that the Mande merchant classes, particularly the Soninke and later the Dyula, were steadfastly Muslim.[44] As such, for example, they brought Islam as well as international trade to Hausaland in the

---

[42] This dating is now generally accepted; see Ivor Wilks, "The Northern Factor in Ashanti history", *Jour. Af. Hist.*, II, 1961, 28-29; R. Mauny, *Tableau Géographique de l'Ouest Africain au Moyen Age,* Mém. d'I.F.A.N., No. 61, 1961, 300; Eva L. R. Meyerowitz, *Akan Traditions of Origin* (London, 1952), 29-44.

[43] Monteil, "Les Empires", 311.

[44] See, for example, Trimingham, *History*, 31, 143.

fourteenth century. One might have expected, therefore, that both the growth of trade and the growth of empire should together have led to a much deeper and more permanent islamization of the empires and of their peoples. However there would seem to be both particular and general reasons why this did not happen. On the particular side, it must be remembered that although Sundiata was emulating an example set by the Soninke (i.e. the northern Mande) of Ghana, who had been islamized, he himself represented *southern* Mande who were breaking up a Soninke commercial dominion by establishing a new riverain Niger trade route. Thus it would be politic for him to appeal to pagan loyalties. Similarly, it has been suggested, Sonni Ali was using the pagan coherence of the Songhai to wrest control of this riverain route from islamized Mande.

On the general side, there might seem to have been good political reasons for the imperial rulers trying to establish their dominion as Muslim princes. One of their greatest problems, and one which never seems to have been solved satisfactorily, was how to secure enduring allegiance from other subjected pagan clans which possessed totally different ancestor and land cults from that of the ruling clan. A universal allegiance of Muslim individuals to a Muslim king might well have seemed a suitable solution. But in fact the pagan cults were too strong. Thus *Askia* Muhammad's islamizing policy soon brought a pagan reaction (and in fact his own downfall). More importantly, perhaps, most of the Sudanic emperors seem to have recognised that the social upsets resulting from an active campaign of Muslim proselytization would have been bad for trade, and so would have weakened the economic mainspring of empire. Thus we are told that, initially at least, the Muslim merchants of Ghana dealt with the Wangara gold-miners by dumb-barter.[45] Later on, al-'Umarī says that *Mansa* Musa had no wish to destroy paganism among the gold-miners lest by so doing the supply of gold might be reduced.[46] There may have been advantages for *traders* in being Muslim, but to try and impose the new and alien religion upon *producers* was apt to upset the intimate and particular relations which the ancestors of each

---

[45] E.g. Maçoudi, *Les Prairies d'Or*, ed. and trans. by C. Barbier de Meynaud and P. de Courtelle (9 vols., Paris, 1861-1877), IV, 92-93.

[46] Al-Omari, *L'Afrique*, 58-59.

individual pagan kinship group had established with the spirits of the land which they tilled or mined, and of the water which fed the land and which occasioned the deposits of alluvial gold. From the economic point of view, therefore, there were limits beyond which it was not good policy to push Islam.

It is at least possible to argue also that from the *political* point of view, in the western Sudan Islam was more a destructive than a constructive force. The period considered in this paper both begins and ends with an invasion of Muslims which either immediately (as in the case of the Moroccans) or ultimately (as Ibn Khaldūn clearly states in the case of the Almoravids[47]) led to the destruction of a pagan system of peace and prosperity. Furthermore, Jean Rouch gives grounds for believing that *Askia* Muhammad's Islamic policy seriously weakened the Songhai empire established by *Sonni* Ali.[48] On the other hand, however, it would seem that Delafosse was going too far when he suggested that the apparent stability of the Mossi-Dagomba states was due to their continuing paganism.[49] It seems more probable that this stability was due in part to the fact that these states remained relatively small, so that their rulers were not faced with the problem of seeking allegiance from pagan groups that were not assimilable into their own.

---

[47] Ibn Khaldoun, *Histoire,* II, 110.

[48] Rouch, *Contribution,* 209.

[49] Delafosse, *Haut-Sénégal-Niger,* II, 124.

III.

European Sources for Tropical African History

by

GRAHAM IRWIN

Associate Professor of History, Columbia University, New York City

THE PURPOSE OF THIS PAPER is to provide a generalized description of the nature and extent of the known European sources for tropical African history, and of the ways in which scholars have employed these sources up to the present time. It also seeks to show, using the Dutch-language records as an example, how, in conjunction with other types of evidence, European archival materials may be called on to help solve problems in "African" as opposed to "colonial" history.

I. DESCRIPTION OF THE EUROPEAN SOURCES

The documentary sources in European languages for the history of tropical Africa are to be found partly in Europe and other places outside Africa, and partly in Africa itself. Official archives currently held in Africa are in many cases extensive, since most of the states which gained their independence after the Second World War inherited the local records of their former colonial masters. In Dakar, for example, are housed the archives of the *Gouvernement-général de l'A.O.F.*, without reference to which research into the modern history of any part of former French West Africa could hardly be attempted. At independence both Ghana and Nigeria took over substantial collections of documents from the colonial governments of those territories, and have since set up efficient national archives services. In Guinea there were some losses of material, due to a policy of destruction and removal adopted by the departing French, and the records of German East and West Africa, which were transferred to Tanganyika and Ruanda-Urundi and to British and French Cameroons and Togoland respectively, also suffered from dispersion and neglect. But, in general, all territories which evolved directly from colonial to independent status took over the archives of the retiring colonial governments more or less intact.[1] The same will presumably happen in Kenya,

[1] Philip D. Curtin, "The Archives of Tropical Africa: a Reconnaissance," *Journal of African History*, I, 1 (1960), 129-47.

Nyasaland and the Rhodesias and, it is to be hoped, in Angola and Mozambique also.

Source materials for tropical African history are also to be found in the home archives of the ex-colonial powers. In part these metropolitan holdings duplicate the records preserved in Africa. Where the home material is unique it normally relates to "colonial" history and to the history of "European activities in Africa" rather than to "African" history as the term is now understood. On the other hand the survival rate for documents has been higher in the metropoles than in their colonies, and many sources which might be expected to exist in Africa have decayed or been lost and may today be consulted only in Europe. The two sets of records, African and European, are therefore complementary, and for research purposes recourse must normally be had to both.

Where colonial rule in Africa was abandoned some time ago—as, for example, when a colony was transferred from one European state to another—the records of the abdicating power were usually repatriated to Europe in their entirety. Thus the local archives of the Dutch establishments on the Gold Coast, sovereignty over which was transferred to the British in 1872, are to be found not in modern Ghana but in the Netherlands. The same is true of the records of the commercial companies which operated in Africa at the time of the slave trade and of the archives of most of the missionary societies. In consequence, European-language sources for African history, many of them of great value, exist today in several European countries, such as Holland, Denmark and Sweden, which have had no colonial connection with Africa since the nineteenth century or earlier.

Taken as a whole, the European-language documentary records are very voluminous, complex and difficult to use. This was recognized in a practical way in 1954, when a committee of scholars convened by the Institute of Historical Research, University of London, set in motion a scheme for the production of guides to the European archives for the benefit of historians of Africa. Up to now this committee has confined its attention to the materials known to exist for West African History, but it is hoped that in time other areas of the continent will be dealt with also. The present plan is for one volume each on Belgium and Holland, France, Portugal, and Scandinavia and Germany. This West African series is being modelled on the "Guides to the materials in foreign archives relating to the history of the United States," published by the Carnegie Institute in Washington, D.C. Each volume will catalogue all relevant documents class by class in institution by institution in country by country, and will supply brief notes on the location, origins and function of each holding institution, on the overall nature of its holdings and on the rules governing their use.[2] The West African guides are not intended as calendars. They will, however, give enough detail to enable a research worker to track down a likely source and order it from the stacks of a repository with a minimum of difficulty. The first in the series, *Materials for West African history in the archives of Belgium and Holland,* by Patricia Carson, was published in early 1962.

Miss Carson's work lists materials in the archives of Antwerp, Brussels, Ghent and Tervuren in Belgium, and of Amsterdam, Gouda, Haarlem, The Hague, Leiden, Middelburg, Rotterdam and Utrecht in the Netherlands. This wide geographical coverage is the most valuable, and perhaps the most unexpected, feature of her book. Most students working on the history of the Dutch overseas, particularly those from foreign countries, stay in The Hague, where they rely on the *Rijksarchief,* or State Archive, for their manuscript, and the National Library, Colonial Ministry Library, Library of the Royal Institute, etc. for their printed sources. They normally have neither the time nor the money to comb through the various provincial and municipal archives. Indeed, one would hardly expect to find material on African history in, say, Ghent in Belgium, or Middelburg in the Netherlands. Yet, as Miss Carson's guide shows, the writing of a definitive work on the overseas trade of West Africa in the eighteenth century would be impossible without reference to the Ghent Public Archive's *Collection d'Hoop,* which contains the papers of the great slaving entrepreneur, Pierre van Alstein. Similarly, the log-books of ships which visited the West Coast of Africa often contain valuable information about the peoples of the coastal

---

2 Patricia Carson, *Materials for West African History in the Archives of Belgium and Holland* (London, 1962), Editor's preface.

states. The most extensive Dutch collection of these log-books is not in the *Rijksarchief* in The Hague, but at Middelburg in Zeeland.[3]

Nevertheless, the bulk of the Dutch-language manuscripts which relate to the history of Africa are to be found in the main Netherlands state repository, the *Rijksarchief.* These manuscripts fall into four main categories. To begin with there are the records of the first Netherlands West India Company, 1621-1674, which are of limited value only, partly because the Directors of this Company were more concerned with fighting Spain and Portugal at sea and with their colonizing ventures in North America and Brazil than with Africa, and partly because a contemporary historian, Joannes de Laet, destroyed a portion of the Company's official correspondence on the grounds that, since he had used it himself, it could be of no interest to posterity.[4] Next, there are the records of the second Netherlands West India Company, 1674-1791, which are more extensive. In addition to a very large body of material relating to ships, cargoes, manifests, invoices, account books, muster rolls, armaments, and the design, repair and upkeep of forts, they contain copies of all inward and outward correspondence passing between the Directors of the Company at Amsterdam and their subordinates in Africa, and the minutes of the Directors' *resolutiën,* or decisions, regarding policy and trade. After the demise of the second Company in 1791 and the establishment of the Kingdom of the Netherlands in 1814, the Dutch possessions in Africa ceased being the agencies of a trading company and became colonies of the Dutch Crown. From 1814 onwards, in consequence, the Dutch home records bearing on Africa are organized as are their counterparts in Great Britain, with sub-divisions corresponding to the various ministries concerned, Trade and Colonies, Foreign Affairs, Admiralty, and so on. This, the third section of the *Rijksarchief* collection, is useful mainly for the diplomatic history of Africa. Lastly, there is the vast series known as the *Archief van de Nederlandse bezittingen ter Kuste van Guinee* (Archive of the Dutch settlements on the Guinea Coast). This is the set of records kept at Elmina Castle, the headquarters of the

---

3 *Ibid.*

4 But see Engel Sluiter, "The Dutch Archives and American Historical Research," *Pacific Historical Review,* VI (1937), 31-32, who warns against exaggerating the extent of de Laet's vandalism.

Dutch administration on the Gold Coast, down to 1872, the year of the transfer of all Dutch possessions in West Africa to Great Britain. At the time of the transfer the entire Dutch archives, which as currently bound run to some thousands of volumes, were moved from Elmina Castle to The Hague.

From this description it will be clear that the total volume of Dutch manuscript material for African history is very considerable indeed. Yet to date surprisingly little use has been made of it. Charles R. Boxer,[5] J. G. Doorman,[6] Nicolaus Hadeler,[7] J. K. J. de Jonge,[8] W. R. Menkman,[9] and K. Ratelband[10] have drawn on the manuscript resources of the *Rijksarchief* for various purposes, chiefly for the elucidation of problems of colonial history. Ivor Wilks[11] and Douglas Coombs[12] have used parts of the same collection for work on Ghanaian history in the 17th-18th and 19th centuries respectively, and a number of scholars are looking into the Dutch sources at the present time. But so far only the surface has been scratched. The same is true, in still greater degree, of the materials for African history in the archives of Denmark, Germany and Scandinavia, while the records of the major colonial powers of

---

5 Charles R. Boxer, *Salvador de Sá and the Struggle for Brazil and Angola, 1602–1686* (London, 1952).

6 J. G. Doorman, "Die Niederländisch-West-Indische Compagnie an der Goldküste," *Tijdschrift voor Indische Taal-, Land- en Volkenkunde*, XL, 5-6 (1898), 390-496.

7 Nicolaus Hadeler, *Geschichte der holländischen Colonien auf der Goldküste, mit besonderer Berücksichtigung des Handels* (Bonn, 1904).

8 J. K. J. de Jonge, *Oorsprong van Nederlands Bezittingen op de Kust van Guinee in Herinnering Gebragt uit de Oorspronkelijke Stukken* ('s-Gravenhage, 1871).

9 W. R. Menkman, *De West-Indische Compagnie* (Amsterdam, 1947).

10 K. Ratelband (Ed.), *Vijf Dagregisters van het Kasteel Sao Jorge da Mina* (*Elmina*) *aan de Goudkust* (*1645–1647*) ('s-Gravenhage, 1953).

11 Ivor Wilks, "The Rise of the Akwamu Empire, 1650–1710," *Transactions of the Historical Society of Ghana*, III, 2 (1957), 99-136. Margaret Priestley and Ivor Wilks, "The Ashanti Kings in the Eighteenth Century: a Revised Chronology," *Journal of African History*, I, 1 (1960), 83-96.

12 Douglas Coombs, "The Place of the 'Certificate of Apologie' in Ghanaian History," *Transactions of the Historical Society of Ghana*, III, 3 (1958), 180-93. Douglas Coombs, *The Gold Coast, Britain and the Netherlands, 1850–1874* (London, 1963).

tropical Africa, Great Britain, France and Portugal, though better known, still contain whole areas of untouched material.

II. Employment of the European Sources to Date

This general neglect by professional historians of the European sources is a reflection of the misconceptions which they, in common with other observers of the African scene, held until quite recently about the continent they sought to study. Before the Second World War the approach of nearly all historians of Africa—there were some exceptions, such as Delafosse, Monteil, Palmer—was firmly "colonialist." Writers of that period concerned themselves with "European activities in Africa" to the exclusion of almost everything else. They saw the events in their narratives through the eyes of the administrator and soldier, the settler, trader and missionary. As a subject for academic inquiry, colonial history is, of course, entirely respectable, and there need have been nothing objectionable about the works these authors produced. But they made the mistake of equating the history of the colonizers with that of the colonized and assumed that, since the peoples of tropical Africa were non-literate, the history of the area could be written only from the records of the literate foreigners who discovered, penetrated, conquered, partitioned and occupied it. The colonial historians were unaware that tropical Africa had any past—or at least any past that could be dignified by the name "history"—before Europeans appeared on the scene.

The first to make a coherent and effective protest against the misconceptions and wrong emphases of colonial history were those exponents of African nationalism and Pan-Africanism who began expressing themselves in writing after the end of the War. Justifiably, the nationalists resented the stereotype of the continent which they read again and again in European history books, "the familiar idea," as Melville J. Herskovits put it, "of undifferentiated Africa as mostly jungle, overrun by great herds of wild animals, inhabited by human beings classed as 'savages.'"[13] They objected to the way in which the colonial historians portrayed the actions of

[13] Melville J. Herskovits, *The Human Factor in Changing Africa* (New York, 1962), 20.

Europeans as consistently good, and the actions of Africans as consistently bad. They saw that Africa must discover its own past and be proud of it, or else cultural independence from Europe would be unattainable even though political independence might be won. They demanded proof that the generally held view of tropical Africa as a primitive and barbarous land until touched by the magic wand of European civilization was false. This desire on the part of the nationalists to free African history from the strictures of colonial history was, and remains, a major preoccupation of those engaged in the search for the African Personality.[14]

By a natural swing of the pendulum some of the nationalists' early claims were hasty and exaggerated. There was a tendency to over-emphasise the contribution of ancient Africa to the mainstream of civilization, as, for example, in the ascription of an impossibly advanced technology to the Empire of Ghana.[15] But this was a passing phase, and the hard core of nationalist criticism of colonial history was entirely sound. The colonial historians failed to see any dynamic in African history because they did not expect to find one. They thought of Africans as passive agents in a process by which externally-sponsored economic, religious and educational innovations would in time produce results, but they did not expect that these results would be spectacular or quickly achieved. As late as 1951 Margery Perham could write in a *Foreign Affairs* article that it was "not a very bold speculation to believe" that the then British colonial territories in Africa would become "fully self-governing nation-states *by the end of the century*."[16] Because they saw no prospect of rapid development in the future, the colonial historians tended in their writings to subscribe to the myth of an unchanging African past.

It has not only been the African nationalists who have protested

---

[14] Joseph K. Zerbo, "Histoire et Conscience Nègre," *Présence Africaine*, 16 (Oct.-Nov. 1957), 53. See also I. Wallerstein, "La Recherche d'une Identité Nationale en Afrique Occidentale," *Présence Africaine*, 34-35 (Oct.-Jan. 1961), 79-91.

[15] On the general point see Herskovits, *Human Factor*, 458-59. My reference is to the well-known Earl Sweeting paintings, reproduced as picture-postcards by the Ghana National Archives.

[16] Margery Perham, "The British Problem in Africa," *Foreign Affairs*, XXIX, 4 (July 1951), 637. (My italics.)

against the presuppositions of colonial history. In the years following the War the colonialist emphases have been challenged from two other, and separate, points of view. In the first place, there has been a sustained assault on the moral perspective of the colonial historians. This attack has come mainly from Marxist writers, who are here following in a direct line from Lenin and other foes of economic imperialism. The current Marxist anti-colonial school uses substantially the same evidence as the colonial historians, but interprets it in a different, often totally contradictory, way. The result is a history of Africa with a different moral perspective, to be sure, but the approach adopted is still essentially "Eurocentric." European activities, policies and problems continue to occupy the centre of the stage, the difference being that these are now regarded as uniformly bad instead of uniformly good. In many ways the impact of the anti-colonial school has been healthy. It has helped to overthrow—more quickly, perhaps, than might have happened otherwise—some of the more offensive complacencies of the colonial historians. But its publications are as far from being true "African history" as were those it so violently attacks. In anti-colonial Marxist writings on Africa it is apparent, at any rate to the non-Marxist, that one systematic bias has merely been exchanged for another.[17]

Secondly, the colonialist approach has been rejected by those historians of Africa who criticize it for its failure to penetrate beyond the barrier which the absence of written records appears to impose. As their starting-point these writers have assumed that, if the past of the non-literate peoples of Africa is to be uncovered, the historian of the area must look to unwritten evidence. This type of source the colonial historians either disregarded or knew nothing about. Exponents of the "ethno-history" of Africa have thus been led to make a re-assessment of oral tradition, and have devised new methods for checking and controlling it.[18] Increasingly, they have sought aid from allied disciplines, such as archaeology, comparative anthro-

---

[17] For an example of the writings of the Marxist anti-colonial school see D. T. Niane et J. Suret-Canale, *Histoire de l'Afrique Occidentale* (Paris, 1961).

[18] See J. Vansina, "Recording the Oral History of the Bakuba—I. Methods," *Journal of African History*, I, 1 (1960), 43-51, and the same author's *De la Tradition Orale: Essai de Méthode Historique* (Tervuren, 1961).

pology, musicology, linguistics, botany, zoology and the history of art. In their attempt to go beyond the written word, they have made their greatest contributions so far in the pre-colonial period and, in more modern times, in areas where contact with Europeans has been non-existent or minimal.

A weakness of historical writing on tropical Africa to date has been its disparate or compartmentalized nature. Distinctions have been drawn between the prehistorical, protohistorical and historical eras, and between the pre-colonial period and the colonial. Like all time divisions of this kind, the periodization is arbitrary, yet in most works no easy transition from one period or era to another is made. The various types of African history, moreover, have up to now been largely written by different types of writers, the specialist training of the individual determining his choice of subject-matter. Few writers, for example, are equally at home in both the European-language records and the oral traditions and archaeology of the area of their study. Yet it is only by a successful tieing together of all types of inquiry that many of the problems of African history will be solved,[19] and the ideal achieved of a smoothly flowing narrative without the jolts and jars that at present characterize transitions from one type of evidence to another.

The key to the attainment of a truly autonomous and integrated history of tropical Africa is undoubtedly to be found in the proper use of the written sources, and it is not only European-language sources that are here involved. Recent research shows that materials in Arabic relating to tropical (as opposed to Sudanic) Africa are very much more numerous than was once supposed.[20] It is being discovered, moreover, that Arabic or Arabic-type script has in the

---

[19] Good examples of the simultaneous use of European sources and oral tradition are the article on "The Ashanti Kings in the Eighteenth Century," by Priestley and Wilks, already cited, and D. P. Abraham, "Maramuca: an Exercise in the Combined Use of Portuguese Records and Oral Tradition," *Journal of African History*, II, 2 (1961), 211-25.

[20] H. F. C. Smith, "A Neglected Theme of West African History: the Islamic Revolutions of the 19th Century," *Historians in Tropical Africa* (Proceedings of the Leverhulme Inter-Collegiate History Conference, Salisbury, Southern Rhodesia, 1962), 145-58, and the same author's frequent contributions from 1959 onwards to the *Bulletin of News* of the Historical Society of Nigeria.

past been used to write down several African languages previously thought to have either no literature at all or an inconsiderable quantity of it. In Northern Ghana, for example, documents at present being unearthed are in Dagbane, Mamprusi and even Guan, as well as in Arabic, Hausa and Fulani. Kings of West African forest states like Ashanti, it appears, made use from time to time of Muslim scribes in order to carry on diplomatic negotiations with their neighbour monarchs in the Islamic lands to the north. Some of this diplomatic correspondence is now turning up in Ghana. More may be found in the court archives of states like Segu, which were conquered by the French at the end of the nineteenth century and whose written records were removed to Paris at that time.[21]

So far as the European-language sources are concerned, those that have already been examined (in part, and for their own particular purposes) by the colonial historians must be studied again. Those that have never been used at all must be intensively investigated. Properly employed, the archives of the ex-colonial powers can be made to yield a wealth of information which the authors of the individual documents comprising those archives did not know they possessed. It is as true of African historiography as of any other that what one learns from a piece of historical evidence depends on the questions one puts to it.

III. The Potential of the European Sources

There are many different kinds of documents in the European colonial archives from which material for autonomous African history may be obtained. The following is an example of one such document. It is the text of a letter written (through an amanuensis) by Nana Osei Tutu Kwamina, King of Ashanti, to Herman Willem Daendels, the Dutch Govenor-General at Elmina Castle on the Gold Coast. At the time of writing (1816) a "palaver," or matter of contention, had arisen between Ashanti and the neighbouring state of Wassa, whose king was named Eltifor. A war had recently been fought between the Ashantis and the Fante people of the coast, who were under the half-hearted and largely ineffective protection of

[21] Ivor Wilks, in a communication to the Conference on the Teaching of History in Ghanaian Schools and Training Colleges, Legon, Ghana, April 1963.

British merchants residing at Cape Coast, Commany (modern Kommenda) and other places. The people of Elmina, traditionally hostile to the Fantes and allies of the Ashantis, were also under European protection, in this case that of the Dutch. The Wassas, who in the past had acknowledged the overlordship of Ashanti, had taken advantage of the general confusion to desert their Ashanti alliance, join the Fantes and attack Elmina.

The King of Ashanti thus found himself in a difficult situation, and his letter shows the incisive manner in which he dealt with it. He dictated his instructions to Willem Huydecoper, a First Assistant in the Dutch administration at Elmina, who had been sent to Kumasi, the Ashanti capital, in order to greet the King on behalf of the Governor-General, and propose to him, among other things, that a highway should be cut by Ashanti labour from the capital to the coast for the convenience of trade and that the Governor-General should pay a state visit to Ashanti as soon as possible. Huydecoper was a mulatto and spoke Twi, the language of the Ashantis, fluently. One can therefore be certain that he understood exactly what was in the King's mind when he took down the royal instructions. The original text is in Dutch.

Koemassie,
29 November 1816.

The King of Ashanti
to
His good friend the
Governor-General H. W.
Daendels, etc., etc.,
at Elmina.

My good friend,

Your honourable letter has been very well explained to me by W. Huydecoper. Your presence here will crown everything with success and good results will flow from your visit. Everything here will be at your service.

The highway will, according to your order and request, be begun next week. Eight days after the work has started, I will send you a report on how far it has proceeded. It is not intended, however, to carry the road farther than Insadjoesoe, for I await a reply from you concerning the Wassas. On receiving this I will continue the road to Great Commany. From here to Insadjoesoe is four days, and from that place to Elmina is nine days. We are leaving Denkyera on the right hand, since if we let the road go through Denkyera it would be much too long. It is now planned to go through Bekkwai, which is best.

Now we will speak about Tando. I sent this person to the Wassas to fetch my prisoners of war, and did not send him for any other purpose. I therefore repudiate all that he has done, and look to you to arrange matters for me in the best possible way. All the swearing and oath-drinking that has taken place I count as nothing.

With the Wassas I used not to have any palaver. When I last went out against the Fantes to exterminate them, my sister Adomma drank oath with these Wassas, and swore that there was no palaver between me and them, and that in consequence they must not go and ally themselves with any other people in order to fight against me. Then, when I was engaged in fighting the Fantes, I took a number of prisoners of war, amongst whom I found, to my surprise, various soldiers of Eltifor's. I did not make much of this, however, but rather sent the Wassas a slave and some jaw bones as a present, and in the end forgave them.

Then, when I was on my way back and had halted for the night at Assikoema, messengers came to me from Eltifor to thank me for the present of the slave and the jaw bones. I took these messengers with me to my capital, gave them various presents and bade them farewell. But after they had gone, other messengers came, one from Elmina and one from Accra. The Elminas gave me the following message:

> "That the Elminas greet the King, and wish to inform him that, while they were carrying some presents for him through the Wassa country, the Wassas stole away their presents and threatened them with death; that they had therefore gone to Accra by sea and had come from there hither; that the Wassas were now allied to the Fantes and Commanys and had attacked Elmina; that Elmina's sufferings were due to its Ashanti connection; and that the King of Ashanti had been insulted by these Wassas and he must come with his army and punish them."

I thereupon fitted out an army and sent all my generals with it to go and fight the Wassas. Then the Akims, who at that time were my subjects, allied themselves with the Aquapims. I had to recall the army, but I fitted it out again and sent it to fight the Fantes and afterwards to destroy English Commany and the Wassas. When this army of mine was at Abra, Your Excellency told it not to go against Commany, and out of respect for you I turned my army back and thus complied with your request. [I have also since refused to aid the Elminas with troops.]

But you will be able to read everything in Huydecoper's journal.

I pray you will forgive and forget all bad things, and our work will prosper. I expect your friendship above all else. The Wassa and Commany palavers I request you to settle for me: each of them for 190 perequins besides the 99 slaves and the powder and lead which the Commanys have taken from the Elminas.

My good friend, if the Commanys will not settle this palaver with you, I will supply men to the Elminas and they will put [the town of] Commany to death.

Praying God to grant you health, I name myself,

Your sincere friend
This is X the mark of
Say Quamin, King of Ashanti.

In our presence,
(Signed) W. Huydecoper,
P. Woortman.

P.S. My name is Say Toetoe. Quamin is the name of my birthday. The oldest Kings of Ashanti have always been good friends to the Hollanders. So never forget me, and I also will never forget you. Say Toetoe, Poekoe Tintin, Kwesie Boaroem, Say Coedjo[22]—these kings were like brothers to the Hollanders, and I am no less.

This document shows clearly that a state like Ashanti, for all that in the early nineteenth century it maintained few written records, nevertheless conducted its foreign relations at that period with sophistication and subtlety.

It would be misleading to imply that all Dutch-language manuscript materials possess a degree of interest for the modern historian of Africa comparable to this letter from the King of Ashanti of November 1816. Most of the Dutch documents are concerned with "European activities in Africa," usually of a petty, humdrum type. The Dutch, moreover, never controlled more than a small strip of territory along the western section of the Gold Coast, and Dutch agents were few, and less enterprising, in terms of places visited and distances travelled, than either the British or the French. Yet historians are finding increasingly that the Dutch sources can be made to yield useful information in ways that are often unexpected.

In the first place, the records are full of detailed reports on controversies between rival fort commanders and accounts of court

---

22 The Ashanti kings here referred to are Osei Tutu, Opoku Ware, Kusi Obodum and Osei Kojo who, according to the traditional accounts, were the first four kings of Ashanti after the union.

cases involving, say, a European on one side and an African on the other. The matters being argued may have lost their interest, but the details of the arguments, the evidence of the witnesses and the grounds of the judgments may be extremely significant. Here, for example, is what Miss Carson's guide says about Volume 62 in the "Register of letters despatched to the Directors of the West India Company, 1700-1789":

> Papers about the despatch of cargoes. Papers about the difficulties with the Portuguese. Papers about the despatch of slave ships . . . Records of the advice given by old natives about questions of ownership, etc.[23]

This source has not been examined, but a fair inference seems to be that the "advice given by old natives" might provide useful material for a historian of Ghanaian land tenure and inheritance.

Secondly, "official reports" by Dutch commercial agents and colonial servants often contain information of a scope far wider than is suggested by the word "official." The Dutch are, and were, a meticulous people. Every outgoing holder of a senior executive post had to provide for the benefit of his successor a *memorie van overgave,* or "handing-over report." In this he recorded not only an inventory of the guns, stores, buildings, etc., responsibility for which he was now transferring, but also any observations on local politics and practices which he felt might guide the officer taking over from him.

Thirdly, officials of the Dutch Gold Coast administration sent on diplomatic missions had to report frequently to their superiors and maintain a complete diary of day-to-day events. An ambassador to the court of an African king, for example, was obliged not only to keep a record of his official negotiations but also set down precisely what presents and "dashes" he gave and received during his stay. The fact that presents were exchanged is of small consequence, but from the lists of the presents themselves and, in particular, from their size and type, can often be deduced the relative power and

---

[23] Carson, *Materials,* 42. For a detailed description of the local Dutch archives at Elmina see R. Bijlsma, "Het Archief der Nederlandsche Bezittingen ter Kuste van Guinea," *Verslagen omtrent 's Rijks oude Archieven* ('s-Gravenhage, 1923), XLIV, Eerste Deel, 1921, Bijlage XI, 337-82.

standing in the community of the chiefs, linguists, army commanders, etc. surrounding the king. From this information, in turn, the historian can determine exactly who were the men that counted in a particular African state at a particular time, and is thereby assisted in working out such matters as the processes of state formation, transitions from military to civil type government, and the like.

This question of lists of presents is a good illustration of the general point that a European source may be of little value in itself, but takes on increased significance when used in conjunction with other types of evidence. The written document, normally the product of a foreign, non-African pen, may not contain much that is directly relevant to African history. But what it lacks in relevance it makes up for in chronological precision.[24] The simple statement in a European source that "so-and-so was destooled today" may provide a peg on which a whole pattern of oral tradition may be hung. Dutch and English, French, Danish, German or Portuguese reports of the same event can be compared and, in the case of Ghana history, the Dutch reports can sometimes even be compared with one another. For long periods at a time Dutch agents were stationed at Axim and Accra as well as at Elmina. The accounts provided by these agents of a happening in the interior of the Gold Coast may often be proved to have been influenced by the attitudes of the indigenous inhabitants of the towns where the agents resided. Thus in favourable cases a variety of checks on oral tradition can be obtained by juxtaposing written materials from different areas and in different languages.

Fourthly, not too much should be read into the fact that Europeans, until the nineteenth century, lived only on the coasts of Africa and did not, except occasionally, penetrate into the interior. These European residents were traders, and in competition with other traders.[25] The profit margins of the companies for which they worked were often small. No factor on the Guinea coast, for example, could build a new fort or open a new trading station

---

24 Abraham, Maramuca, 217.

25 See E. C. Martin, *The British West African Settlements, 1750–1821* (London, 1927), 45-46.

without permission from his principals at home, and such permission was not given unless a strong case could be made out. As part of their normal duties, therefore, agents of European commercial companies in West Africa were constantly writing appreciations of the total trading situation, not only in the areas they knew intimately on the coast, but also in the interior since, especially in the eighteenth century, a large part of West African purchasing power was centred on the states of the forest. From the European records, therefore, can be learnt a great deal about areas which no European ever visited, and the coastal factors were much better informed about the situation in the interior than has sometimes been supposed.[26]

Finally, it must never be forgotten that for the world of scholarship as a whole Africa has long been under the wing of its neighbour, Asia. The International Congress of Africanists has only recently broken free from its parent, the International Congress of Orientalists,[27] and several famous European booksellers still list their "Africa" books in catalogues marked "Orientalia." This situation is not only a reflection of the comparative newness of African studies. It finds a parallel in the relationship that used to exist in the era of European expansion between Europe on the one hand and Africa and the more distant parts of the world on the other. In the days of sailing ships the West Coast of Africa was a frequent port of call for vessels going to the Caribbean and South America, and to India, Southeast Asia and the Far East. From European descriptions of "the world beyond" written from the fifteenth to the eighteenth centuries, therefore, one can often glean information about Africa, even though the title of the work to hand may contain no reference to the continent at all. This is particularly true of travellers' accounts, encyclopaedic compilations and the reports of explorers and navigators. A work entitled "Voyage to the East Indies," or "Exact description and narrative account of the Dutch (French, English,

---

[26] Margaret Priestley, "Trade and Politics on the Gold Coast in the Eighteenth Century: a Survey of Contemporary Evidence," *Historians in Tropical Africa* (Proceedings of the Leverhulme Inter-Collegiate History Conference, Salisbury, Southern Rhodesia, 1962), 287.

[27] See I. I. Potekhin, "Toward the First International Congress of Africanists," *African Studies Bulletin*, V, 3 (Oct., 1962), 34-35.

etc.) possessions in the East and West Indies," or even "The great and famous voyage round the world performed in the years such-and-such by the honourable Captain so-and-so" often proves to contain useful, and sometimes unique, material on Africa.

These are only some of the ways in which the European-language sources can be made to yield information for the new-style, autonomous history of tropical Africa. As suggested above, the reaction against a Eurocentric and biassed colonialist approach produced on the one hand nationalistic and anti-colonial history anxious to "set the African record straight," and on the other an intensive quest for a new methodology and new tools of research with which to uncover a past which it was believed conventional historical inquiry could not penetrate. The stage has now been reached when the European sources can, as it were, come into their own again. They provide, above all, the time-scale, the precise chronology without which the results of ethno-historical inquiry must necessarily remain vague, and the controlling framework of hard, unassailable fact into which the findings of research in other disciplines can be fitted.

IV.

African Colonization in the Nineteenth Century: Liberia and Sierra Leone

by

JOHN D. HARGREAVES

Professor of History, King's College, Aberdeen, Scotland

SIERRA LEONE AND LIBERIA[1] are the two outstanding examples of attempts to found on the African coast settlements of Africans who had been expatriated as slaves, and of descendants of such.[2] Both countries have been subjected to much derogatory criticism from foreign observers, though both have at various times found warm defenders. On the whole, most observers since 1870 (at least until recent years) have tended to judge the British colony of Sierra Leone a greater success than the Liberian Republic. The last three or four decades of the nineteenth century saw Sierra Leone Creoles exercising commercial and cultural influence through very extensive areas of west Africa; their far-ranging presence is attested by the very witnesses who judged them unfavourably. But in these years the range of Liberian influence became if anything restricted; even the survival of the Republic seemed doubtful.

A number of historians have recently worked to make the Sierra Leonean achievement more widely understood and appreciated.[3] But surprising little research on Liberian history has been published[4] (surprisingly in view of the flowering of African studies in the United States, where so many of the documentary sources may

---

[1] The work on which this paper is based was begun in the United States during the summer of 1961 with the assistance of a grant from the Carnegie Trust for the Universities of Scotland, to whom I wish to express my most sincere gratitude. An earlier version of the paper appeared in *Sierra Leone Studies*, No. 16, June 1962.

[2] The French settlement of recaptives at Libreville was on a very much smaller scale. B. Schnapper, *La Politique et le Commerce Français dans le Golfe de Guinée de 1838 à 1871*, (Paris & La Haye, 1961), 97 ff. Some Liberated Africans were also settled in the Gambia, but these settlements were much more varied in composition.

[3] Above all C. H. Fyfe, *A History of Sierra Leone* (London, 1962).

[4] But see D. F. McCall, "Liberia: An Appraisal," *Annals*, CCCVI, American Academy of Political and Social Science, July 1956, I am indebted to Professor McCall and to other members of Boston University's African Studies Program, for searching criticism of a draft of this paper.

be found). The present essay (based, on its Liberian side, solely on a selective reading of printed material), attempts to draw some comparisons between the experience of the two settlements up to about 1870, and to suggest possible explanations for their divergent fortunes thereafter.

The Common Background

The coast along which both states were founded lies within the tropical forest-belt, south and west of the highlands where the Niger, Gambia, and Senegal rivers rise. The early European contacts appear to have occurred towards the close of a period of migration and dispersion of peoples; in this area the units of political authority were generally small, and there seemed to be great heterogeneity of language and culture. The appearance probably exaggerated the reality; societies like Poro provided some bonds of unity across political and even linguistic boundaries, while itinerant Muslim traders provided contact with the states of the western Sudan. As the coastal trade with Europe developed, ivory, gold and hides came down from the interior, while dye-woods were cut in the coastal forest and trade in pepper led Europeans to coin the name of "Grain Coast." But by the eighteenth century the economy of the region was dominated by the slave trade, although both the total numbers exported and the proportion of slaves to total exports were smaller than in other parts of west Africa.

The existence of a subsidiary trade in African produce on a thinly populated and supposedly fertile coast helps to explain the development of African colonization in this particular region. During the later eighteenth century schemes for commercial and agricultural development in Africa became increasingly popular with European businessmen, philanthropists and statesmen. Some of these schemes included the planting of colonists; and—especially after the disastrous Bulama enterprise of 1792—many people believed the most suitable colonists would be free or liberated Negroes from outside Africa. Sierra Leone, promoted by the increasingly active anti-slavery lobby of English Evangelicals, was the first successful application of this idea of associating colonization with the diffusion of commerce, civilization and Christianity.

THE AMERICAN BACKGROUND TO LIBERIA

Parallel ideas were current in the newly independent United States. From 1786 onwards there were suggestions that American Negroes should be sent to joint the Colony of Sierra Leone: in 1817 a Congressional Committee urged the newly formed American Colonization Society to investigate this possibility.[5] That Society preferred an independent settlement of its own; after an unsuccessful attempt on Sherbro Island in 1820, it secured its site at Cape Mesurado in December 1821. But some of its more earnestly Evangelical sponsors regarded the new colony as a parallel enterprise to Sierra Leone; its growth was expected to assist the civilizing of Africa, as well as offering Negro emigrants opportunities which they could not hope to enjoy in the contemporary United States.

Yet these were not the whole purpose of the colonization movement in America, and the complexity of the domestic background created peculiar difficulties for the Liberian settlements. Granville Sharp had first promoted colonization in Sierra Leone out of concern for Africans left impoverished in London; but the problems of free Negroes in the United States soon developed on a far larger scale. In 1790 there were 59,527, but by 1820 they numbered 233,634 out of a total Negro population of 1,771, 656, and a United States population of 9,618,000; they were most heavily concentrated in mid-Atlantic states, north and and south of the Mason-Dixon line, and to a growing extent in parts of the Middle West.[6] It was in hope of removing this unassimilated and discordant element from

---

[5] Letters from W. Thornton to J. C. Lettsom, 1786-1789, in T. J. Pettigrew, *Memoirs of Lettsom* (London, 1817), II, 497-540. E. L. Fox, *The American Colonization Society, 1817–1840* (Baltimore, 1919), 40-42, 52, 67. C. J. Foster, "The Colonization of Free Negroes in Liberia," *Journal of Negro History* XXXVIII (1953), 43. Report of Congressional Committee on the Slave Trade, Feb. 11, 1817, printed in *A View of Exertions Lately Made for the Purpose of Colonizing the Free People of Colour in the United States, in Africa or Elsewhere* (Washington, 1817). On the Colonization Society the best general source of information, published since this paper was first drafted, is P. J. Staudenraus, *The African Colonization Movement,* 1816–1865 (New York, 1961).

[6] For general discussion of the problems of free Negroes in this period, see J. H. Franklin, *From Slavery to Freedom* (New York, 1948), ch. XIV.

United States society—if not to Africa, then to Haiti or some remote quarter of the American continent—that influential Southerners like Jefferson, Clay and Randolph (and many Northerners and Westerners too) supported plans for colonization.[7] While some colonizationists sincerely hoped to encourage the manumission of slaves by providing facilities for their expatriation, others were chiefly anxious to be rid of potential trouble-makers.

The American Colonization Society therefore found itself trying to achieve varied and even contradictory aims, among which the hope of developing and civilizing Africa was inevitably pushed into a subordinate role. Bostonians might support missionary work in Liberia, and equip colonists with farm implements, books, tools and printing materials;[8] the officers of the Society were largely pre-occupied with retaining nation-wide support in the United States. Too much hostility to slavery would doom the Society throughout the South; too open an acquiescence would damage its reputation with Northern reformers. Its compromise position—"neither to destroy nor to perpetuate"[9]—was actually less morally equivocal than it sounds; only through such ambiguity could Northerners and Southerners be drawn to seek a gradual reduction of slavery. There seemed a genuine possibility that in those border-states where slavery had already served its economic purpose, the attractive power of overseas colonies of freed slaves might encourage, not merely manumissions by individual proprietors, but the gradual undermining of slavery itself.[10]

This was probably illusory. Even in the border states, support for colonization seems to have been strong only at periods of racial tension, such as slave revolts. Such a boom followed Nat Turner's insurrection of 1831, which killed more than fifty white Virginians; even here, it was notably stronger in the non-slave-holding sections of the state. But soon afterwards the great rise in slave-prices in the cotton states provided a far more profitable channel for

---

[7] Report of inaugural meeting of A.C.S., Dec. 21, 1816, in *A View of Exertions* . . . see B. Dyer, "The Persistence of the Idea of Negro Colonization," *Pacific Historical Review,* XII (1943); Foster, "Colonization," *passim.*

[8] Staudenraus, *Colonization,* 121-24.

[9] *Ibid.,* 174.

[10] Cf. Fox, *Society,* 11-12, 113.

disposing of surplus slaves.[11] At the same time, the impassioned attacks of W. L. Garrison, who denounced Colonization as a hypocritical plan for making the slave system even more secure, swung many earnest Northern supporters over into the Abolitionist movement, dividing the critics of slavery along partially sectional lines. During the tensions of the 1850's and the Civil War itself there was a somewhat despairing revival of interest, though more in schemes for re-settlement within the Americas than in specifically African colonization. Lincoln himself hoped that these might provide the basis for some humane form of apartheid.[12]

In retrospect, all these plans for exporting American racial problems seem to have been unrealistic, for three good reasons. The first—the physical and financial problems of providing transport and reception facilities for a really substantial part of the Negro population—might theoretically have been overcome, though practically this never seemed likely. The second reason—the continuing demand for slave labour in the cotton states, and the consequent great increase in America's Negro population—might alone have been decisive. The final crippling difficulty was the reluctance of free Afro-Americans to leave the country which, despite all their handicaps and humiliations, they had come to regard as their own. As early as 1817 Philadelphia Negroes (who had earlier shown readiness to support "any commercial enterprise desirable for the purpose of civilizing Africa"), firmly rejected colonization as a "circuitous route" back to bondage;[13] and later Negro leaders in the Northern cities, with exceptions like the Reverend Alexander Crummell,[14] joined the Abolitionists in charging the Colonization

---

[11] S. M. Elkins, *Slavery* (Chicago, 1959), 209-12.

[12] See especially his "Address on Colonization to a Deputation of Negroes," Aug. 14, 1862, in R. P. Basler (ed.), *The Collected Works of Abraham Lincoln* (5 vols., New Brunswick, 1953), V, 370-75. J. G. Randall, *Lincoln the President* (London, 1945), II, 137-41. For Mid-Western support for colonization, see D. Christy, *Ethiopia: Her Gloom and Glory* (Cincinnati, 1857), esp. 250-55, Memorial of March 1, 1855.

[13] Staudenraus, *Colonization*, 34.

[14] A. Crummell, *The Relations and Duties of Free Colored Men in America to Africa,* (Hartford, 1861); see G. Shepperson, "Notes on Negro American Influences on the Emergence of African Nationalism," *Journal of African History,* I (1960), 301-02.

Society with self-interested hypocrisy.[15] Meanwhile Southern freedmen "voted with their feet"—in the negative. Voluntary emigrants to Liberia were usually difficult to obtain, though the number increased after 1831 (out of fear of reprisals for Turner's insurrection), and again in mid-century.[16] The American Colonization Society estimated that, of 11,909 emigrants sent up to 1866, 4541 were born free, 344 purchased freedom, and 5957 were emancipated on the express condition that they emigrated.[17]

Differences in Immigrant Population

Apologists for Liberian failings have sometimes pointed to the difficulties of this latter group, suggesting that men suddenly and perhaps involuntarily transferred from plantation life could hardly be expected to prove energetic and enterprising citizens of a new frontier colony in Africa. This may be true; even so, Liberia received more immigrants with experience of personal freedom in a western country than Sierra Leone. The most important such group there was the 1131 Nova Scotians, who arrived together in 1792: they were an independent-minded community, largely ex-servicemen of the American war, deeply Evangelical in religion, British in allegiance, yet suspicious of British promises. The 550 Maroons who arrived in 1800 came from a community which had resisted the Jamaican government intermittently but with success over 140 years; though noted for their discipline and cohesion, they had known colonial society chiefly as its enemies. The only other Sierra Leoneans to arrive from outside Africa during the nineteenth century came in small groups. Of the "Black Poor" sent by Sharp from London to the abortive settlement of 1787, Kuckzynski estimates that no more than 65 survived to join the Colony of 1792; the

---

15 E.g., S. E. Cornish & T. E. Wright, *The Colonization Scheme Considered in Its Rejection by the Colored People. . . .* (Newark, N. J., 1840).

16 Foster, "Colonization," 55-56. H. H. Bell, "The Negro Emigration Movement, 1849–54," *Phylon,* XX (1959). Annual emigration figures are reprinted by Staudenraus, *Colonization,* 251.

17 C. H. Huberich, *The Political and Legislative History of Liberia* (N. Y. 1947), I, 41. This does not include 1227 sent by the Maryland Colonization Society to its settlement near Cape Palmas, which was separate until 1857. On emancipations, see Fox, *Society,* ch. IV; Staudenraus, Colonization, 114.

Afro-American Paul Cuffee took 38 freedmen to Freetown in 1816; and throughout the century there was a small trickle of immigrants, some of them gifted, from the West Indies.[18]

Descendants of these settlers long retained some sense of social superiority; but on the whole it was not they who played the greatest roles in Sierra Leone's nineteenth century development. After Parliament began to legislate against the slave trade, the Colony received a stream of new settlers in the shape of recaptives or Liberated Africans; 60,000 arrived up to 1840, Kuckzynski estimates, although only 37,000 were still living there at that date. Some settled in the new villages of the Sierra Leone peninsula; others prospered in commerce, not only in Freetown, but along the whole West African coast; their children, the Creoles, largely provided West Africa with its first professional class. In Liberia only 5722 recaptives were landed at all, more than 3000 of them in somewhat difficult circumstances in 1860-61.[19] Some of the earlier arrivals were settled in the village of New Georgia, near Monrovia, described by the Agent in 1832 as "the most contented and independent of any in the colony . . . rapidly improving in intelligence and respectability." Though they inter-married with Americo-Liberians, and adopted many of their customs, they retained distinctive institutions too; in 1834 Agent Pinney agreed that Iboes and Congoes should elect their own headmen.[20] Their role in Liberian history has never been studied; but clearly as a community they do not compare with the dynamic recaptives of Sierra Leone.

One last difference in population was that, whereas Sierra Leone usually contained something of the order of one hundred European civilians, there were few white men in Liberia except missionaries and, in early years, the Colonization Society's Agents. It is true

---

[18] R. R. Kuckzynski, *Demographic Survey of the British Colonial Empire*, I (Oxford, 1948), 154. On all these groups see C. H. Fyfe, *History*, *passim*.

[19] Cf. W. D. Boyd, "The American Colonization Society and the Slave Recaptives of 1860–61 . . . ," *Journal of Negro History*, XLVII (1962), Appendix.

[20] Huberich, *Liberia*, ch. XVI. A. Alexander, *A History of Colonization on the Western Coast of Africa* (Philadelphia, 1846), 378-79, report by Mechlin, 1832. S. Wilkeson, *A Concise History of . . . the American Colonies in Liberia* (Washington, 1839), 56-57, 82. J. W. Lugenbeel, *Sketches of Liberia* (2d ed., Washington, 1953).

that these pious and dedicated men often played dominant roles: but after J. J. Roberts became Governor for the Society in 1841, the settlement was administered by Americo-Liberians. There is mention of one white American settler, married to a Negro woman, and later in the century there were Europeans in charge of German, Dutch and British trading establishments; but to a greater extent than their neighbours, Liberians were free from the competition, advice, and example of resident white laymen.[21]

Agriculture and Reasons for its Failure

These, broadly, are some of the differences in origin and background between the two colonies. How did their actual development compare? The sponsors of both attached great importance to the development of agriculture,[22] which they hoped would provide a secure livelihood for the colonists, and a sound Jeffersonian foundation for society: also a flourishing export trade from which some of them hoped to profit. Jehudi Ashmun, the zealous young clergyman who guided Liberia through some of its early difficulties, found time to write *The Liberian Farmer*, a pamphlet of simple practical advice on agricultural methods and the care of possible crops.[23] Though tropical agricultural science was nowhere well developed at this time, much of Ashmun's advice seems to have been quite well adapted to Liberian conditions. In particular, there seemed to be good prospects of extending the cultivation of the indigenous variety of coffee; but it was only when the Ceylon coffee-leaf disease spread through Asian plantations after 1869 that Liberian coffee was able to make much headway in the world market. Exports then rose rapidly, according to figures obtained by the Colonization Society's Agent in 1892:—

---

[21] Kuckzynski, *Survey*, 178-87. H. Bridge, *Journal of an African Cruiser* (N. Y. & London, 1845), 33. For an estimate of the number of Europeans in trade see *Liberia* (Bulletin of the American Colonization Society), No. 6, Washington, 1895; letter of Clement Irons.

[22] In both countries iron deposits were known to exist from the early nineteenth century, but these were left commercially undiscovered and undeveloped until well into the twentieth century.

[23] Reprinted as Appendix 7 to R. R. Gurley, *Life of Jehudi Ashmun* (Washington, 1825). Also see 128-33 of the Appendix; Huberich, *Liberia*, I, 365-66.

1855: under	5000 lbs.
1865:	23,400 lbs.
1875: over	100,000 lbs.
1885: over	800,000 lbs.
1892: over	1,800,000 lbs.

"There are at present few male citizens who do not own and operate a coffee plantation," he reported.[24] But this was bonanza development; a few years later Indonesian producers had re-stocked their plantations, and the vast development of the Brazilian coffee industry was under way, supported by foreign capital. Meanwhile Liberians seem to have done nothing to improve the efficiency of their plantations or their marketing organization: as so often when African farmers have sought direct access to world markets, there were complaints of inadequate or careless preparation of the crop. As world prices fell from around twenty cents a pound to as low as five cents, Liberian exports collapsed once more to under 500,000 lbs.[25]

This is a familiar story in West Africa, very similar indeed to that of Sierra Leonean ginger. The instability of world prices and market conditions, rather than physical difficulties or human failings, have been the chief cause of that failure of peasant agriculture which foreign observers so regularly regretted.[26] Even so, failure has never been total. Visitors to Liberia in the 1830's frequently referred to the spread of cultivation; even in 1849 R. R. Gurley of the Colonization Society, visiting Liberia as government Commissioner, observed "substantial farmhouses surrounded by well-cleared and cultivated plantations of from ten to thirty and fifty or seventy acres," along the St. Paul's River and elsewhere.[27] But peasant agriculture was not particularly rewarding. Since many African food crops were unattractive to America-bred palates, even the

---

[24] Report by Rev. E. E. Smith, *Liberia*, No. 1, Nov. 1892.

[25] Report by G. W. Ellis, Jr., *ibid.* No. 26, Feb. 1905. Cf. H. H. Johnston, *Liberia* (London, 1906), Vol. I, 602-03; G. W. Brown, *The Economic History of Liberia* (Washington, 1941), 158, where different figures are cited.

[26] Cf. Fyfe, *History*, 259, 353-54, 466-67.

[27] Gurley to Clayton, Feb. 15, 1850 (U.S. Congress; 31st Congress, 1st Session. Executive Document No. 75). Cf. Huberich, *Liberia* I, 666 ff; Buchanan, to A.C.S., May 17, 1839.

local market was not secure; rice could sometimes be bought more cheaply from local African producers.[28] As in Sierra Leone, far greater rewards could be achieved by success in commerce. "In agriculture," Gurley was told, "little more is done than to supply ourselves with the necessaries and a few of the conveniences of life."

Agriculture might have been made more remunerative by greater applications of capital and technical skill to sizeable plantations; but since the available land was limited (especially in Sierra Leone), this would have involved encouraging social inequalities, and possibly undue dependence on foreign capitalists. (Liberia finally decided to face these risks after the first World War). Nevertheless, even in Sierra Leone the nineteenth century saw a few attempts at larger-scale farming, all more or less abortive: at first with European capital, later by wealthy Africans like Moses Pindar Horton and Samuel Lewis.[29] In Liberia, where land was less scarce, immigrants could apparently obtain large holdings more easily and there may have been ideas of introducing the plantation system as they had known it in the American South; in 1838 Lewis Sheridan, a wealthy freedman from North Carolina, was granted a long lease on six hundred acres. But here the labour needed for the care of crops cost up to sixty cents a day, and was not easy to come by.[30] The reasons for agricultural failure deserve more study; but clearly no attempt at large-scale farming in either country achieved sustained success in the nineteenth century.

Transportation: The Steamship

No export trade in perishable agricultural produce could be expected to flourish without regular transportation facilities to overseas markets and sources of credit. In this respect Sierra Leone, an established port of call for British and other African shipping,

[28] J. W. Lugenbeel, *Liberia,* 15.

[29] N. A. Cox-George, *Finance and Development in West Africa; the Sierra Leone Experience* (London, 1961), 131-36. See Fyfe, *History,* 354, 422, 490, 506, 525, 536; J. D. Hargreaves, *A Life of Sir Samuel Lewis* (London, 1958), 26-28.

[30] Wilkeson, *History,* 74. Huberich, *Liberia,* I, 345-46; 414-17. Bridge, *Journal,* 44 ff, 96.

had certain advantages over Liberia. Voyages to Liberia from American ports were quite frequent in the early years of the settlements, but many seem to have depended on business provided by the Colonization Societies on the outward journey, and the absence of predictable schedules must have impeded any Liberian attempts to find regular outlets for their exports in the United States.[31] As early as 1822 Ashmun proposed that the Colonization Society should grant a monopoly of Liberia's foreign commerce to the Baltimore Trading Company (in whose service he then was): they could then stipulate for four regular annual voyages, which would carry produce, supplies and new colonists on the Society's behalf, as well as bringing home camwood from the forests and produce from the farms. But the Society, anxious to retain its support from merchants in New York, Philadelphia and Boston as well as in Baltimore, could not agree to exclude any of these ports from that Liberian trade whose prospects it was depicting so favourably.[32] In 1846 the Chesapeake and Liberian Trading Company was founded in Baltimore—evidently as a semi-philanthropic venture, for there were hopes of attracting Negro capital and employing Negro crews; but its voyages were somewhat irregular, and it apparently did not survive the wreck of its ship in 1853.[33]

By this time, steamship promoters were preparing to enter the west African trade. In August 1850 the Naval Committee of the House of Representatives supported a proposal from the Colonization Society that the United States should subsidize the development of quarterly steamship service to West Africa from New York, Baltimore, and New Orleans, on the grounds that this would both encourage steamship construction in the United States and assist colonization and American commerce in Liberia.[34] But it was the African Steamship Company which, in 1852, included Liberian

---

[31] Mr. G. H. Brooks, Jr., although he does not discuss trade with Liberia in his doctoral thesis on "American Legitimate Trade with West Africa, 1789–1914" (Boston University, 1962), suggests that many American merchants avoided the settlements because of doubts as to their credit-worthiness.

[32] Gurley, *Ashmun,* 117, 161; App., 39-44. Staudenraus, *Colonization,* 158-61.

[33] G. S. Stockwell, *The Republic of Liberia* (New York, 1868), 222-27.

[34] U.S. Congress. Report of the Naval Committee to the House of Representatives, August 1850.

ports in the slower of its new scheduled steamship services from Britain; after 1879 the house of Woermann, already active in Liberian trade, introduced steam services from Hamburg and with their help developed a commanding position in Liberian trade.[35] This orientation of Liberian trade and communications towards Europe may have tended to discourage the inflow of commercial capital, and possibly immigrants, from the United States.

These steamship voyages began about the time when Liberians were beginning to build their own sailing ships, capable not only of coastal voyages but of reaching Liverpool and New York; and it has been argued that the steamers ruined this most promising development of Liberian enterprise.[36] But, even if it is assumed that these new products of Western technology might have been permanently excluded from Liberia, it is difficult to see that these enterprising local shippers could ever have secured more than a limited share of their own country's carrying trade, or that the re-investment of their profits would have been sufficient to trigger off real economic growth in other sections of the Liberian economy. On the other hand, the new cheap and regular transport services lowered the costs of taking Liberian produce to world markets, and, in the short run at least, made it easier for small African traders to compete directly in that trade. If prices to producers fell at this time, this was not due to the steamers—logical though it might seem locally to blame them—but to the instability of world market prices, already identified as perhaps the major handicap to West African economic development.

Comparison of African Commercial Enterprise

This point is underlined if the progress of Liberian commerce is compared with that of Sierra Leone. Many friends of the Liberians were confident that they would prosper more than their neighbours, since their independent status enabled them to protect themselves against foreign competition. By the constitution of 1847, citizenship in Liberia was restricted to "persons of colour," and

[35] P. E. Schramm, *Deutschland und Übersee* (Braunschweig, 1950), 237-43, 372-73.

[36] Brown, *Liberia,* 118, 134-35, 141-42; McCall, *Liberia,* 90.

restrictions were placed upon the commercial activities of foreigners. At first the external trade of Sierra Leone had indeed been virtually a British monopoly. But after the failure of Macaulay and Babington in 1827, few European firms of any size traded directly in Sierra Leone until late in the century; instead, foreign capital was used to extend commercial credit to independent Freetown merchants. Liberated Africans, prospering by their enterprise in retail trade, increasingly moved into larger operations and used steamships to develop direct connections with European exporters. The very dependence of the Sierra Leone economy upon Great Britain thus assisted the rise of a well-to-do African commercial class, who played such a notable part in diffusing the cultural and commercial influence of the Colony not only in the immediate vicinity, but on the lower Niger and through much of West Africa.[37]

It seems that the Liberians may have got off to a quicker start than the Sierra Leoneans in reaping what Ashmun called "the precarious gains of this country traffic." In 1831 a new colonist commented on how quickly young settlers learned "drive as hard a bargain, as any roving merchant from the land of steady habits, with his assortment of tin ware, nutmegs, books or dry goods." The sentiment will be familiar to any student of nineteenth century Sierra Leone but hardly at such an early date. There are references to substantial fortunes made by such men as J. J. Roberts, first President of the Republic; the Reverend C. M. Waring, a Baptist preacher turned trader; Sheriff Francis Devaney, who declared in 1830 that he would not accept $20,000 for his business; and Colonel Hicks, a former slave from Kentucky turned commission merchant, who in 1844 impressed American naval officers by his gracious hospitality.[38] But it is notable that these names rarely appear among the prominent Liberians of later generations. (If Liberian history were studied with the painstaking attention to biographical and family history that Mr. Fyfe has devoted to

---

[37] C. H. Fyfe, History, 266-67 & *passim*; also his "Four Sierra Leone Recaptives," *Journal of African History*, II (1961); "The Life and Times of John Ezzidio," *Sierra Leone Studies*, IV (1955); "European and Creole Influences in the Hinterland of Sierra Leone before 1896," VI (1956).

[38] Staudenraus, *Colonization*, 153-55; Alexander, *Colonization*, 338 ff; Bridge, *Journal*, 96-98.

Sierra Leone, we might learn a great deal about the subsequent decline).

Trade figures are too unreliable for precise comparison; but in 1831 and 1832 Liberian exports were estimated, respectively, at $125,549 and $88,911, compared to figures for Sierra Leone of £81,000 and £58,920. Moreover, much of the profit of Sierra Leone's trade still went to Europeans. Very roughly, Sierra Leone was exporting over three times as much as Liberia, though her settled population was more than ten times as large. Since literary evidence suggests that agriculture for the local market was at this time more productive in Liberia, it seems that settlers there still enjoyed appreciably higher standards of income per head. As outward signs of this, Monrovia, during the 1830's and '40's, was building churches and schools, public offices and frame-houses of distinctive architectural style. There were libraries and debating societies; the *Liberia Herald* was well-established as a newspaper at a time when Sierra Leone's *Gazette* had ceased publication. Comparing the two colonies in 1834, F. H. Rankin concluded that "the American settlement is decidedly far in the advance with regard to intellectual cultivation." But he noted that the Liberians, unlike the majority of Sierra Leoneans, had brought with them from America "a stock of civil and social knowledge, as well as an impulse to improvement," and rightly foresaw changes in the relative condition of the two settlements.[39]

During the second half of the century, these changes were reflected in comments by foreign observers. Though reliable figures are hard to find, it seems clear that Liberia's foreign trade developed slowly after 1850, while Sierra Leone's increased appreciably though erratically.[40] By the 1870's visitors were no longer praising the enterprise of Liberian traders; they rather tended to complain that a commercial oligarchy was controlling the trade and government of the state. Winwood Reade, in 1870, was well-disposed towards the Liberians, and he conceded that their settlements were "respectable and well-ordered": but he feared that their economy was stagnant and that

---

[39] F. H. Rankin, *The White Man's Grave* (London, 1836), 1, 36-40.
[40] Cox-George, *Finance*, 142-44.

> Nothing can save them from perdition except the throwing open of the land; the free admission of European traders and of negro settlers from Sierra Leone; or in other words, the free admission of capital and labour.[41]

External Support and Finance

Some conditions which may explain why Liberia fell behind nineteenth-century Sierra Leone in wealth and influence have already been mentioned; but possibly the most important was her ambiguous relationship to the United States. The original aim of the Colonization Society was to win substantial financial support from the Federal government; hence its efforts to appease all sections of the country, so that it could claim nation-wide public approval. But its purpose was too controversial to succeed; not only was its attitude to slavery unacceptable both in New England and in the Deep South, but the proposals for Federal aid touched off controversies about the proper power of the Federal government. Subsidies were indeed secured for the re-settlement of Liberated Africans, totalling $264,710 in the years 1819-29. Thanks to the efforts of W. H. Crawford, President Monroe's Secretary of the Treasury, these funds were used indirectly to assist the settlement of Americo-Liberians also; in particular they subsidized the fortification of Monrovia, and military operations against slave-dealers which made the colony's power respected in the 1820's. But not until 1858, on the eve of the Civil War, were new Federal funds obtained by the Society; these were to assist emigration, and could not be applied directly to support the government of Liberia. State governments at various times gave some assistance to emigration; Maryland voted its State Colonization Society a total of $443,883 over the period 1831-57. But essentially the Society's funds depended on private contributions, which they always knew to be "inadequate to the consummation of our design." Hence from the 1830's the Liberian settlements found they had to bear the expenses of their own government—not as a matter of principle, but because little American money was available.[42]

---

[41] W. W. Reade, *The African Sketchbook* (London, 1873), 11, 260; see his letter encl. in C.O. 267/313, Foreign Office to Colonial Office, Feb. 28, 1871.

[42] Staudenraus, *Colonization,* 24 ff; 50-58; 150-51; 178; 242-46; 118; 224-25.

It may be objected that the government of Sierra Leone too was expected to be financially self-supporting. This was certainly the ruling principle of the nineteenth century Treasury, but it was not completely applied. The Liberated African Department received grants totalling over £350,000 during the century; the ordinary civil budget received substantial subsidies during the early years of Crown Colony government; and even after Treasury control was tightened in the 1860's, it could still exact a reluctant grant-in-aid if that seemed the only means by which a respectable government could be carried on. Larger still was the British government's military expenditure in Sierra Leone; as Dr. Cox-George has pointed out, this represented a substantial injection of purchasing power into the economy, as well as a direct reinforcement of governmental power.[43] Finally, there were concealed subsidies not appearing in the colonial accounts—notably the cost of local naval operations against slave-traders and in support of legitimate commerce. In all these ways, the British government contributed heavily to the establishment of ordered government and the expansion of Sierra Leonean influence.

Lacking such support, the Liberians could hope to finance a government capable of protecting an expanding trade only by imposing customs duties. It was the reluctance of foreign merchants to recognize the validity of duties imposed by a government sponsored only by the American Colonization Society which prompted the proclamation of Liberia as an independent Republic in 1847.[44] But this solved no problems. Merchants trading on the long coastline claimed by the new state would not willingly accept taxation without some return, notably in the form of protection against those coastal Africans who had long regarded it as their prescriptive right to plunder vessels wrecked or stranded on their shores. Yet the Liberian government could not provide effective protection without receiving funds to build up military, police and preventive services. As a beginning, it attempted in 1865 to confine foreign trade to six "ports of entry"; predictably, chiefs and traders alike

---

Fox, *Society*, 57 ff. J. H. T. MacPherson, *History of Liberia* (Baltimore, 1891), 31 ff.

[43] Cox-George, *Finance*, ch. 6 and p. 164.

[44] Cf. Huberich, *Liberia*, I, ch. V.

resented and evaded this restriction, (which some alleged was designed to strengthen the "merchant oligarchy" in these six Liberian ports).[45] Foreign merchants continued to trade outside Liberia's fiscal control; but they nevertheless held the Liberian government responsible when their property was violated, sometimes invoking the coercive power of their own governments. To escape from this financial deadlock, President Roye in 1870 sought a loan in London; but the inexperienced Liberians were cheated by unscrupulous financiers, and received little concrete return for the new embarrassments brought by a public debt.[46]

Liberian Relations with Indigenous Africans

Given better and stronger government (and the stimulus of more readily accessible export markets), Liberia might have hoped to achieve at least as much as Sierra Leone in the way of commercial and cultural penetration of its hinterland. The political fragmentation of the hinterland created especial difficulties for both settlements, but from early times Liberians were trying to overcome them. Ashmun believed that missionary schools for aboriginal children might provide an effective instrument of "civilization," and substantial numbers of boys do seem to have attended such schools. Even more important as a channel for the communication of techniques and beliefs was the practice, early established in Liberia as in Sierra Leone, by which settler families would receive local children into their homes. Enemies of the settlement claimed that this relationship could become tantamount to slavery, and undoubtedly it was exploited as a cheap form of labour; but the A.C.S. Agent, Rev. E. E. Smith, warmly defended the practice in 1892:

> In the families of the Liberian farmers native boys are brought up to manual labour and become efficient farmers; the girls are taught

45 Johnston, *Liberia*, I, 248, 350-2. Reade, *Sketchbook*, 11, 257.

46 Johnston, *Liberia*, I, ch. XV; R. L. Buell, *The Native Problem in Africa* (N.Y. 1928), 11, 796-97. A critic suggests that, in view of Liberia's "low credit-rating," this loan was actually "a regular business transaction conducted according to the standards of the time." I accept the point, but see no reason to modify the language used above. Sierra Leone, though it did not find loans easy to come by, was of course protected from such "regular business transactions" by the dependence of its government on Whitehall.

> housework. A small proportion of these young people are taught to read and write, and some of them become prominent citizens of the State.

Smith estimated that there were over 3,000 youths in settler homes, and that they remained there for an average period of seven years, after which some would start farms of their own.[47] It seems clear that a study of social intercourse and inter-marriage between settlers and indigenous peoples might surprise many who generalize about supposedly superior settler attitudes; and this might apply to Sierra Leone as well as to Liberia.

Early Agents of the Colonization Society sponsored some exploratory journeys inland, and signed treaties, notably with the chief of the "Condo" confederacy at Boporo, north of Monrovia.[48] At the same time the Colonization Society was building great hopes on the arrival in Liberia of Abdul Rahman, an elderly slave who claimed descent from the founder of the Fula state in Futa Jalon.[49] Abdul Rahman died without leaving the coast, and Boporo became hostile in the 1830's; but some commercial contacts continued, and bred hopes of finding mines and great markets. From the 1860's Liberian governments, like their Sierra Leone neighbours, began to encourage exploring journeys; the most notable, that of Benjamin Anderson, reached a Mandinka town called Musardu in the highlands now in southern Guinea.[50] E. W. Blyden, already a prominent though controversial figure in Liberia, was at that time preaching in both countries the importance of developing relations with the Muslim states of the western Sudan.

Liberia's International Weakness

But it was along the coast, where revenue might be quickly collected, that the Liberians (like British colonial governments later), were most active in claiming sovereignty. Ashmun's vigorous

---

[47] Report of Rev. E. E. Smith, *Liberia,* No. I, Nov. 1892.

[48] Gurley, *Ashmun,* 364; App. 26-38, 80-89. Alexander, *Colonization,* 260-61; Johnston, *Liberia,* I (Nov. 1892), 148.

[49] Staudenraus, *Colonization,* 162-64.

[50] B. Anderson, *Narrative of a Journey to Musardu,* (N.Y., 1870). Mr. Svend Holsoe of Boston University has identified Musardu as Moussadougou, north of Beyla.

assaults upon neighbouring slave-traders had initially given Liberia a good name among British anti-slavery men, though this was tarnished for some by Garrison's attacks. In the early 1830's a British African Colonization Society planned to plant its own sister colony of American Negroes at Cape Mount; in 1850 Lord Shaftesbury and Samuel Gurney helped collect £1,000 to assist Liberia to buy the coastline between Cape Mount and Sherbro Island.[51] As late as 1865 the prospects for a Liberian "pax" seemed good enough for the Chairman of a British Parliamentary Committee to toy with the notion of transferring the Sherbro to her flag.[52] But when the Liberians tried to assert their authority in 1860 they were resisted by the most influential ruler on this coast, Manna of the Gallinas, with strong encouragement from J. M. Harris, a British trader who was beginning to develop trade there. Manna's resistance encouraged the government of Sierra Leone to exert more active influence on this coast; after prolonged and sterile negotiations, they used the power of the Royal Navy to impose a settlement unfavorable to Liberia in 1884.[53] It is doubtful whether Sierra Leone's claim to these countries was better grounded in treaties and consent than Liberia's; the decisive factor was naval power. A period in African history was opening when local disputes were sometimes decided by armed strength on the spot; in such strength Liberia remained notably deficient.

American friends of Liberia claimed that its settlers enjoyed a freedom, under government of their own people, such as they could not hope to secure in the contemporary United States. "The adult male inhabitants consider themselves *men*, and know how to enjoy the blessings of a free institution," a ship's captain reported in 1830; and it was no liberated slave but a former barber from upstate New York who wrote in 1865 "the ponderous weight of human bondage

---

[51] T. Hodgkin, *An Enquiry into the . . . African Colonization Society . . . an Account of the British African Colonization Society* (London, 1833), Johnston, *Liberia,* I, 226-27; Christy, *Ethiopia,* 177-79.

[52] Parliamentary Papers, 1865, Vol. V: Adderley's questions, and replies of Burton (2534-42); Wylde (2767-71); Wildman (3706-28); Chinery (5128-39); Bradshaw (6906-17).

[53] For this boundary dispute, see John D. Hargreaves, *Prelude to the Partition of West Africa* (London, 1963), 45-47, 85-88, 240-43.

has rolled off from my soul."[54] Nineteenth century Sierra Leoneans too enjoyed important liberties—in theory, the liberties of British subjects: but in practice these were often very restrictively defined by colonial legislation, and they never included the basic liberty of self-government. For Liberia, however, the price of freedom was political and economic weakness. And by the end of the nineteenth century, weakness had become so dangerous that only the counter-balancing forces of inter-power rivalry (sometimes brought skilfully into play by Liberian governments intent on survival), saved that freedom from being lost.

---

[54] Capt. W. E. Sherman to E. Hallowell, 10 May 1830, in *Third Annual Report,* Connecticut Colonization Society (New Haven, 1830), appendix; H. W. Johnson, Jr., quoted Stockwell, *Republic,* 193-96. Buell, II, 733-34.

V.

The United States African Squadron 1843-1861

by

ALAN R. BOOTH

Graduate Student in History (African Studies Program), Boston University

THE STORY of the involvement of the United States Navy in the suppression of the African slave trade is not generally known. It is the purpose of this paper to describe its role in the fight against that trade on the west coast of Africa. On June 5, 1843 the frigate *Saratoga* left New York under the command for Commodore Matthew Perry, later commander of the first U.S. Naval Mission to Japan, 1852-1854.[1] The *Saratoga* was the first flagship of the newly-commissioned United States African Squadron.[2]

The hopes of many men went with the *Saratoga.* To some in Washington, the ship symbolized the fulfillment of a dream to place the United States in the van of the battle against the slave trade. For the *Saratoga* this was the maiden voyage, and nearly all signs pointed to a successful one. The ship sailed across the Gulf Stream logging prodigious distances for such a heavily gunned frigate (once in twenty-four hours it made two hundred and fifty miles[3]). On June 23, the frigate rounded the headlands of the Cape Verdes and anchored off Teneriffe.[4] On July 13, Perry took the *Saratoga* to meet the other ships of the Squadron, the *Macedonian,* the *Decatur,* and the *Porpoise,* to cruise off the Guinea coast.[5]

I

The commissioning of the African Squadron was an event with a considerable history. In 1807 President Jefferson had signed the

---

1 E. M. Barrows, *The Great Commodore* (New York, 1935), 160-61, 212 ff.

2 Perry to Upshur, June 5, 1843, in M. C. Perry, Letters to the Secretary of the Navy, Apr. 10, 1843—Apr. 29, 1845 (Washington, National Archives Microfilm, FM 89, Roll 101, 1949); Barrows, *Great Commodore,* 161. Hereafter, first references to the microfilmed letters of the respective squadron commanders to the Secretary of the Navy will be cited as LSN, followed by inclusive dates, then WNAM, followed by FM and Roll numbers. Succeeding references will cite the Squadron Commander, followed by the word "Letters."

3 Barrows, *Great Commodore,* 161.

4 Perry to Upshur, June 29, 1843, in Perry, Letters.

5 Perry to Upshur, July 13, 1843 and Aug. 3, 1843, in Perry, Letters.

Slave Importation Prohibition Act;[6] but like most laws, the Act was merely a scrap of paper without the willingness and means to enforce it. Jefferson's policy of a small coastal Navy left America with little power on the high seas, and the slave trade continued almost unabated. Indeed, President Madison found it so serious that he mentioned the continuing problem in his Annual Message of 1810.[7] In 1816, the African Society of London estimated that 15,000 slaves were being taken annually from Africa to America, a quarter of the total number taken from that continent each year.[8]

The explanation for this prolonged defiance of the law in the United States was simple. After the Revolution, the American South had turned from growing rice, tobacco and indigo to cotton, which far more than the former staples required slave labor to make it economically successful. Consequently, after 1807 the trade in African slaves continued by smuggling, which (as had been true in Colonial New England) was winked at by almost everyone. In 1819, for instance, three American schooners were captured coming back from the "Havana run" with one hundred and seven slaves. However, the Federal Judge at Mobile, after condemning the ships, "reserved" for future order the disposition of the slaves—which involved placing them indefinitely in the hands of three bondsmen who happened to be friends of his. Nothing was done to the slave-traders.[9]

Great Britain, meanwhile, had not been idle in its efforts to stop the slave trade. By 1820 it had, by treaty and convention, bound nearly every major maritime power in the world to suppress the trade; and from many of them it had gained the right to stop and search their merchant vessels for slaves.[10] Most of the major maritime powers had in addition joined in the establishment of

---

6 W. E. B. DuBois, *The Suppression of the African Slave-Trade to the United States of America 1683-1870* (Cambridge, 1896), 108.

7 *Ibid.*, 111.

8 *Ibid.*, 110.

9 *Ibid.*, 117.

10 H. G. Soulsby, *The Right of Search and the Slave Trade in Anglo-American Relations 1814-1862* (Baltimore, 1933), 14; DuBois, *Suppression*, 133-35; C. Lloyd, *The Navy and the Slave Trade* (London, 1949), 62.

mixed courts.[11] In all of these agreements, however, the United States was conspicuously absent.

Smarting from the Treaty of Ghent (where no mention had been made of the issue of impressment, over which it had avowedly fought the War of 1812), the United States refused to sign a treaty involving the "right of search." It found little meaning in Castlereagh's distinction between "belligerent" right of search (impressment) and "reciprocal" right, limited to the detection of slavers. This dispute over the right of search was to affect Anglo-American relations for nearly fifty years; one of its offspring was to be the African Squadron.

The differences of view were fundamental. It was obvious to British statesmen that unless every nation granted a right of search, all slavers would merely flock under the wings of those who refused. The United States, on the other hand, had an economy based on agriculture, not machines. In addition, it had a chip-on-the-shoulder attitude characteristic of short men and emergent nations. It had lost face in the recent war over a demand which Britain now wanted it to accede to in peace, in order to stop a practice which many interests did not *want* to stop.[12] When John Quincy Adams was asked by George Canning whether he could conceive of a more atrocious evil than the slave trade, he replied:

> Yes. Admitting the right of search by foreign officers of our vessels upon the seas in time of peace; for that would be making slaves of ourselves.[13]

---

[11] Soulsby, *Right of Search,* 14. A "mixed court" was a special tribunal staffed by citizens of the treaty signatories to adjudicate cases arising from the capture of slavers.

[12] Even John Quincy Adams himself had once said: "Slavery in a moral sense is an evil, but in connection with commerce it has its uses." S. F. Bemis, *John Quincy Adams and the Foundation of American Foreign Policy* (New York, 1949), 122.

[13] Adams to Channing, June 29, 1822, in J. Q. Adams, *Memoirs of John Quincy Adams* (Philadelphia, 1875), VI, 37. On another occasion, Lord Palmerston had expressed the British point of view with equal candor: ". . . to appoint a commission to inquire whether the right of search is essential for the suppression of the slave trade is about as rational as appointing a commission to enquire whether two and two make four." Quoted by Soulsby, *Right of Search,* 25.

Consequently, the negotiations between the two countries over the issue were hardly fruitful. When the Foreign Secretary, Castlereagh, in 1823 raised the subject of a mutual right of search treaty, Adams, then Secretary of State, replied with a denunciation of the practice of boarding on the high seas in peacetime.[14] Castlereagh for his part had refused even to renounce the principle of impressment.[15]

While these negotiations were proceeding, developments within the United States were altering the character of the Law of 1807. Already the internal slavery question was becoming a heated issue, dividing the country along sectional lines. Commercial and farming elements in the North, who were to wink at conditions amounting to virtual slavery forty years later, were in 1818 horrified at the Southern practice and determined that it should not spread. The colonization movement to return freed slaves to Africa was well developed, fostered by Northern humanitarians and Southerners who feared the influence of the freedmen on the slave population. In 1819, therefore, the Slave Trade Act was passed directing the President to use armed cruisers on the coasts of the United States and Africa in order to suppress the slave trade. At the same time the foundation of the future state of Liberia was provided for, to serve as a haven for the "safe keeping, support and removal beyond the limits of the United States" of all slaves freed by the cruisers.[16] An initial appropriation of $100,000 was made to enforce the Act. In 1820 an amendment was added making slave trading an act of piracy, punishable by death.[17]

The Americans were, therefore, in a position to "show the flag" and with it their determination to stop the trade at its source. But

[14] Adams to Hugh Nelson, U.S. Minister in London, Apr. 28, 1823, in J. Q. Adams, *The Writings of John Quincy Adams* (New York, 1917), VII, 398-99.

[15] Soulsby, *Right of Search,* 18.

[16] DuBois, *Suppression,* 121.

[17] For the Act's provisions, see *Statutes at Large of the United States* (Boston, 1855), III, 532-34. While Congress passed this "Piracy Act," the United States never signed a treaty to this effect; such an action would have submitted it to a "law of nations" and made its ships subject to search. See Squadron Order dated Jan. 17, 1849, in B. Cooper, LSN, Nov. 22, 1848—Sept. 3, 1949 (WNAM, FM 89, Roll 104).

this precursor of the African Squadron hardly showed that determination. Only occasional cruisers were despatched to the coast of Africa, where they remained for only a few weeks at a time.[18]

In addition, international complications hindered suppression of the trade. American and foreign slavers, heretofore accustomed to fly American colors with immunity, merely switched to Spanish colors when the American cruisers appeared. The first cruiser reported what was to become the common pattern:

> . . . we [the ship *Cyane*] have made ten captures, some by fair sailing, others by boats and stratagem. Although they are evidently owned by Americans, they are so completely covered by Spanish papers that it is impossible to condemn them. . . . The slave trade is carried on to a very great extent. There are probably no less than three hundred vessels on the coast engaged in that traffic, each having two or three sets of papers.[19]

When the cruiser *Cyane* captured and sent to New York a Spanish slaver, the Spanish Minister lodged a stiff protest. Even worse, when in 1821 the *Alligator* captured and sent to New York four slavers under French colors but which she strongly suspected were Americans, the French Minister raised such a tempest that Adams gave the French in February 1822 a blanket repudiation of America's intention to commit such acts again in peacetime.[20] Indeed, the instructions to the Commanders before leaving for the African coast had been from the beginning very explicit in that respect:

> Whatever well-grounded suspicions you may entertain [that a vessel had been fitted out and intended for piracy] you will not molest her, unless you have satisfactory evidence that she has either *attempted* or *actually commited* some piratical aggression on some merchant vessel of the United States.[21]

Meanwhile, the Congress was proving more cautious than the Executive over the slave suppression issue. In 1824, negotiations

---

[18] List of cruisers and captures in Appendix A. The Schooner *Alligator,* for instance, remained on the Coast from November to December 1821, while the Schooner *Shark* was there only from September to November of the same year.

[19] Captain Edward Tranchard, Captain of the Ship *Cyane,* to the Secretary of the Navy, Apr. 10, 1820, in *American State Papers, Foreign Relations,* V, 95.

[20] Soulsby, *Right of Search,* 23. In spite of this, 600 slaves were retaken and eleven slavers captured through the end of 1821: DuBois, *Suppression,* 126.

[21] Navy Department to Perry, May 29, 1819, cited by Bemis, *Adams,* 424n.

between Secretary Adams' Minister and George Canning, the new British Foreign Secretary, resulted in the Anglo-American Treaty, which for the first time included a carefully circumscribed right-of-search provision.[22] But the Senate, still jealous of American rights on the high seas, altered the treaty by so many amendments to which the British could not possibly agree, that it was never ratified.[23] Shortly thereafter, the American cruisers were recalled from the African coast.[24]

Within a decade President Jackson placed the final capstone on this policy of intransigence. In 1834 his Secretary of State informed the British Minister, Sir Charles Vaughn, that the policy had been formed "not to make the United States a party to any convention on the subject of the slave trade."[25]

The results of this policy were soon evident. The slave trade gradually became an American business. One authority estimates that between 1820 and the repudiation of the Treaty of 1824 the annual slave traffic to the Americas never exceeded 40,000; but by 1837, the American importation had reached as high as 200,000 a year.[26] As all the maritime powers, one after another, submitted to the British power of search, and as the first countries began signing equipment treaties, the American flag was becoming the last haven of the pirates.[27] Even Governor Thomas Buchanan of Liberia was moved to say:

---

22 Bemis, *Adams,* 432-33.

23 *Ibid.,* 434-35. Desire on the part of some Senators to deprive Adams of a diplomatic triumph in a Presidential election year also played a part.

24 Lloyd, *Navy,* 52. An occasional cruiser was sent to show the flag, however. See *African Repository and Colonial Journal,* CXXVII (Sept. 1835), 265-66.

25 Forsyth to Vaughn, Oct. 4, 1834, cited in Soulsby, *Right of Search,* 45.

26 DuBois, *Suppression,* 143. American apathy was not the only reason for the increase. Cotton supplied the growing market for slaves, and the increasing risk of slaving supplied the incentive to staggering prices and profits. Slaves brought anywhere from $500 to $1200 in the period 1840-1860. (*Ibid.,* 162; Soulsby, *Right of Search,* 43n.) As a slaver himself pointed out: "It was an old maxim of the British excise men that no trade could be prohibited when its profits were more than thirty percent. The profits of a successful slaving voyage were a hundred and fifty, two hundred, two hundred and fifty percent." B. Mayer, *Adventures of an African Slaver* (New York, 1928), xviii.

27 DuBois, *Suppression,* 143; Soulsby, *Right of Search,* 46. "Equipment

> The chief obstacle to the success of the very active measures pursued by the British Government for the suppression of the slave trade on the coast, is the *American Flag*. Never was the proud banner of freedom so extensively used by those pirates upon liberty and humanity. . . .[28]

Toward the end of the 1830's, it became apparent that the British were determined to stop the wholesale flight of slavers to the Stars and Stripes. American names began to appear on British prize lists. It was an entirely unofficial affair; British officers simply took matters into their own hands and boarded American vessels which looked suspicious. If nothing was found, the result was usually an indignant protest to the British government when the Yankee captain reached home waters. It did no good, for the British had followed up their blunt use of naval power with a tidy diplomatic theory. The distinction, they maintained in 1841, lay between the "right of search," which they no longer demanded, and the "right of visit," which they claimed was a just and proper method of veryifying, by inspection of papers only, the nationality of a vessel. It involved no more than a single British officer, of the rank of lieutenant at least, entering only the cabin of the subject vessel.[29]

In American minds there was no difference between the two, but in the British view, there was a world. In a note to our Minister in 1841, Lord Aberdeen wrote that Great Britain renounced

> . . . all pretension to visit and search American vessels in time of peace. Nor is it as American that such vessels are ever visited; but it has been the invariable practice of the British Navy . . . to ascertain by visit the real nationality of merchant vessels met with on the high seas, if there were good reason to apprehend their illegal character.[30]

Treaties" allowed the naval ships to seize suspected slavers if they possessed the equipment for transporting slaves (uncommon numbers of fresh water casks, chains, etc.). Heretofore, only the presence of slaves on board had made seizure legal.

[28] Quoted by A. H. Foote, *Africa and the American Flag* (New York, 1854), 152.

[29] R. W. Van Alstyne, "British Right of Search and the African Slave Trade," *Journal of Modern History*, II (1930), 37.

[30] Cited in *ibid.*, 38. This was no idle statement. In 1816 the British

The right of search issue was not the only point of friction between England and the United States, however. There was in addition a serious dispute over the sinking of the American steamer *Caroline* in 1837, as well as the controversies over the Maine boundary and the Oregon Territory. Indeed, Mr. Andrew Stevenson, the American Minister in London in 1841, wrote to the State Department that "there seems to be a general impression that war is inevitable."[31]

II

While statesmen were quibbling over the semantics of "search" versus "visit," two more practical men were solving the problem of the right of search in a simple but effective way. Their solution was to have far-reaching consequences.

In 1840 Lieutenant Paine of the United States Ship *Grampus* had been sent as a token patroller on the African coast, as specified by the Act of 1819. But Paine looked on the assignment not as a symbol, but rather as an opportunity to help rid the Atlantic of an infamous trade. The ship made for Sierra Leone, where Paine signed an agreement for a joint-cruising expedition with Commander Tucker of the Royal Navy. It was established that each should be authorized

> . . . to detain all vessels under American colors, found to be fully equipped for, and engaged in, the Slave Trade; that, if proved to be American property, they shall be handed over to the United States' schooner Grampus, or any other American cruiser, and that if proved to be Spanish, Portuguese, Brazilian, or English property, to any of Her Britannic Majesty's cruisers employed on the West Coast of Africa for the suppression of the Slave Trade.[32]

The agreement was a success. In the days before underwater cables, it took weeks at best for a message to be answered. The

---

Admiralty had issued a circular to all its cruisers to the effect that the right of search, being a belligerent right, had ceased with the war. H. Wheaton, *Enquiry into the Validity of the British Claim to a Right of Visitation and Search of American Vessels Suspected to be Engaged in the African Slave Trade* (Philadelphia, 1842), 35.

[31] Stevenson to Forsyth, Mar. 9, 1841, *ibid.*, 52.

[32] Quoted in E. D. Adams, "Lord Ashburton and the Treaty of Washington," *American Historical Review, XVII* (July, 1912), 771.

American government, of course, gave orders to put a stop to the venture as soon as it heard of it, fearing that it conceded too much of the British claim.[33] But the orders did not come until several vessels had been captured, and both governments had come to be fully aware of the value of joint cruising. Therefore, when the British government sent Lord Ashburton to Washington in 1824 to negotiate the differences between the two governments, he was prepared to suggest a compromise which he knew would be successful—because it had already been tried on the African coast. Moreover, he had an understanding of a changed situation. The last thirty years, he knew, had seen the United States grow into a formidable naval power. The issue of impressment had died,[34] and Ashburton was not one to live in the past. His American counterpart, Daniel Webster, was equally aware of the implications of the new balance of power: "We are no longer a minor commercial power, nor do we know that we have any particular exemption from war, if war should again break out," he told the British Minister.[35] Both negotiators had studied the Paine-Bell Report suggesting joint cruising on the African coast,[36] and this became the basis of discussion and final agreement in the Webster-Ashburton Treaty of 1842. The negotiations led to the formation of the African Squadron as one of the provisions of that Treaty.

Specifically, Webster committed his country to the principle of

---

33 Soulsby, *Right of Search,* 56.

34 Adams, "Lord Ashburton," 775, quotes the minister in a letter to Aberdeen explaining his stand: "Impressment as a system, is an anomaly hardly bearable by our people. To a foreigner it is undeniable tyranny, which can only be imposed on him by force. Our last war . . . may perhaps have justified violence. America was comparatively weak, and was forced for some years to submit. . . . But the proportions of power are altered. The population of America has more than doubled since the last war, and that war has given her a Navy. . . . Under these circumstances can impressment ever be repeated? I apprehend nobody in England thinks it can."

35 Lloyd, *Navy,* 55-56.

36 "We are of the opinion that a squadron should be kept on the coast of Africa to cooperate with the British or other nations interested in stopping the slave trade; and that the most efficient mode would be, for vessels to cruise in couples, one of each nation. . . ." Quoted in Adams, "Lord Ashburton," 774. The Bell of "Paine-Bell" was Lieutenant Paine's second-in-command during the cruise in 1840.

joint cruising between an American squadron and a corresponding British force, in substitution for the principle of the right of search. Each country was to supply a squadron whose force totalled eighty guns at all times on the African coast. Article VIII stipulated that the two squadrons were to be independent of each other, but the two governments were to "give such orders to the officers commanding their respective forces, as shall enable them most effectually to act in concert and cooperation, upon mutual consultation, as exigencies may arise."[37]

In theory, the Webster-Ashburton Treaty was the perfect solution. But theory turned out to be quite different from the fact, and even before Commodore Perry sailed, the first troubles had begun.

III

It had been evident since the first few years after the passage of the 1807 Act that the South was interested in continuing the slave trade, not in stopping it.[38] Only a handful of plantation owners—those owning exhausted land in the tidewater areas of Virginia and South Carolina—were in favor of upholding the law. These men, whose depleted land had been made valuable by using it for slave-breeding, had an obvious interest in an end to slave importation. But the great majority of Southern farmers and plantation owners favored the illicit trade, for just the opposite reason.

Such sentiment, however, was not confined to the South. New York, as one authority points out, was "almost as dependent upon southern Slavery as Charleston itself," especially as the century wore on, for the chief cargo of the merchant vessels going east was cotton. New York money financed the plantations, shipped the cotton, and manufactured it. In line with their interests, toward the middle of the century, New York supported a good number of the American slavers on the African coast. It is not strange, then, that the New York interests joined the South in fighting all attempts to stop the slave trade.[39] Between them, these pro-slave trade interests

---

[37] Soulsby, *Right of Search,* 86.

[38] See above, p. 80; and also, G. M. Dallas IV, "The African Squadron, 1843-1861" (Cambridge, Harvard Senior Thesis, unpublished, 1956), 34. I am indebted to Mr. Dallas for permission to cite from his work.

[39] P. Foner, *Business and Slavery* (Chapel Hill, 1941), 4, 6, 164, 167.

in both the north and the south held immense political power in Washington; if not in the House, then certainly in the Senate and the Administration.[40] It was unfortunate, but not unusual, that the Secretary of the Navy in 1843 was a Virginian and a staunch advocate of slavery.[41] And he had friends in New York.

The unfortunate fact is that the Treaty of 1842—so carefully and sincerely negotiated by Webster and Ashburton—was thwarted in its implementation by Abel P. Upshur. As Navy Secretary, he had certain powers over the policy set for the new Squadron, and he used them. In his orders to the first Commander of the Squadron, Commodore Perry, on 30 March 1843, Upshur wrote:

> The rights of our citizens engaged in lawful commerce are under the protection of our flag, and it is the chief purpose as well as the chief duty of our naval power to see that these rights are not improperly abridged or invaded. . . . It is to be borne in mind, that while the United States sincerely desire the suppression of the slave trade, and design to exert their power, in good faith, for the accomplishment of that object, they do not regard the success of their efforts as their paramount interest, nor as their paramount duty. They are not prepared to sacrifice to it any of their rights as an independent nation; nor will the object in view justify the exposure of their own people to injurious and vexatious interruptions in the prosecution of their lawful pursuits. Great caution is to be observed on this point.[42]

Secretary Upshur had immediately changed the primary goal of the African Squadron from the suppression of the slave trade to the protection and fostering of American commerce on the coast. Justifying his attitude, he argued to President Tyler:

> The want of such a force heretofore has enabled the English to exclude us from the most valuable part of the trade of the Gambia and Sierra Leone, and the French to exclude us entirely from Senegal. The trade in palm oil, already very valuable, and rapidly increasing from year to year, is so conducted, that the articles with

---

[40] It was a House Resolution, passed by a majority of 131 to 9, which prompted President Monroe to initiate the negotiations with Great Britain which led to the Anglo-American Treaty of 1824. See note 22 above; see also Soulsby, *Right of Search*, 26-27.

[41] Dumas Malone, ed., *Dictionary of American Biography* (New York, 1936), XIX, 127.

[42] Soulsby, *Right of Search*, 129.

> which it is purchased must be landed and placed in the hands of native chiefs and trade agents. The American trader has nothing to rely on but the integrity and honor of these people—a precarious dependence, which renders the trade of very little value to him. The English, on the contrary, keep a sufficient naval force constantly on the coast, and being thus in a position to enforce their contracts, the natives do not venture to break them. Hence, this trade is nearly engrossed by the English, and is very valuable to them, although most of the articles necessary to carry it on can be more cheaply furnished by the United States than by them. It is in vain to hope that our commerce with Africa can be maintained even in its present condtion, and still more vain to hope that it can be greatly extended, unless we offer it the protection which it would derive from the constant presence of our ships of war.[43]

It is clear from their letters that the commanders of the African Squadron were under no illusions with respect to their primary responsibility on the Coast. Commodore Perry's first official act upon reaching the Coast was to chastise the natives of Little Berebee, eastward of Cape Palmas, for the murder of the captain and crew of the American merchant brig *Mary Carver*. Eventually, four towns were burned, and the chief and several of his subjects were killed.[44] Shortly before this incident, Perry had written that the slave trade had been reduced by the British to such an extent that there was little left of it: "I cannot hear of any American vessels being engaged in the transportation of slaves, nor do I believe there has been one so engaged in years."[45] Later he reported that he was despatching the *Decatur* of the Squadron to travel southward along the coast to touch "at the settlements lying between Cape de Verde and Sierra Leone with a view of looking after the American trade in that quarter."[46] In an effort to encourage commerce, Perry wrote at length about the type of goods desired and the benefits to be gained:

> This trade is, in a prospective point of view, of much more importance to the interests of the United States than is generally supposed. . . .

---

[43] Upshur to Tyler, Dec. 27, 1842, in Soulsby, *Right of Search*, 121.

[44] Foote, *Africa and the American Flag*, 236-37. Perry's account of the expedition in Perry to Upshur, Jan. 15, 1844, in Perry, Letters.

[45] Perry to Upshur, Sept. 5, 1843, in Perry, Letters.

[46] Perry to Upshur, Oct. 1, 1843, *ibid.*

> The cargoes of vessels trading to Africa are made up almost entirely of American productions; one of the great staples of the U. States, *tobacco,* being an indispensible item in all trading cargoes under whatever Flag. . . . The inferior kinds of Virginia and Kentucky & Maryland tobacco are the most profitable.
>
> The profits on the cargo are great and the articles of African produce received in return contribute to the wealth, comfort and convenience of the people of the United States. . . . [Later he enumerates gold dust, palm oil and coffee. The cotton grown, he says, is distinctly inferior.]
>
> Most of the articles composing the cargo of a trading vessel are becoming indispensible to the comfort or convenience of many of the Native Tribes such as tobacco, cotton cloths, hardware, muskets, gunpowders, all of which may be supplied from the U. States. . . .
>
> But there is another argument in favor of an increase of the lawful trade to Africa and that is its tendency to check the exportation of slaves from that country.[47]

Continually Commodore Perry complained about the restrictive duties at Sierra Leone, stated the need for United States consuls at the major points of trade, and reported several reprimands to British officers for boarding American vessels—principally at Whydah and Lagos.[48] During Perry's entire two years on the Coast as Commander of the Squadron, only one American slaver was taken by his ships.[49]

Captain Isaac Mayo, Squadron Commander from 1853 to 1855, shared Perry's interest in commerce. Perhaps it was because Mayo was himself a slaveholder,[50] but in any event matters in the newly independent Republic of Liberia commanded a good part of the efforts of his small squadron. As settlements were established farther and farther away from Monrovia, the encroachments were

---

[47] Perry to Henshaw, Jan. 29, 1844, in *ibid.*

[48] Perry to Henshaw, Jan. 22 and 29, and Feb. 2, 1844, in *ibid.*

[49] The Brigantine *Uncas,* taken off the River Gallinas on Mar. 1, 1844 by the USS *Porpoise.* No slaves, merely suspicious equipment, were found. Perry to Henshaw, May 18, 1845, in *ibid.* Peter Duignan and Clarence Clendenen in *The United States and the African Slave Trade, 1619-1862* (Stanford, 1962), 40, by dating the capture of the *Pons* and other ships in 1843 rather than about Dec., 1845, exaggerate the part played by Perry, who was no longer in command in Dec., 1845. The evidence suggests that Perry regarded the protection of trade as his primary responsibility.

[50] Dallas, "African Squadron," 56.

resisted by the indigenous tribes. In addition, intertribal wars increasingly disrupted peaceful trade. Perry had settled the *Mary Carver* incident, and now Mayo was called upon to use the power of the Squadron to restore trade:

> On my arrival at Cape Palmas it was represented to me by Gov. McGill, the Chief Magistrate of the American Colony at that place, that a vexatious and somewhat sanguinary war had, for the last three years, existed between one of the Barbo tribes on the left branch of the Cavalla River and a Grebo tribe upon the opposite branch. This war had interrupted the usual trade of the coast, had created alarm and distrust among the coastal vessels, and had in various ways proved injurious to the interests of American Colonists in that quarter.
>
> Governor McGill in the most urgent terms solicited my interference to bring about a cessation of hostilities and the chiefs of some of the native towns also sent me a petition to the same effect.
>
> Moved by these applications and by my own desire to prevent unnecessary bloodshed, I proceeded in this ship [the *Constitution,* which had won fame in the War of 1812] to the Cavalla River (about fifteen miles from Cape Palmas) on the 4th inst., and immediately sent boats to communicate with the contending parties. The Grebo tribe gladly accepted my intervention, but the more warlike Barboes rudely repelled my messenger, threatening to put him to death.
>
> On the morning of the 5th, I left the ship with five armed boats bearing a white flag and went as near the beach as the heavy surf would permit. Again sending a messenger with a white flag (the head Krooman of this ship) I urged this fierce people to consent to an adjustment of their quarrel, but they again rudely repelled my messenger and defied my power; daring me to land, and using terms which among themselves, are considered equivalent to a declaration of war. Finding it necessary to intimidate them, I threw a few light signal rockets over their town, to drive the women and children to the shelters of the neighboring forest, and then from the launch's gun, threw a few shells over their houses. Being wholly unused to such projectiles, and very much alarmed by their explosion, they gladly swung out a white flag, and sensibly expressed their willingness for peace.
>
> On the following day it was again impossible for our boats to land, but I succeeded in getting a deputation on board the "Constitution" from each tribe, whereupon a "Grand Palaver" was held and peace agreed upon. On the morning of the 6th [7th?] other deputations came on board. The peace was ratified with all the formalities peculiar to this country, and I sailed for the Gulf of Guinea most happy to have terminated this affair without bloodshed.

With the restoration of peace, Mayo continued, came the resumption of normal trade.[51]

It is to be noted, however, that after the initial effects of surprise and terror of the ships' guns had subsided, such actions would no longer always suffice to bring the Africans to terms. Members of the American Mission Station on the Gabon River, for instance, saw quite a different outcome from a similar set of circumstances in July, 1845. On the 12th of that month, the Captain of the French Brig *Tactique* demanded that King Glass raise the French Flag on every occasion that the ship did. The King coolly-refused, even under the threat of bombardment; for he was quite familiar with men-of-war, and knew that he could quickly rebuild his huts after the attack. King Glass merely moved his people out of the coastal village and waited; an American missionary, John L. Wilson, described the incident:

> At 8 o'clock a.m. the Ensign was raised on board the Man of War, but it met with no response from the shore; a blank cartrage was fired over the town, but no Ensign was raised aloft. Another was fired, but still the flag lay snugly folded up at the foot of the staff, and there it continued for a week afterwards . . . the French kept up a desultory firing from day to day, at such of the natives as went out to fish or were seen walking on the beach, their balls sometimes passing over our premises, but never so near as to endanger our safety . . . until the Sabbath the 20th, when we could not mistake the intention to disperse the Congregation which had assembled at our Church for worship.

The *Tactique* finally departed, wrote Wilson, shortly before the U.S. Ship *Truxton* arrived to protect American interests.[52]

Returning to Captain Mayo; in addition to his concern over coastal unrest, he also saw a threat to American commerce in the series of treaties which the British and French had been signing along the Coast. Not to be outdone, the Squadron Commander kept his country from being excluded from the palm oil trade of Lagos by signing a most-favored-nation treaty with its British puppet-King, Docemo:

---

[51] Mayo to Dobbin, Sept. 14, 1853, in Mayo, Letters.

[52] J. L. Wilson, to Bruce, Captain of the *Truxton,* Aug. 2, 1845, in C. W. Skinner, LSN, Jan. 14, 1845—Aug. 8, 1846 (WNAM, FM 89, Roll 102).

Flag Ship Constitution
Princes Island (Bight of Biaffa)
Aug. 9th, 1854

Sir:

I have the honor to enclose a duplicate of a letter addressed to the King of Lagos, to which is appended his reply, and a solemn pledge given by him and his chiefs for themselves and for their people, that citizens and property of the United States shall henceforward in Lagos be placed on the same footing with the citizens and property of the most favored nation with which they already have, or hereafter enter into a treaty. You will perceive that while this concession is so full on their part, I have carefully avoided making any pledge whatever on the part of the United States.

Lagos is one of the most important ports on the Bight of Benin, and is destined to become a place of much commercial importance. For many years it was one of the two ports most largely engaged in the Slave Trade, Whydah being its rival.

In 1851 the English Government having in vain tried the effect of negotiation and threats, proceeded to more stringent measures, and an expedition from its Squadron consisting of twenty three armed boats made in November a demonstration against the town which was repulsed by the natives. In this affair the English lost in killed and wounded fourteen Officers and men. In December of the same year the attack was renewed by a much larger force, the boats of the Squadron being supported by two small steamers which succeeded in getting into the river. This assault was made with desperate gallantry, and the natives were forced to abandon their town after having killed and wounded ninety two of their British assailants. The British then replaced upon his throne the lawful King Akitoye, who had been driven into exile by his cousin Kosoko, a fierce and warlike chief wholly devoted to the Slave Trade. Akitoye readily bound himself by a treaty with his English allies, to suppress the Slave Trade in his dominions, to put an end to the shocking practice of offering human sacrifices, to afford protection to all Christian Missionaries, and to throw open his country to foreign trade. An English Consulate was established, and the stipulations of the treaty have been faithfully observed both by Akitoye and by Docemo his son, who has succeeded to his throne.

The town in which this King resides contains about eighteen thousand inhabitants and must from its position become the centre of a very valuable trade. It is situated at the mouth of the river Ogu, which extends far into the interior, and affords a direct communication with Abeocuta, a city of eighty thousand inhabitants. It passes through a country of the richest fertility, supplying to commerce Palm Oil, Ivory, Cotton, Indigo and Ginger, and is inhabited by a people which will gladly till the soil when relieved from the desolating wars which have been constantly undertaken to supply the slave trade and the demand for human sacrifices. Vessels drawing ten feet can pass into this river from the sea, and from it there is a safe, continuous and invaluable communication along the coast both to the Westward and to the Southward, by a chain of lagoons which will bring to it the produce of a great extent of the country.

The exportation of Palm Oil alone is already very valuable, it must increase and attract the attention of our Merchants, to whom the pledge I now forward will secure every desirable priviledge.

The French as well as the English have made a treaty with the King of Lagos, and this pledge which I have secured may prove particularly valuable if they should at any time attempt to obtain exclusive privilege. The King still feels insecure in the possession of his authority, for his rival Kosoko with about three thousand armed men and a well appointed flotilla of War canoes, still infests the Lagoons, and is ready to renew hostilities whenever a favorable opportunity may be offered. It is this fact that made the King so willing to enter into the terms I proposed. His strength is chiefly derived from his relations with civilized nations, and we will doubtless magnify his free concessions to me into an alliance, the report of which will have an effect on his enemies. The willingness with which the British Consul encouraged the King to take this step, probably sprung from the same cause, for the British Naval force on this station has been so much reduced, that the arrival of a large Ship like the Constitution was very opportune and friendly relations between its officers and the authorities on shore, could not fail to exercise a salutory influence.

I received a visit from the King on the 31 of July. He came on board in great state with a large retinue, and was received with a salute and other tokens of distinction.

I have the honor to be Very Respectfully Your Obd. Serv.

/s/ I. Mayo
Comm. in Chief,
U.S. Naval Forces
West Coast of Africa

To the
Honb J. C. Dobbin
Secretary of the Navy
Washington

PS. I have in my possession a specimen of the cotton produced near Lagos, it is of short staple and inferior quality.[53]

[53] Mayo to Dobbin, Aug. 9, 1854, in Mayo, Letters.

Captain Mayo was indeed a man of initiative. Ever since Commodore Perry had made his first requests, every Squadron Commander had seen the need for American consuls at the major ports along the Coast. Mayo finally took the step of appointing some. The first was Captain Ira E. Taylor at Sierra Leone,[54] followed by Mr. D. G. Welles at Loando.[55] In these cases, apparently, Captain Mayo was acting on his own:

> I have appointed Mr. Archibald Forsyth to act as Consul of the United States for the English Colony of Bathurst until the pleasure of the Government can be known.[56]

The actions of Commodore Perry and Captain Mayo were hardly unique among the squadron commanders. All of them, it seemed, took their responsibility towards American traders and settlers more seriously than their duty to uphold the provisions of the Webster-Ashburton Treaty. An example is the instruction given by Captain LaVallette, Squadron Commander from 1851 to 1853, to Commander Benson of the sloop *John Adams*. In 1851 a settlement had been established at Bassa Cove, with almost immediate resistance from the Fishmen.[57] LaVallette wrote to Benson:

> I am informed by Commander William Pearson of the Dale that on the 15th Nov. last the natives inhabiting the Coast of Africa near Grand Bassa had risen upon the Emigrant Settlements there and massacred a number of the Emigrants, that they had been repulsed with a loss of about forty killed, and had meditated another attack had not, as is supposed, the opportune arrival of the Dale with President Roberts and reinforcements prevented the parties from putting it in execution. . . .
>
> You will proceed in the U.S. Sloop "John Adams" under your command . . . to Mesurado, Coast of Africa, and communicate with Mr. Roberts, President of Liberia, and arrange the course which will be proper to attain the objects in view.
>
> It would seem to me that if you were to proceed with the President to all the principal settlements on the Coast, landing at each of them, calling the Chiefs or Kings together and representing to

54 Mayo to Dobbin, Nov. 17, 1853, in *ibid.*

55 Mayo to Dobbin, Apr. 5, 1854, in *ibid.*

56 *Ibid.*

57 Roberts to American Colonization Society, Nov. 6, 1851, in *The African Repository and Colonial Journal,* XXVII (March, 1852), 92.

them the inevitable consequences of punishment in any case of future injury to the settlers it would have the desired effect. . . .

After adjusting affairs in the settlements of the Emigrants on the coast of Liberia, you will be governed in your subsequent movements by circumstances. We are charged with the protection of our commerce in this quarter, as well as with the suppression of the slave trade.[58]

The *John Adams* did forestall another attack, and restored normal trade to the area.[59]

The American squadron commanders were quite open about their desire to foster trade rather than to chase slavers, for they were convinced that the British and French were up to the same tricks. One American commander declared that:

> Under the pretence of suppressing the slave trade, I have not a doubt that it is the intention of both England and France to make as many settlements on the coast as they can, for the purpose of monopolising the trade of the continent. . . .[60]

Another complained that:

> It is the policy of the British ship masters on the coast to represent the Americans as engaged in the slave trade; for if, by such accusations, they can induce British or American men-of-war to detain and examine the fair traders, they thus rid themselves of troublesome rivals.[61]

The result of this attitude was predictable. While the American Squadron devoted its time to protecting the infant settlement of Liberia, looking for commerce, and sending warning notes to British Captains, the slave trade began to increase.[62] While the first reac-

---

[58] LaVallette to Benson, Dec. 12, 1851, in E. LaVallette, LSN, Jan. 23, 1851—Mar. 30, 1853 (WNAM, FM 89, Roll 106).

[59] Benson to LaVallette, Feb. 7, 1852, in *ibid.*

[60] Read to Mason, Dec. 11, 1846, in G. C. Read, LSN, May 27, 1846—Oct. 11, 1847 (WNAM, FM 89, Roll 103). Cited by Soulsgy, *Right of Search,* 119.

[61] H. Bridge, *Journal of an African Cruiser* (New York, 1845), 53. Cited by Soulsby, *Right of Search,* 119. It is of course clear that at least part of the reason for the desire to encourage American commerce was to accomplish what the British had as their goal—to replace the slave trade with legitimate commerce. See Skinner to Henshaw, Mar. 16, 1845, in Skinner, Letters.

[62] See Skinner to Commodore Jones (RN), May 7, 1845, in Skinner, Letters.

tion to the Webster-Ashburton Treaty had been for slavers to scurry for protection under Brazil's flag,[63] they soon learned that they had less to fear from the Americans than they did from British illegal boardings. The old game of dual flags, dual logbooks, even dual crews was resorted to, with the slaver running up either an American or a Brazilian flag depending on who was after him.[64]

The British government had signed the Webster-Ashburton Treaty to avert such practices, yet the only thing it seemed to have gained on the African coast was a few American cruisers more interested in commerce than in the suppression of slaving. But to their angry complaints the U.S. commanders remained impervious:

> The Flag which a vessel wears is prima facie, altho' it is not conclusive evidence of her nationality. It is a mere emblem which loses its character when it is worn by those who have no right to it. On the other hand those who lawfully display the flag of the United States will have all the protection that it supplies. Therefore when a foreign cruiser boards a vessel under this flag, she will do it upon her own responsibility.[65]

The American commanders, then—avowedly on the Coast to protect the U.S. flag from misuse—were not concerned about British actions if the boarded vessel was flying the flag illegally. But if the vessel was proved to be American, the U.S. squadron commanders launched an immediate protest, which was often followed by a stiff note from the State Department.[66]

If the Navy Department was acting to impede the effectiveness of slave suppression on the African coast, its efforts were no less effective than those of the American judiciary. The Law of 1820

The British, it is clear from this letter, were playing their own game of "dual flags." On the complaint of Captain Richard Lawlin of the U.S. merchantman *Madonna,* Skinner accused the British of flying the American flag on patrol in order to induce American ships to heave to to be searched. In this instance the Union Jack was raised only after the *Madonna* had been boarded and searched.

63 Brazil had no right of search treaty with Britain.

64 Foote to Gregory, Sept. 14, 1850, in F. Gregory, LSN, Oct. 11, 1849—June 25, 1851 (WNAM, FM 89, Roll 105).

65 Foote to Hastings (RN), Apr. 17, 1850, in Gregory, Letters.

66 Such was the case of the boarding of the *Roderick Dhu* in 1843. Soulsby, *Right of Search,* 104.

required that a captured slaver must always be returned for adjudication to the port whence it had sailed.[67] It was quickly established in these courts that "absolute proof" was required to designate a ship as a slaver, and that the only acceptable evidence was the presence of slaves on board, since the equipment and rigging used for the palm oil trade was often identical to that used in the slave trade. It was an easy matter, therefore, for the Americans to jettison their human cargo and thereby avoid prosecution.[68]

Yet in spite of all the obstructions, it must be said that the United States, for the first few years at least, was living up to the letter of the Treaty.[69] In 1844 the sloop *Saratoga* was joined by the frigate *Macedonian*, the brig *Porpoise*, and the sloop *Decatur*. The force totalled 82 guns, two more than called for. The Treaty also embodied the principle of joint cruising, but this was soon proved to be impractical. To cover the entire West African coast with four ships was asking a great deal of the Navy.

The British, whose squadron from 1843 to 1857 average nineteen ships and 148 guns,[70] could cover the Coast more systematically and thoroughly. Therefore, it was obviously impractical for the Americans to cruise jointly in a few small areas and leave most of the Coast free for the American flag. In addition, as will be detailed later, the American ships were too deep-drafted to move close-in to the slave-trading areas and pounce on the anchored ships, yet too slow to apprehend the fast slave brigs and clippers on the open sea. The British, naturally, were reluctant to cruise jointly: they had faster, smaller ships—in many cases steamers—and their captains resented being held back to keep company with the American laggards. In practice, then, the American and British squadrons merely worked "in close cooperation," a euphemism for each going his own way, exchanging information only when they

67 DuBois, *Suppression*, 121. The reason was, DuBois points out, to ensure that Southern slavers would face Southern juries.

68 J. R. Spears, *The American Slave Trade* (New York, 1900), Chapter 3, *passim.*

69 1844 to 1847. See Appendix B.

70 *United States Documents*, Senate Executive Document No. 49, 35th Congress, 1st Session, 15, 28, 29.

chanced to meet.[71] Consequently in the late 1850's, the British began to detain vessels which claimed immunity under the American flag until an American cruiser appeared, but this practice was immediately resisted.[72]

IV

If the Americans complied with the terms of the Webster-Ashburton Treaty, they did so only for the first few years. After 1847, for nearly half the years for which we have records, the Americans failed to maintain their stipulated 80 guns on the Coast.[73] And if they had complied with the letter of the law for a while, they seldom complied with the spirit. While the British and French were keeping upwards of twenty-five ships on the Coast, the Americans seldom kept more than five. It is clear that there was a deliberate attempt on the part of the Navy Department to comply only technically with the Treaty by over-gunning a minimum number of ships and sending them. Captain Cooper, commanding officer of the *Yorktown*, complained bitterly of this policy, which at times led to dangerous consequences:

> We have had a long and very disagreeable passage to this Island [Porto Praya, Cape Verde Islands]. The present battery is much too heavy for the ship, twelve guns would have made the ship much easier and more efficient than the sixteen. . . . The ship rolls very deep and returns with a quick heavy jerk straining the ship in every part. We have not had since we left Boston, a dry plank in any part of her.[74]

But over-gunning was only part of the story. It seemed also as

---

[71] Lloyd, *Navy*, 178.

[72] Cass to Napier, Apr. 10, 1858, in *United States Documents*, 35th Congress, 1st Session, Senate Executive Document No. 49, 47-48.

[73] See Appendix B. Because of maintenance problems, even these ships were sometimes unavailable for duty even though shown on the roster. One commander wrote: "The Squadron, for the last eight months, has never consisted of more than three efficient vessels, mounting 48 guns; it is now reduced to two, mounting 38. . . ." Skinner to Henshaw, Oct. 20, 1845, in Skinner, Letters.

[74] Cooper to Mason, Dec. 20, 1848, in B. Cooper, LSN, Nov. 22, 1848—Sept. 3, 1849 (WNAM, FM 89, Roll 104). The Navy Department had been aware of the numbers problem from the first. Commodore Perry had written that the American ships were too few and the area too large for the patrol to be effective. Perry to Henshaw, May 20, 1844, in Perry, Letters.

if it were the policy of the Navy Department to send the wrong kind of ship to the Coast, and usually a decrepit one at that. While the British furnished their squadron with small cruisers (good for shallow coastal patrolling) and a large proportion of fast steamers,[75] the American practice was quite different. As soon as he reached the coast of Africa, Commodore Perry had to order the ship *Consort* home because it was unseaworthy.[76] Two years later, Commander Bell, captain of the *Yorktown*, complained that both its rigging and its hull were rotten.[77] In 1851 the United States brig *Bainbridge* had to be sent back before its tour was up because its sails were falling to pieces and the copper was coming off its hull, causing it to leak dangerously.[78] The pattern soon became clear: the Commodore was usually sent out in a spanking new ship, but his unfortunate juniors were often given what were fast becoming the deadwood of the Navy.

But not even the Commodore was safe at times. When the *Constellation*, the flagship of the Squadron, left Boston in 1859, its commanding officer, Flag Officer Inman, had to turn back within a week because it was rotten and taking water as it rolled. But the Navy neither replaced it nor patched it up. Loading sixty tons of iron ballast in the *Constellation*, the Navy once again put it to sea![79]

The ships were not only in bad condition: they were also wholly unsuited to their task. Slavers were pirates by law, and indeed they had many things in common with them. One of these was speed, which was the major weapon of both professions. Pirates needed speed to catch up, but slavers needed it to get away. Since speed and guile were their methods, slavers carried few guns and almost never tried to shoot it out. When overhauled they would submit

---

75 *United States Documents*, 35th Congress, 1st Session, Senate Executive Document No. 49, 15-16.

76 Perry to Henshaw, Aug. 5, 1843, in Perry, Letters.

77 Skinner to Henshaw, Mar. 16, 1845, in Skinner, Letters.

78 Gregory to Graham, Feb. 16, 1851, in F. H. Gregory, Letters. These conditions reported are not in themselves unusual, for these were the days of poor maintenance and corruption in the Navy yards. What is unusual is the percentage of such unseaworthy ships.

79 Inman to Toucey, July 18, 1859, in W. Inman, LSN, May 28, 1859—Feb. 13, 1860 (WNAM, FM 89, Roll 110).

to an 8-gun schooner as readily as to a 44-gun frigate.[80] It was obvious from the first to the squadron commanders that ten small vessels could patrol five times as much coast as could the two frigates which would answer the gun requirement. The British realized this early, and manned their squadrons accordingly. The American Navy, repeatedly made aware of the problem by its commanders, never did. As early as September of 1843, the Secretary of the Navy was told that the wrong kind of ships were being sent to the Coast;[81] they were too slow, too unwieldy, and too deep-drafted. Four years later the steady drumming of commanders' protests had accomplished nothing. In 1846 one commodore wrote:

> The Brigs *Dolphin, Boxer* and sloop *Marion* are not at all Calculated for the service. They cannot sail sufficiently well to overhaul a slaver, nor can the two brigs carry provisions for a sufficient time to let them remain on a distant station for more than a very limited period. If it be not intended to increase the number of vessels on this Coast, I beg leave to suggest a change of the species of force now employed, which would be better suited for this particular service. The frigate is certainly too large for a cruizer to chase small slavers in shore, and the coast being without harbors make it necessary to anchor at inconvenient distances from the land.[82]

In 1855 Captain Mayo requested that the eighty-gun stipulation be annulled and instead the United States send out a fleet of schooners each manned by a junior officer and a crew of 20, mounting a pivot gun.[83] In spite of all their entreaties, there was no hint of a steamer until 1859. When Commodore Conover wrote to Secretary Toucey: "I take the opportunity of submitting to the Department my experience of the absolute inefficiency of this Squadron, comprised as it is entirely of sailing vessels, for any effectual suppression of the slave trade,"[84] he was only expressing a sense of frustration of long standing. Yet it was three years more before the first

---

80 J. C. Furnas, "Patrolling the Middle Passage," *American Heritage*, IX (Oct., 1958), 7.

81 Perry to Upshur, Sept. 5, 1843, in Perry, Letters.

82 Read to Bancroft, Sept. 18, 1846, in Read, Letters.

83 Mayo to Dobbin, cited by Dallas, "African Squadron," 52.

84 Conover to Toucey, Oct. 13, 1857, in T. A. Conover, LSN, June 9, 1857—Aug. 31, 1859 (WNAM, FM 89, Roll 109).

steamer, the *San Jacinto*, appeared. There were never more than four.[85]

If equipping the African Squadron had been less than desirable, the support of its was abominable. Commodore Skinner complained in 1846 of the case of the *Boxer*. As usual its sails and rigging were rotten—so rotten that on more than one occasion a sail had been ripped from the masts into the sea. But even worse, it had been discovered that the grape-shot loaded on the *Boxer* was twelve-pound caliber, while her guns were nine-pounders.[86] In addition, provisions sent out to stock the Squadron bases were often stored incorrectly and carelessly, with the result that when they were opened for use they were found mouldy, rotten, and alive with insects. One commander wrote of his attempts to remedy the problem:

> I directed a quantity to be selected and passed through the oven, which process, by killing the insects, and drying the bread, will render it eatable.[87]

The Squadron base was another source of frustration and inefficiency. Porto Praya was chosen as the main supply and repair base in the beginning because it was reasonably close to one of the main haunts of the slavers, the Windward Coast around Liberia.[88] But it did not remain handy for long. As the British (even the American commanders gave the credit to the British),[89] forced

---

[85] For a list of Squadron ships and commanders, see Dallas, "African Squadron," Appendix B.

[86] Skinner to Bancroft, May 8, 1846, in Skinner, Letters.

[87] Skinner to Bancroft, May 16, 1845, in *ibid.*

[88] Another reason was that there was an American consul there, who would aid in the Squadron's fostering of trade along the Coast. Dallas, "African Squadron," 52-53.

[89] Cooper to Mason, May 4, 1849, in Cooper, Letters. The Africans themselves were no less quick to discern between the English and other white men along the Coast. Witness the story of one freed slave (originally from Bornu) to an American Captain: "My years were eighteen. There was war. At that time my mother died. My father died. I buried them. I had done. The Foulahs [Fulani] caught me. They sold me. The Housa bought us. They brought us to Tomba. We got up. We came to the Popo country. The Popos took us. To a white man they sold us. The white man took us. We had no shirts. We had no trousers. We were naked. Into the midst of the water—into the midst of a

the slave trade farther and farther down the Coast the problem of distance became acute. For a base to be 800 miles from the Gallinas was bad enough, but by the late 1850's most of the traffice had moved to the vicinity of the Congo River mouth—2000-odd miles from Porto Praya. The only concession made, in spite of repeated entreaties to change the site of the base, was to put a small stock of supplies at Monrovia. But this did nothing for the repair problem, and as we have seen, the ships were in constant need of repair. In the mid-1840's—in the relatively easy days of cruising, that is—the brig *Truxton* spent only 181 days cruising on station out of a total West African tour of 468 days.[90] As the distances increased, a brig or sloop (which carried supplies for six weeks' cruising at best) had to turn around and go home for supplies nearly as soon as she reached the Congo.

By the early 1850's, the situation was so bad that commanders' letters showed some exasperation. Commodore LaVallette wrote that the British steamers were doing such a fine job in the Bight of Benin that the trade was now almost wholly centered between Cape Lopas and Loanda. Repeatedly he asked that the base be changed to St. Helena, which was directly in the path of the southeast trade winds. By such a move, he argued, the cruisers could reach Loanda in ten days as against fifty from Porto Praya. Moreover, he made a scathing denunciation of the choice of Porto Praya in the first place:

> Porto Praya is as unhealthy as any place on the coast. Its anchorage is unsafe. It furnishes very indifferent supplies of beef and vegetables. The water is bad. The climate causes rot in the provisions, and the moth is very destructive to clothing. The island itself has a very inconvenient position as regards . . . being in a region subject to tornados, almost constant rains, calms and currents

---

ship they put us. Thirst killed somebody. Hunger killed somebody. By night we prayed. At sun-time we prayed. God heard us. The English are good. God sent them. They came. They took us. Our hunger died. Our thirst died. Our chains went off from our feet. Shirts they gave us. Trousers they gave us. Hats they gave us. Everyone was glad. We all praised the English. Whoever displeases the English, into hell let him go." Quoted by W. F. Lynch to J. C. Dobbin, Oct. 17, 1853, in *United States Documents,* 33d Congress, 1st session, Senate Executive Document No. 1, 335-36.

[90] Furnas, "Patrolling," 7.

> which present more obstacles to the navigation in making passages from thence to Monrovia and back than are encountered on any other point along the coast.[91]

But no action was taken. Only under Flag Officer William Inman, the last Squadron Commander, was the problem partially solved. Supply ships were stationed off the Congo to provision the cruisers, enabling them to extend their cruises, not indefinitely, but at least for several weeks. Inman's record of prizes during his two-year tenure nearly matched the combined records of all the commanders who came before him.

In the face of such obstruction it is not difficult to see why duty in the African Squadron was so thoroughly hated. Furthermore weather and disease added a threat to life. The first man died on Perry's cruise to take up station.[92] Scores died thereafter. Perry spoke for many when he observed that it seemed that "the Almighty had interdicted this part of Africa to the white race."[93] In 1844 there was such an epidemic aboard the *Preble* that it had to be manned by an almost entirely new crew from other ships.[94] Unfortunately the value of quinine was not appreciated until ten years later, so that only the crudest measures were employed to keep fever down. Perry ordered his sailors to keep in dry clothing and to build fires between decks during the rainy season.[95] After the *Preble* epidemic, ships generally anchored well off shore, out of range of the mosquito and hence the yellow fever and malaria.[96] To meet the shortage of men Perry added Africans, usually Kroomen, to his crews. When the ships were relieved to return to the United States, the Kroomen were simply transferred to the new ships.[97]

But such measures were totally inadequate: Perry's fears were

---

[91] LaVallette to Graham, Nov. 18, 1851, in LaVallette, Letters.

[92] Perry to Upshur, June 29, 1843, in Perry, Letters.

[93] Perry to Henshaw, Jan. 4, 1844, in *ibid.* Two months later he asked to be relieved because on the Coast "few constitutions can hold out longer than eighteen months."

[94] Perry to Henshaw, Nov. 22, 1844, in *ibid.*

[95] Barrows, *Great Commodore,* 173.

[96] J. C. Furnas, *The Road to Harpers Ferry* (New York, 1959), 178. The *Preble* had contracted the fever chasing a slaver upriver, anchoring for the night near a swamp.

[97] Skinner to Mason, Mar. 4, 1845, in Skinner, Letters.

echoed and reechoed with greater vehemence by his successors. One wrote:

> In conclusion, Sir, I give it as my decided opinion, that this Ship will be of no more service as a Cruiser on this coast, until she can obtain an entire new crew of men who have not the seeds of that scourge the African fever ready to sprout out on the slightest exposure. . . .[98]

Another called the African Station "cheerless and debilitating."[99] As the situation became more desperate, so did the letters. Commodore Crabbe admitted that they were "all desirous of leaving this cheerless and health destroying station."[100] Like every single other commander with the exception of Inman, Crabbe was anxious to get home as fast as he could by whatever means, pleading "pressing family affairs."[101] Commodore Mayo proved himself to be an agile "name-dropper." Since he had been Perry's right-hand man in many a battle, he argued, he thought it to be for the good of the service that he be assigned Perry's second-in-command in his forth-coming Japanese expedition.[102]

The junior officers and men of the Squadron were not in a position to appeal so easily to Caesar. Court martials took up a great deal of the commanders' time. Duelling among the officers—even in some cases between officers and men—was not uncommon. Drunkenness was rife. Officers feigned sickness in order to escape the Squadron. One officer, all recourse gone, abandoned command of his ship and fled aboard a merchant vessel to the United States.[103]

But even when the Squadron chanced to get such a conscientious and energetic a commander as Flag Officer Inman, his efforts were invariably frustrated by the Navy Department. Ships were not replaced; bases were not furnished; prize crews sent to the United States were not returned; steamers were few and far between.

---

98 Skinner to Bancroft, Mar. 4, 1845, in *ibid.*

99 Quoted in Skinner to Bancroft, Mar. 30, 1845, in *ibid.*

100 Mayo to Dobbin, Nov. 17, 1854, in Mayo, Letters.

101 Crabbe to Dobbin, Oct. 9, 1856, in T. Crabbe, LSN, Jan. 17, 1855—June 7, 1857 (WNAM, FM 89, Roll 108).

102 Crabbe to Dobbin, Feb. 17, 1856, in *ibid.*

103 Perry to Upshur, Aug. 5, 1843, in Perry, Letters.

Inman did his best—which was far superior to anything seen before—but at last he could stand the obstruction no longer. To Secretary Toucey he wrote:

> The African Squadron under my command has performed its whole duty. I must be permitted to say, this has been done in the face of positive discouragement from the Department. I have never exceeded my instructions, yet I have been rebuked, by countermand of my orders, in every case of transfer or appointment. No commander-in-chief should be placed in such a position, nor the flag of his country, thus discredited in his person.[104]

Inman might have added another reason for his frustration. In all the years since the Webster-Ashburton Treaty, not a single conviction had been handed down by an American court against any of the slavers taken by the American squadron. Captains and crews went to jail only long enough to post bail—which was always so low that they could easily afford to jump it—or to be acquitted quickly on some technical flaw in the evidence against them. Not one slave captain was executed for piracy under the Act of 1820 until Lincoln's presidency.[105] When the slaver *Casket* was released at New York after being taken there by a prize crew, a reprimand was sent to the Squadron Commander for interrupting "lawful commerce."[106] The bark *Emily* was seized in the late 1850's on suspicion of slaving and then released, only to be caught red-handed on the coast of Africa; but when it appeared at New York, it was entrusted to a notorious slave captain who had previously been acquitted in Key West in spite of convincing evidence as to his guilt.[107]

V

By the late 1850's, a crisis was near over the suppression of slavery within the United States. The Fugitive Slave Law had roused the North, while to the South, slavery had become an institution of positive good. The African Squadron was becoming something of a political football. In the Senate, the slave interests used two different

---

104 Inman to Toucey, Apr. 14, 1860, in Inman, Letters.

105 Spears, *Slave Trade,* 219; Soulsby, *Right of Search,* 134.

106 *Ibid.*

107 DuBois, *Suppression,* 185.

tactics. The first was to try to kill the Webster-Ashburton Treaty by pressure and legislation. In 1854 Senator John Slidell of Louisiana, on the Committee on Foreign Relations, reported to the Senate a bill to abrogate Article VIII of the Webster-Ashburton Treaty because it was expensive, fatal to the health of the sailors, and had proved useless. This, and a measure to substitute life imprisonment for the death penalty, were not enacted.[108] But the interests were more successful in their attempts to undermine the Squadron by cutting its appropriations. In 1853, for example, the requested $20,000 was reduced to $8,000.[109]

Meanwhile, the attitude of the Navy Department had not changed. While he had finally seen fit to supply four steamers to the Squadron, Secretary Isaac Toucey instructed his commodore, as before, that the protection of American vessels against foreign interference rather than the suppression of the slave trade was the primary consideration.[110]

The British, long disillusioned, were now losing their patience. To them it was becoming clear that Squadron or no, the slave trade was now being financed and carried on principally by the Americans.[111] In spite of the addition of American steamers, one British officer expressed what was probably the universal sentiment among British officers when he wrote:

> No vessel has been seen here for one year certainly; I think for nearly three years there have been no American cruizers on these waters. . . . I cannot, therefore, but think that this continual absence of foreign cruizers looks as if they were intentionally withdrawn, and as if the Government did not care to take measures to prevent the American flag being used to cover Slave Trade transactions. . . .[112]

Britain, because of the Crimean War, had reduced its squadron

---

108 *Ibid.*, 183.

109 *Ibid.*

110 Toucey to Inman, July 6, 1859, in *United States Documents,* 36th Congress, 1st Session, Senate Executive Document No. 2, 87-89.

111 DuBois, *Suppression,* 162.

112 *Ibid.*, 186-87. And in truth, the yearly slave trade to America since the arrival on the Coast of the U.S. Squadron in 1843 had more than trebled. *Ibid.*, 143.

during the middle 1850's,[113] but by 1858 it was back at strength and determined to show that it meant business. That year saw the British Squadron commence a series of seizures of suspected American slavers; and instead of sending them under prize crews to the United States, it burned them or disposed of them at Sierra Leone.[114] When the American Minister protested this violation of the Webster-Ashburton Treaty, Lord Clarendon, the British Foreign Secretary, coolly announced that if the Americans were derelict in their responsibilities, the British would be forced to do their duty for them.[115] Furthermore, the Royal Navy poured salt in the wound by detaining several American vessels off Cuba. Public opinion in the United States became thoroughly aroused. A group in the South even demanded the repeal of all acts prohibiting the slave trade acts;[116] while the United States Senate angrily passed a resolution denouncing the British actions, prompting a stiff note of protest by Secretary of State Cass.[117] Once again open conflict seemed possible.

However, the solution of the issue was to be found not in war, but in men. America had the laws and the machinery to stop the slave trade; what it needed was the leaders who would use them. And finally, it found two such men. The first was Flag Officer William Inman; the second was Lincoln.

When Secretary Toucey had dispatched the steamers to the African Coast in 1859, he had also sent a new Squadron Commander to lead them. Whatever Toucey expected, he did not have to wait long before he realized that he had appointed a man of Lieutenant Paine's stamp. From Inman's first General Orders, it became obvious that he meant to act. Soon he had deposited coal and secure supply caches along the coast, provided supply ships to alleviate the

---

113 Van Alstyne, "British Right of Search," 38.

114 *United States Documents,* 36th Congress, 2nd Session, House Executive Document No. 7, 316-18, 400-14.

115 Clarendon to Dallas, Oct. 8, 1857, cited by Soulsby, *Right of Search,* 157-58.

116 The Commercial Convention at Vicksburg, Mississippi, on May 19, 1859. W. J. Carnathan, "Proposal to Reopen the African Slave Trade," *South Atlantic Quarterly,* XXV (1926), 410.

117 Cass to Napier, Apr. 10, 1858, *United States Documents,* 35th Congress, 1st Session, Senate Executive Document No. 49, 52.

cruising problem, and collected accurate charts of the Coast from the British consuls and officers, forwarding them to Washington for reproduction. While other commanders had stood in port, complaining about equipment and disease, despatching requests for relief, Inman wrote:

> My vessels are constantly at sea. . . . The Flag Ship has been less than a month in any port in marked contrast with any that preceeded her.[118]

The results were significant. Within less than two years of his arrival on the Coast, Inman was able to boast:

> It is but truth to say, that since I assumed this command, a check upon the slave trade, by capture of slavers and intended slavers, has been given by the Squadron, greater in number and effect, than by the whole of the Squadrons combined that have preceded me. No less than eleven vessels and two thousand seven hundred and ninety-three (2793) slaves (the latter landed at Monrovia) have been seized and sent to the United States.[119]

But no one man in Inman's position could stop the trade. He might catch a dozen slavers a year; there were scores more to take their places. And the fact remained that, after a short stay in New York or some other port, the condemned ship with its crew might soon again be on the Guinea coast.

While Inman was using his full powers at sea, for the first time an American President was using his full powers to enforce the laws which the Congress had provided. Execution of the slave-trade laws in the United States were placed directly under the Secretary of the Interior, who was given ample funds to prosecute the slavers. Within a year, more slave-trade convictions were obtained than the total for all the years since 1808.[120] Captain Nathaniel Gordon of the slaver *Erie* became the first man to be hanged for piracy under the long-dormant provisions of the Law of 1820.[121] After the beginning of the Civil War, the Union blockade became in-

---

[118] Inman to Toucey, Aug. 14, 1860, in Inman, Letters. Inman was never one to hide his light under a basket. His letters total three times the number normal for his tenure.

[119] Inman to Welles, Mar. 6, 1861, in *ibid.*

[120] DuBois, *Suppression,* 192.

[121] Furnas, "Patrolling," 102. The date of the hanging was Feb. 21, 1862.

creasingly effective at stopping the slave trade at its ultimate destination. In short, the trade after 1860 dwindled more because of conditions in the United States than because of those on the coast of Africa.

As the War continued and the Union reverses dominated the headlines in London, President Lincoln became increasingly concerned about the possibility that the British would come to the aid of the Confederates.[122] Since this obviously would have been critical for the Union, it seemed to Lincoln that it was high time for mending fences. On March 23, 1862, the Secretary of State, Seward, proposed that the two countries sign a right of search treaty. The British jumped at the chance. The Treaty for the Suppression of the African Slave Trade, which included everything the British had sought to negotiate for the past fifty years, was signed fifteen days later. Its terms included the mutual right of search, an equipment article, and the establishment of mixed courts at New York, Sierra Leone, and Cape Town. The Senate ratified it unanimously.[123]

VI

The African Squadron did not survive the first year of the Civil War. Flag Officer Inman, the last Squadron Commander, was recalled in September of 1861, and the other ships soon followed; all were needed for the Union blockade. The next year saw the Squadron's official demise, when it was merged under the command of the European Squadron.[124]

As an instrument of suppression of the slave trade, the Squadron can hardly be termed a success. During its eighteen years on the Coast, it had captured only twenty-four ships, liberating a total of 4945 slaves.[125] Remembering that Britain and the United States were bound by the Webster-Ashburton Treaty to maintain the same

---

[122] Indeed, it was an African Squadron ship which almost precipitated this very thing. It was the *San Jacinto,* on return from Africa, which stopped the British mail steamer *Trent* and removed the Confederate Ministers Mason and Slidell in Nov. of 1861.

[123] W. L. Mathieson, *Great Britain and the Slave Trade 1839-1865* (London, 1929), 175.

[124] R. G. Albion, "Distant Stations," *United States Naval Institute Proceedings,* LXXX (Mar., 1954), 268.

[125] See Appendix D.

minimum number of guns on the Coast, these figures are a sorry contrast to the British effort. During the same period, the British West African Squadron captured 595 slave ships, liberating 45,612 Africans.[126]

The evidence suggests that the principal reason for the Squadron's failure lies with the Secretaries of the Navy, who deliberately changed the Squadron's prime mission from slave suppression to the encouragement of commerce, and who (as all the commanders intimated and Flag Officer Inman openly stated), thwarted its efforts by giving it inferior ships and haphazard support. Until Flag Officer Inman took command, the commanders' letters to the Secretaries dealt far more with the activities of the Squadron in protecting trade, and aiding the American colonists in Liberia, than they did with slave-catching. Most men tend to write what they know their superiors want to hear: Commodore Perry could hardly have believed that, as he wrote, there had been no American slavers on the Coast for years.[127] Nor would it have been natural for Captain Mayo to appoint consuls on his own unless he were sure that his superiors would approve of such boldness.

Yet there is no evidence that the Squadron was consciously used as an agent of political expansion. It is true that its ships regularly stopped at Monrovia and aided the young republic, yet the United States government was constantly opposed to giving Liberia its official protection. Indeed, the United States did not even recognize the Liberian Government until 1862—fifteen years after its establishment. But as long as America was required by treaty to maintain a squadron on the Coast, it is evident from the Navy Secretaries' instructions that they intended to subordinate its stipulated purpose to that of "protecting the American flag."

Most of the Navy Secretaries during the period 1843-1861 were not personally interested in stopping the slave trade. Of the nine Secretaries who held office during the period, six came from the South.[128] Of the three Northern Secretaries, only one, George

---

126 For a listing of British captures, see Lloyd, *Navy,* Appendix A.

127 See note 45 above.

128 From *Dictionary of American Biography, passim.* The Navy Secretaries were: Abel P. Upshur, 1843-1844 (Virginia); David Henshaw, 1844-1845 (Massachusetts); George Bancroft, 1845-1847 (Massachusetts); John Y. Mason,

Bancroft (who is perhaps better known as an American historian than as a politician), actively supported abolition. The other two were Southern sympathizers. David Henshaw of Massachusetts, who served from 1844 to 1845, drew his political support from the Tyler-Calhoun faction in the South, and was a close friend of many slaveholders.[129] Isaac Toucey, although from Connecticut, was an active supporter of slave interests. He had supported both the Fugitive Slave Law of 1850 and the Kansas-Nebraska Bill of 1854. Indeed, it was suggested by a Congressional Report that Secretary Toucey's despatch of the streamers to the Squadron in 1859-60 was prompted by his intention not so much to strengthen the Squadron as to disperse the naval forces of the Union as the South moved towards secession.[130]

In conclusion: the obstructive attitudes of successive Secretaries of the Navy before the Civil War made it impossible to achieve the avowed objects of the African Squadron.[131] Although the Navy played a notable part in preserving order on the Liberian coast, and in protecting and encouraging American trade, the Squadron's role in the suppression of the slave trade was small, especially when considered in relation to the cost in lives and money.

1848-1850 (Virginia); William B. Preston, 1850-1851 (Virginia); William A. Graham, 1851-1853, (North Carolina); John P. Kennedy, 1853-1854 (Maryland); John C. Dobbin, 1854-1858 (North Carolina); and Isaac Toucey, 1859-1861 (Connecticut).

129 *Ibid.*, VIII, 563.

130 *United States Documents*, 36th Congress, 2d Session, House Report No. 87, 1-6.

131 Two recent studies suggest additional factors: Warren S. Howard in *American Slavers and the Federal Law, 1837-1862* (Berkely, 1963), 42, 124-41, claims that many officers were inept "misfits" who spent too much time in Madeira; Duignan and Clendenen in *Slave Trade*, 40-42, suggest that the Navy was short of ships, and that American statesmen were suspicious of the objects of the British squadron. However, both studies reject the frequent charge—see e.g. Daniel P. Mannix, *Black Cargoes* (New York, 1962), 223—that Southern officers in the U.S. Squadron were to blame.

APPENDIX A*

List of American African Cruisers, 1820–1822

Vessels	Guns	Commanders	Dates on Coast	Captures
Cyane (ship)	24	E. Trenchard	Mar. 1820–1822	4 schooners: *Endymion* *Esperanza* *Plattsburg* *Science*
Hornet (ship)	18	G. Read	1820–1822	*Alexander* (brig)
John Adams (ship)	24	A. Wadsworth	1820–1822	(none)
Alligator (schooner)	12	R. Stockton	May–Dec., 1821	4 schooners: *Jeune Eugene* *Mathilde* *Daphne* *Eliza*
Shark (schooner)	12	M. C. Perry	Sept.–Nov., 1821	(none)

* From *American State Papers, Foreign Relations*, V, 141.

APPENDIX B*

AMERICAN SQUADRON—TOTAL NUMBER OF SHIPS AND GUNS ON THE COAST OF AFRICA, 1843–1857

Year	Vessels	Guns
1843	2	30
1844	4	82
1845	5	98
1846	6	82
1847	4	80
1848	5	66
1849	5	72
1850	5	76
1851	6	96
1852	5	76
1853	7	136
1854	4	88
1855	3	82
1856	3	46
1857	3	46

* From *United States Documents,* Senate Executive Document No. 49, 35th Congress, 1st Session, 29.

APPENDIX C*

BRITISH AFRICAN SQUADRON—TOTAL NUMBER OF SHIPS AND GUNS ON THE COAST OF AFRICA, 1843–1857

Year	Vessels	Guns
1843	14	141
1844	14	117
1845	20	180
1846	23	245
1847	21	205
1848	21	208
1849	23	155
1850	24	154
1851	26	201
1852	25	174
1853	19	117
1854	18	108
1855	12	71
1856	13	72
1857	16	84

* From *United States Documents,* Senate Executive Document No. 49, 35th Congress, 1st Session, 28.

APPENDIX D*

List of Slavers Captured by the American Squadron

Name of Vessel	Date Captured	Vessel Making Capture	Remarks
Uncas	Mar. 1, 1844	*Porpoise*	No slaves.
Merchant	Dec. 3, 1845	*Jamestown*	Seized by HMS Brig *Cygnet*, Aug. 28, 1845, handed to *Jamestown* at Freetown. No slaves.
Pons	Jan., 1846	*Yorktown*	Off Kabenda. 913 slaves aboard; 150 died in 14 days, 763 landed at Monrovia.
Panther		*Yorktown*	No slaves.
Robert Wilson	Jan. 15, 1846	*Jamestown*	In Puerto Praya Bay. No slaves.
Chancellor	Apr. 10, 1846	*Dolphin*	No slaves.
Casket	Aug. 2, 1846	*Marion*	No slaves.
Martha	June 6, 1850	*Perry*	No slaves.
Chatsworth	Sept. 11, 1850	*Perry*	Off Ambriz. No slaves.
Advance	Nov. 3, 1852	*Germantown*	Caught landing slave supplies. No slaves.
Rachael P. Brown	Jan. 23, 1853	*Germantown*	Boarded in Puerto Praya Bay. No slaves.
H. N. Gambril	Nov. 3, 1853	*Constitution*	1000 mi. south of Congo. No slaves.
Glamogon	Mar. 20, 1854	*Perry*	Congo River. No slaves.

* From Letters to the Secretary of the Navy (WNAM, FM 89, Rolls 101-112).

APPENDIX D* (*Continued*)

Name of Vessel	Date Captured	Vessel Making Capture	Remarks
Delicia	Dec. 21, 1859	*Constellation*	Off Kabenda. No slaves.
White Cloud	May 23, 1860	*Mohican*	No slaves.
Thomas Achorn	June 27, 1860	*Mystic*	No slaves.
Triton	July 16, 1860	*Mystic*	No slaves.
Erie	Aug. 8, 1860	*Mohican*	Off Congo River. 997 slaves landed at Monrovia.
Storm King	Aug. 9, 1860	*San Jacinto*	619 slaves. Off Congo River. Slaves landed at Monrovia.
Cora	Sept. 25, 1860	*Constellation*	705 slaves. 694 landed at Monrovia; 11 died in voyage.
Bonita	Oct. 10, 1860	*San Jacinto*	750 slaves. Landed at Monrovia.
Express	Feb. 25, 1861	*Saratoga*	No slaves.
Nightingale	Apr. 21, 1861	*Saratoga*	Off Kabenda. 961 slaves landed at Monrovia.
Triton	May 21, 1861	*Constellation*	No slaves.
Falmouth	June 14, 1861	*Sumpter*	No slaves.

* From Letters to the Secretary of the Navy (WNAM, FM 89, Rolls 101-112).

VI.

Italian Settlement Policy in Eritrea and its Repercussions 1889-1896

by

RICHARD PANKHURST

Director of the Institute of Ethiopian Studies,
Haile Sellassie I University, Ethiopia

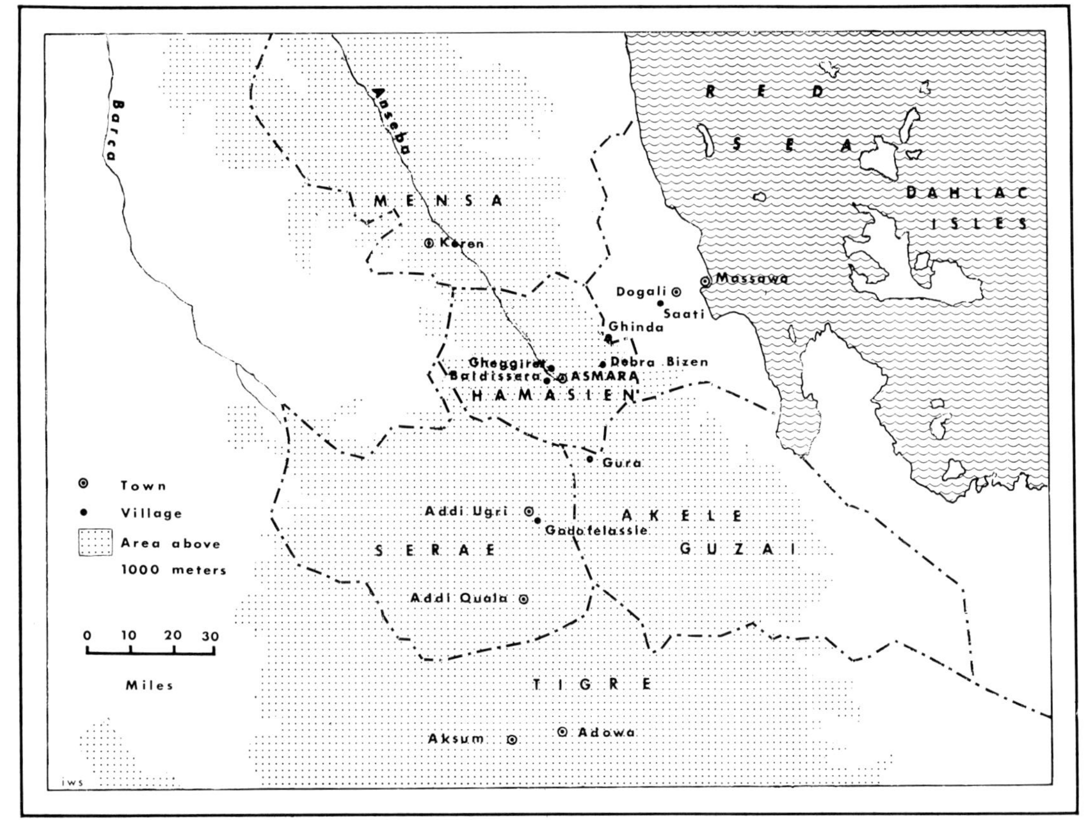

THE ERITREAN PLATEAU

THE IDEA OF EUROPEAN SETTLEMENT in the cool highlands of East Africa played a major role in the theory and practice of Italian colonial activity in the last decade of the nineteenth century. The short-lived Italian project of establishing large numbers of settlers in Eritrea thus occurred early in the era of the scramble for Africa, indeed before the main period of white settlement in Kenya with which it nonetheless affords interesting comparisons and contrasts.

Though the Italian experiment was a complete failure it is of considerable historical interest as it provided one of the main reasons for Italian expansion in this part of Africa, while fear of land expropriation contributed largely in rallying the local population behind the Emperor Menelik II and thereby in assuring his remarkable victory at the Battle of Adowa in March 1896. The patriotism of the Ethiopian people, particularly of the northerners in whose country the campaign was fought, played an important part in deciding the outcome of the war—a critical event in Ethiopian history—and affords an example of national unity seldom equalled in the chronicles of the land.[1] Besides ensuring the continued independence of Ethiopia, the outcome of the war spelt disaster for the Italian settlement schemes which though significant were thus ephemeral.

I

Italian expansion in Africa may be said to have begun for practical purposes in February 1885 when Rear Admiral Caimi seized the port of Massawa which had shortly before been abandoned by the Egyptians on account of the Mahdist revolution in the Sudan. After occupying the port the Italians began to move inland. They were defeated by the Ethiopian commander, Ras Alula, at Dogali in the coastal strip in January, 1887,[2] but succeeded in the summer

---

1 C. Conti Rossini, *Italia, ed Etiopia* (Rome, 1935), 173-74.

2 A. B. Wylde, *Modern Abyssinia* (London, 1901), 49; E. S. Pankhurst, *Eritrea on the Eve* (Woodford Green, England, 1952), 38-39.

of 1889 in making their way up to the plateau in a period of chaos which resulted in part from the death of the Emperor Yohannes, who had been killed while fighting against the Mahdists, and in part from a cattle plague and famine of unprecedented proportions.[3] By the end of 1889 the Italians were thus in possession of an extensive stretch of highlands which seemed climatically ideal for Europeans to live in and contained considerable areas which on account of war, famine and epidemics had at least temporarily been abandoned by their inhabitants.[4] The stage seemed set for European settlement.

Though the existence of the Ethiopian highlands with their cool temperate climate had caused the Swiss adventurer Werner Munzinger to contemplate the possibility of settlement by Chinese as early as 1875,[5] the question of colonisation did not attain practical significance until the Italians actually succeeded in bringing part of the plateau under effective military occupation. Even in the first phase of the occupation there was little talk of settlement as this might not have accorded with the frequent professions of friendship towards the people of the area. The Ethiopians, it should be emphasised, had a plentiful supply of fire-arms and had therefore to be treated with caution.[6] General Baldissera, who occupied the town of Asmara and the neighbouring plateau, was at the time most anxious to avoid provoking popular opposition. Accordingly, he issued a proclamation on August 2, 1889, in which he pardoned criminals, promised to protect all existing interests and even called on people who had earlier been deprived of their land to come to him so that he could afford them justice. The proclamation declared:

> Cultivators, traders. Do not fear. The Government will be the Government of Italy. Come: I will give you what belonged to

---

[3] R. Pankhurst, *An Introduction to the Economic History of Ethiopia* (London, 1952), 230-37.

[4] R. Pankhurst, "The Great Ethiopian Famine of 1889-92," *University College of Addis Ababa Review*, I (1961), 90-103.

[5] E. Cerutti, "Considerazione circa l'Eritrea," *L'Explorazione Commerciale* (1892), 219.

[6] See R. Pankhurst, "Fire-arms in Ethiopian History," *Ethiopia Observer*, VI (1963), 135-80.

your father. You who say that you had *gulti, resti* and *shumet,** and were dispossessed, come and let me know of this. . . . He who has committed murder or robbery in the past is pardoned. He will not be charged.

. . . . Woe to you who in the future make raids, rob the merchants or fail to respect the law. You will be severely punished. I am a Christian. Priests and lay persons continue in the religion of your fathers. I have come to protect and enrich the country, not to destroy it. I have fixed Thursday as the market day and the day for audiences in Asmara. . . .

Do not fear; sell and buy. . . . He who is wronged come to me. This is said by the General who represents the Government of Italy in Hamasien.

(signed) Baldissera[7]

Notwithstanding such words, which might have been taken to constitute a guarantee that traditional ownership of land would be respected, there soon emerged a school of Italian thought which took the view that the territory was ideally suited for European settlement, that the Colony should be made to absorb at least part of the massive emigration from Italy, that State and "abandoned" lands should be put at the disposal of Italian colonists, and that "native" land rights should be curtailed in the interests of white settlement.

To understand this turn of Italian policy it is necessary to recall that northern Ethiopia was at this time suffering from acute economic difficulties unprecedented in its recorded history. The country had been ravaged by the fighting of 1875 and 1876 against the Egyptians and by subsequent Egyptian-inspired banditry. A. B. Wylde, previously British Vice-Consul for the Red Sea, describing the province of Hamasien, observed: "Poor Hamasen! from 1873 to 1878, both years included, it had a bad time of it. This plateau used to be called the Plain of the Thousand Villages. Not one-half of them was now occupied, and some of them have only perhaps five or six families living in them, while others are totally deserted."[8]

---

* *gulti* and *resti,* forms of land tenure; *shumet,* political appointment.

---

[7] A. Mori, *Manuale di Legislazione della Colonia Eritrea* (Rome, 1914), I, 771; A. Omodeo, V. Peglion and G. Valenti, *La Colonia Eritrea* (Rome, 1913), 17n.

[8] A. B. Wylde, *'83 to '87 in the Soudan* (London, 1888), I, 216.

At the beginning of 1889, little more than a decade after that account was written, an epidemic of rinderpest broke out which swept away the great majority of the country's livestock. The virtual non-existence of plough oxen rendered cultivation almost impossible, and an acute famine resulted in which the starving peasants fell easy prey to cholera and small-pox. The population of most parts of the country was decimated, while thousands of famine victims abandoned their homes and farms and made their way to the coast in the hope of obtaining imported grain.[9] The position around Asmara at this time may be seen from the account of the British traveller, Theodore Bent, who observed: "Civil war, famine, and an epidemic of cholera, have, within the last decade, played fearful havoc in Abyssinia, villages are abandoned, the land is going out of cultivation. . . . It is scarcely possible to realise without visiting the country, the abject misery and wretchedness which has fallen upon the Empire during late years."[10]

These calamities, which may be compared with those which preceeded European settlement in Kenya,[11] had profound political and economic consequences. On the one hand they greatly disorganised the ancient Ethiopian State and reduced the possibility of efficient resistance to Italian encroachments, while, on the other, they produced extensive depopulation and provided apparent justification for Italian colonisation of abandoned or semi-abandoned areas. The question of "abandoned lands," which had its parallel in British East Africa settlement history, was to dominate Italian thinking for the next few years; it became a crucial matter after July 1, 1890, when King Umberto of Italy decreed that the Italian Government had assumed the right to make all the Colony's laws, including those relating to land tenure.[12]

The idea of Italian settlement on the Eritrean plateau made rapid progress. Almost everyone who learnt anything of the area was impressed by its salubrious climate, which appeared ideal for

---

9 R. Pankhurst, "Ethiopian Famine," 90-103.

10 T. Bent, *The Sacred City of the Ethiopians* (London, 1896), 11-12. See F. Martini, *Il Diario Eritreo* (Florence, 1946), II, 237.

11 L. S. B. Leakey, *Mau Mau and the Kikuyu* (London, 1952), 9.

12 Mori, *Manuale,* II, 95-97; L. Franchetti, *Mezzogiorno e Colonie* (Rome, 1950), 133.

European colonisation, as well as the good opportunities for agricultural development. It was generally believed that settlement schemes were practicable and certain of success. On March 5, 1890—only 7 months after General Baldissera's proclamation—the Italian Prime Minister, Francesco Crispi, informed the Italian Parliament that settlement in Africa was part and parcel of Italian policy.[13] A couple of months later on May 13, he gave the news that farmers and capitalists from Italy would shortly be sailing for the Colony.[14]

Many Italians at this time were greatly influenced by the extent of emigration from their country and by the feeling that emigrants who settled in foreign lands not under the Italian flag were somehow "lost" to Italy. The rate of emigration was, moreover, growing rapidly, as may be seen from the following figures. No less than 2,207,331 persons had emigrated between 1876 and 1889.[15]

Year	Number of Emigrants
1876	108,771
1877	99,213
1878	96,268
1879	119,831
1880	119,901
1881	135,832
1882	161,562
1883	169,101
1884	147,017
1885	157,193
1886	167,829
1887	215,665
1888	290,736
1889	218,412

At first the Italian authorities thought in terms of giving Italian colonists the land in large estates of 100 square kilometres, some-

[13] Ministero degli Affari Estari, *L'Africa Italiana al Parlamento Nazionale, 1882–1905* (Rome, 1907), 204.

[14] C. Matteoda, "Il Pensiero dei Pionieri sulla Valorizzazione Economico-agraria della Colonia Eritrea," *Atti di Primo Congresso di Studi Coloniali* (1931), VII, 332.

[15] Commissario Generale dell'Emigrazione, *L'Emigrazione Italiana dal 1910 al 1923* (Rome, 1924), 819.

what in the manner which was to be practiced in the "white highlands" of British East Africa. Soon, however, the very different idea of small farms for peasant cultivators gained ground.[16]

II

An important role in the development of Italian settlement in Eritrea was played by Baron Leopoldo Franchetti, who was put in charge of Italian colonisation on June 19, 1890,[17] and who subsequently became head of the *Ufficio per la Colonizzazione*, which was set up on January 25, 1891.[18] A parliamentary deputy from Umbria, and a man of considerable personal wealth, he was also an energetic propagandist expounding his views in the Chamber of Deputies, in journals of opinion such as the *Nuova Antologia* and in his own pamphlet *L'Italia e la sua Colonia Africana.*[19]

In the latter part of 1890, Franchetti established an agricultural experimental station just outside Asmara. No fewer than 96 different types of seed were sown, and in the following year two additional stations were established, one at Gura in Akele Guzai and the other at Godofelassi in Serae.[20] Satisfactory results were announced which were said to prove the practicability of white settlement, though a later Italian writer claimed that the sites were geographically too similar to each other to enable the formulation of a general view of the Colony's potential and that many of the experiments were designed to prove the possibility of colonisation rather than to ascertain which in fact were the best crops to grow.[21] Bent, writing

---

16 Franchetti, *Mezzogiorno,* lx-lxi; *See l'Africa Italiana . . .* , 224.

17 Mori, *Manuale,* II, 90-91; C. de la Jonquière, *Les Italiens en Erythrée* (Paris, n.d.), 187; Matteoda, "Pionieri," VII, 335.

18 Mori, *Manuale,* II, 220-22.

19 The pamphlet first appeared as an article: Franchetti, "L'Italia e la Sua Colonia Africana," *Nuova Antologia* (Rome, 1891), 493, 498-509; Cerutti, "Considerazione," 222.

20 P. de Lauribar, *Douze Ans en Abyssinie* (Paris, 1898), 48-49; B. Melli, *La Colonia Eritrea* (Parma, 1900), 52-53, 73-74; *I Nostri Errori: Tredici Anni in Eritrea* (Milan, 1898), 133-38, 166-72; Franchetti, *Mezzogiorno,* lxxiii; A. de G. Maistre, *Contro la Politica Coloniale* (Milan, 1888), passim; F. Virgilii, "Dall'Emigrazione alla Colonizzazione," *Atti del Primo Congresso,* VI, 188; *Relazione Generale della R. Commissione d'Inchiesta sulla Colonia Eritrea* (Rome, 1891), 35-37.

21 *I Nostri Errori,* 133-35.

a few years later, reported that experiments at Asmara had been a "considerable success" as far as cereals were concerned, but that the climate had not been as propitious as had been hoped for either grapes or olives. Results at the Godofelassi station had "not been very satisfactory," and the olives sent out from Italy had been a complete failure; experiments at Gura, on the other hand, had proved a greater success than elsewhere.[22]

The thesis expounded by Franchetti and his followers of the "colonialist school" was, very simply, that there was an abundance of cultivatable land on the Eritrean plateau, and that at the existing rate of Italian emigration it would be possible to absorb Italian peasant emigrants for a period of two generations. He urged that Italian emigration should be canalised into Eritrea, where settlers should be given free land and credit facilities. He claimed that Italian peasants would find no difficulty in acclimatising themselves, and that the Italian military posts would provide them with guaranteed markets. He therefore recommended that the Italian authorities should increase their agricultural research to build up a body of useful data, and that public lands should be measured and taken over in the interests of settlement.[23]

The idea of Italian settlement which Crispi had propounded in 1890 was accepted by his rival and successor, the Marchese di Rudini on May 5, 1891.[24] It could therefore be considered a matter above party at least as far as the greater part of the political spectrum in Italy was concerned. The project took an important step forward when the Italian Government appointed a Royal Commission of Enquiry on March 11, 1891, which after visiting the territory, produced a report on November 12, 1891.[25] The Commission was an influential body composed of a Senator, Guiseppe Borgnini, five Parliamentary deputies Ferdinando Martini, Giulio Bianchi, Conte Luigi Ferrari and the Marchese Antonino di San Guiliano, and an officer, Lieutenant-General Nobile Edoardo Driquet.

Their report, throws some light on Italian land policy. It was

[22] Bent, *Sacred City*, 20, 88, 206.

[23] Franchetti, *l'Italia e la Sua Colonia Africana*, 31, 34, 37, 39-40, 45; Matteoda, "Pionieri," 336-38; *L'Africa Italiana*, 259, 333, 354, 361, 365.

[24] Cerutti, "Considerazione," 222, 259-66.

[25] Mori, *Manuale*, II, 231-33.

entirely in favour of settlement: "The Colony of Eritrea is able to serve in the future as the vent of part of Italian emigration, and there is reason to hope that little by little it will be able to finance itself."[26]

The Commissioners recalled that Italy was short of capital, had a dense and growing population with a consequent high rate of emigration, and constituted too small a market to allow it by itself to achieve adequate agricultural and industrial development. In these circumstances, it was argued, the object of colonial policy should be twofold: firstly, to obtain cultivatable land with a healthy climate where Italian emigrants could better their position without abandoning their nationality, and, secondly, to acquire secure and permanent markets which would be advantageous to metropolitan Italy. Study on the spot had convinced the Commissioners that the Eritrean highlands were suitable for extensive settlement.[27] They had good soil, adequate rainfall and could yield plentiful agricultural produce. The climate was cool and healthy and therefore ideal for the permanent residence of Europeans. The plateau, moreover, was relatively near to the coast, and, compared with existing areas of settlement, such as Australia, South Africa and Latin America, was not too far from metropolitan Italy. The Eritrean plateau was therefore envisaged as one where Italian agricultural labourers, then earning on average less than a lira a day, would have the opportunity of transforming themselves into peasant proprietors, while at the same time maintaining their Italian nationality which they would be obliged to abandon if they emigrated to other parts of the world.[28]

The Commissioners were also attracted by the fact that the Eritrean plateau was sparsely populated; they had been led to believe that the population had fallen by more than half in the few years prior to their visit.[29]

Turning to the question of land ownership the Commissioners urged the need for flexibility, a principle which they believed would ensure an opening for Italian colonisation. They declared that

---

26 *Relazione Generale*, 204; Matteoda, "Pionieri," VII, 336.
27 *Relazione Generale*, 6.
28 *Ibid.*, 12-40.
29 *Ibid.*, 40.

property rights should "not be subjected to a system incompatible with a rapid increase of agriculture and scientific colonisation," as "would certainly be the case" if the authorities attempted to respect "all the laws and local customs" of the land, or introduced "the rigid concepts" of the Italian civil code and the "ties and fetters" of Italian law.[30]

Having thus devised a formula for land acquisition which would have been impossible under either Ethiopian customary law or the Italian code of law, the Commissioners proceeded to argue that the Colony contained extensive State domains which could be made available to Italian colonists. Enumerating the causes for the existence of such lands the report observed that some lands had always belonged to the State and others had for one reason or another in recent times reverted to it. The latter category comprised three main divisions. Firstly, "lands formerly the property of clans and villages, but abandoned by their inhabitants"; these lands, which were said to include "some of the best in the Colony," had, it was claimed, passed into the possession of the State, "according to Ethiopian law." Secondly, "lands which had become the property of the State through the extinction of the [land-holding] clan." Thirdly lands which had been confiscated by the Emperor Yohannes or his local governor, Ras Alula, prior to the Italian occupation.

Elaborating on their claim that State and other land could be taken over for purposes of settlement the Commissioners presented a number of arguments which constituted little more than special pleading in favour of expropriation. The report declared that expropriation was part of the country's tradition, for the Ethiopian sovereign had always had "the power to do what he wished, the subjects were obliged to obey him, and he was responsible only before God for the injustices he committed." The Commissioners also claimed that Ethiopians "did not have a great attachment to the soil or in general to the place of birth," and that they therefore "migrated easily." An individual proprietor or tribe moved by the Government for the latter's own purposes would submit, they said, "with resignation and perhaps even with pleasure" when the new location was believed to be superior to the old. The report added

---

30 *Ibid.*, 156.

that the Emperors Yohannes and Menelik both frequently transposed entire populations from one place to another, and had carried out expropriations on a vast scale, leaving the proprietors only such land as they could themselves cultivate.

The Commissioners' final argument was that it would not be difficult to find available land in a country where the density of population was only about 4 inhabitants per square kilometre and was tending to fall rather than to increase, and where the cultivatable land greatly exceeded not only the needs of the people but also their possibilities of cultivation. The report concluded that land legislation should be designed "to facilitate colonisation and the progress of agriculture; in other words it must make easier the passage of land into the hands of Italians, and, as between Italians, of those who can cultivate it best."

To achieve this objective the Commissioners recommended an enquiry into the cadestrial register at the ancient Ethiopian city of Aksum and into the archives of the monastery of Debra Bizen, as well as an examination of the memories of the older generation, with a view to establishing the location and extent of the State domains of traditional times. The purpose of this enquiry was to assist the authorities in preventing or eradicating the "usurpation" of such lands by "natives," and, when suitable, to place the land at the disposal of Italian emigrants.

Since State lands even on the most flexible definition were presumed insufficient the Commissioners also recommended a policy of confiscation, but urged that it should be carried out with great caution, little by little, and with a minimum of publicity. They claimed that in most cases no hardship would be involved for every clan possessed much more land than it could use. Nevertheless they again warned against recourse to ordinary legal methods, observing that to use the expropriation laws of Italy, with their complicated terms and formalities, would be a "massive mistake." As for compensation it should be given on the basis of individual circumstances, by payment in money, the provision of land in other parts of the colony, or partial or total exemption from taxes.

The Commissioners also recommended that the authorities should "facilitate in every way the acquisition by Italians of lands belonging to the natives." Up to that time, the report noted, Italian purchase of land had wisely been prohibited in the fear that speculators would buy up extensive stretches of good land at minimal prices and then monopolise them without cultivating them, a course of action alike detrimental to the State and to bona fide colonists. To avoid this danger the Commissioners urged the need to determine exactly which land should be reserved for future development either by the State or by Italian farmers, and proposed that the sale of lands by "natives" to Europeans should not be considered valid unless approved by the Government, the latter having the right to refuse such authorisation or to insist on the modification of agreements contrary to the public interest.

At the same time the Commissioners recommended that traditional systems of land tenure should be modified to facilitate the purchase of land by Italians. The report pointed out that collective ownership presented an almost insuperable obstacle to sales or long-term concessions, as the consent of the entire village or tribe was required before they could be made. The report therefore considered it necessary to encourage the emergence of a system of private property "in order" as it said, "to remove a great obstacle to colonisation."

Finally, the Commissioners urged the need for compulsory land registration, a proposal which clearly supplemented all their other recommendations.[31]

The Commissioners' report, which virtually gave a blank cheque to unlimited settlement and expropriation, had no small effect on Italian colonial policy. Italian thought, as a study mission of the Società Italiana per il Progresso delle Scienze remarked in 1913, was now dominated by three major assumptions all of which were embodied in the report. Firstly, that the ownership of land in Ethiopia was traditionally vested in the sovereign who could allocate it or appropriate it at will. Secondly, that State lands were not needed by the inhabitants who cultivated them and that persons who had abandoned their lands had thereby forfeited to the State all rights of tenure. Thirdly, that the needs of Italian emigrants necessitated and justified the placing of vast amounts of land at their disposal.[32]

---

[31] The above paragraphs are based on pages 178-86 of the *Relazione Generale.*

[32] Omodeo, *Eritrea,* 16.

Though these assumptions largely passed unchallenged at the time, they were open, as the Società Italiana observed, to the gravest possible criticism.[33] In the first place the sovereign's traditional ownership of the land was largely theoretical; the basic feature of the Eritrean plateau, as all authorities agree, was that the greater part of the land was in one way or another vested in the community and could not be alienated except in special circumstances. Thus the modern writer, S. F. Nadel, notes that family ownership (*resti*) "represents the paramount land title in Eritrea . . . the people speak of *resti* as a 'fundamental' right and a 'sacred' possession."[34] In the second place Italians contentions about State lands were considerably distorted. Such lands had been devised to supply the sovereign with provisions, but were nonetheless inhabited by cultivators who lived on a share of the crop. The allocation of State lands to Italian peasant cultivators would therefore necessitate the expropriation of already established Ethiopians, who, though they might not have any theoretical permanence of tenure, would, under the Ethiopian system, seldom or never have been obliged to move. The Italian thesis that abandoned land traditionally became the property of the State and could therefore be used for settlement was also little more than a half truth. It was true that such lands, if really abandoned, were said to revert to the State; on the other hand the principle of clan or village ownership was so strong that descendants could always reclaim their share in ancestral property, even after the passage of many generations. The question whether the land was in fact abandoned or to what extent it was abandoned was, moreover, an important issue which the Italians tended to ignore. Because of the temporary economic dislocation and distress, many areas had been evacuated by their inhabitants, a large proportion of whom had died, but in many cases there were survivors who hoped to return as soon as they

---

33 *Ibid.*, 16.

34 F. Nadel, "Land Tenure on the Eritrean Plateau," *Africa*, XVI (1946), 1-22, 99-109; M. Perham, *The Government of Ethiopia* (London, 1948), 290-92; Balambaras Mahteme Sellassie Wolde Maskal, "The Land System of Ethiopia," *Ethiopia Observer*, I (1957), 290; Gebre Wold Ingida Worq, "Ethiopia's Traditional System of Land Tenure and Taxation," *Ethiopia Observer*, V (1961), 318.

were again in a position to resume cultivation. To the Italians these areas constituted abandoned lands, irrespective of whether any survivors might still be alive. This view ran entirely contrary to Ethiopian tradition which held that rights of ownership were vested in the community and would not be alienated from any descendants who might remain or return to the area even generations later. (It may be argued that Italian awareness of these facts prompted the report's emphasis on the need to reject traditional systems of land tenure.) In the third place the Italian argument that settlers should be given all suitable land which might be available was based on the reiterated assertion that considerable land surpluses existed. Though the economic difficulties of the period had resulted in extensive depopulation, history was to show that within a few generations Eritrea was to become an overcrowded territory and that there was in the long run no room for extensive foreign settlement.[35]

Italian opinion in the early 1890's was in the main favourable to the principle of settlement, the more so as the weaknesses in the Commissioners' case were not yet apparent. The journal *L'Esplorazione Commerciale* published an article in 1892 which revealed that the famous German explorer, Georg Schweinfurth, had pointed out that Eritrea was one of the colonies nearest to Europe and had expressed the view that almost all the Eritrean villages possessed more land than they needed. He believed that hundreds of Italian families could be settled in the vacant land of every village, that the villagers could be persuaded by tax exemptions to look upon this with favour, and that Italian colonists could thus be introduced into the area without the need for expropriation. Another German author, Gerhard Rohlfs, was cited as stating that 100,000 persons could live in the then largely uninhabited Ghinda valley.[36]

III

Settlement began in earnest in the latter part of 1893 when stone houses were built at the foot of the Italian fort at Addi Ugri, four kilometres from Godofelassi. In November and December

---

35 S. H. Longrigg, *A Short History of Eritrea* (London, 1945), 164-65.

36 Cerutti, "Considerazione," 220-21.

a band of 29 Lombard, Venetian and Sicilian peasants with 15 women and 17 children arrived. Each family received 20 or 25 hectares of land, agricultural implements, cattle and the necessary provisions for the period prior to the first crop. These supplies were made available on the basis of 3% loans of 4,000 lire per family, and it was promised that families cultivating the land by their own effort for five consecutive years would be given permanent tenure.[37]

Not long afterwards some 200 Italians were given land at Ghinda on the edge of the plateau where they began cultivation of maize, durra, potatoes, beans and gourds.[38]

Franchetti had sufficient funds to operate a modest settlement programme. His annual expenses were as follows:[39]

YEAR	EXPENSES
1890–1	117,000 lire
1891–2	94,240 lire
1892–3	150,000 lire
1893–4	152,708 lire

Life in Eritrea, however, turned out far less satisfactory than the settlers had been led to expect. The hardships inevitable in the pioneering stage were intensified by the effects of the famine and by incompetence in official quarters. There was an acute shortage of all supplies. The livestock of the Colony having almost all perished, it was necessary to import mules from Italy which though unacclimitised to the country and therefore inferior to the native animal, fetched fabulous prices which the settlers could ill afford. In certain areas drinking water was not available and was therefore shipped from Naples in special boats.[40]

Though the Italian Government and its local administration both favoured colonisation, friction soon developed between Franchetti and General Baratieri, the Governor of the Colony. The Italian

---

[37] de Lauribar, *Abyssinie,* 51; Franchetti, *Mezzogiorno,* lxxvi-lxxviii, 320, 403; *I Nostri Errori,* 133.

[38] de Lauribar, *Abyssinie,* 208; *L'Africa Italiana,* 174, 204, 335, 338, 503-04, 662, 710.

[39] Franchetti, *Mezzogiorno,* 407n; de Lauribar, *Abyssinie,* 52.

[40] *Ibid.,* 500-02; Martini, *Diario,* I, 201.

officials were mainly military men with little knowledge of or interest in agriculture, and seem to have been reluctant to make any thorough surveys of the territory lest this aroused the opposition of the entire Eritrean population; expropriation was therefore often on a haphazard basis. The pioneers moreover had been badly selected. They included factory workers from Milan who were unused to the countryside, old persons too inflexible to adjust their way of life, and peasants from various parts of Italy who spoke local dialects and did not feel any sense of unity or common purpose. It is also said that Franchetti did not allow them sufficient initiative. Unexpected natural calamities also had their effect in destroying morale. The country, as we have seen, had just experienced a severe epidemic of cattle plague, and many of the cows imported by the Italians fell victim to it. Crops also suffered heavily from hail and locusts. The settlers, furthermore, encountered great difficulty in selling their produce as means of transport were rudimentary and the market was very limited. Faced with such unsatisfactory prospects and being in need of ready money a number of the settlers abandoned their land and took work with the Italian Government which, because of the shortage of European labour, was willing to pay higher wages than the average colonist's anticipated earnings from the land.[41]

Wages, however, were by no means attractive, for as Bartolommei-Gioli later observed, the abundance and low price of Eritrean labour inevitably depressed the earnings of the unskilled Italian labourer, though a certain racial differential was normal.[42] The typical wage for an Italian labourer, according to Powell-Cotton, was one and three quarter to two dollars a day, as against a quarter to three quarters for a "native." These figures are confirmed by both Martini and Bartolommei-Gioli.[43] Finally there was no gain-

---

[41] *I Nostri Errori,* 134-36, 167-70; Franchetti, *Mezzogiorno,* 283-310; de Lauribar, *Abyssinie,* 49; *L'Africa Italiana,* 176, 225-26, 347, 454, 514-15, 519; F. O., *Eritrea* (London, 1919), 17.

[42] G. Bartolommei-Gioli, *La Colonizzazione Agricola dell'Eritrea,* (Milan, 1903), 40.

[43] P. H. G. Powell-Cotton, *A Sporting Trip Through Abyssinia* (London, 1902), 520; F. Martini, *Diario,* II, 133, III, 59; R. Paoli, *Nella Colonia Eritrea* (Milan, 1908), 96-97; Bartolommei-Gioli, *Colonizzazione,* 39; R. Pankhurst, "Status, Division of Labour and Employment in Nineteenth and Early

saying that an atmosphere of insecurity prevailed, for settlement was being effected in the face of one of the best armed native people of Africa.[44] This sense of insecurity could not be dispelled until the Italians had made themselves masters not only of Eritrea but also of nearby Ethiopia—as de Lauribar observed the work of the plough could not really begin until the work of the gunpowder had been completed.[45]

The difficulties of life in Eritrea made it impossible to settle any large number of Italian women. Even as late as 1905 the Census of that year recorded that the European population comprised only 309 women over the age of 16 as against 1,684 men of the same age. Of the men, 1,343, or 79.75%, were celibate, while only 94, or 30.42%, of the women were unmarried.[46] This disproportion, coupled with the absence of a strong feeling of racial superiority on the part of the Italians, led to the institution of the so-called *madame* system where by many Italians took Eritrean women, almost invariably Christians, to live with them. De Lauribar says that the Italians tended to be enthusiastic about the Eritrean women and praised their beauty, faithfulness and adaptability.[47] There was also a considerable amount of prostitution, particularly to meet the demand of the Italian soldiers.[48] A sizeable half-caste population soon emerged, the existence of which tended to differentiate the Colony from nearby areas of Anglo-Saxon settlement.[49]

Twentieth Century Ethiopia," *University College of Addis Ababa Ethnological Society Bulletin,* II (1961), 47.

44 Pankhurst, "Fire-arms," passim.

45 de Lauribar, *Abyssinie,* 50.

46 Camera dei Deputati, *Relazione sulla Colonia Eritrea* (Rome, 1913), I, 48-49.

47 de Lauribar, *Abyssinie,* 294-95; Martini, *Diario,* I, 88, 220, 262-63, III, 581, IV, 48-50, 101, 173; Paoli, *Eritrea,* 82, 299; F. Scheibler, *Setti Anni di Caccia Grossa* (Milan, 1900), 372-73; A. Pollera, *La Donna in Etiopia* (Rome, 1922), 73-76; P. G. Jansen, *Abissinia di Oggi* (Milan, 1935), 41-48; G. B. Penne, *L'Africa Italiana* (Rome, 1906), 212-23; A. Sapelli, *Memorie d'Africa* (Bologna, 1953), 199-200.

48 Martini, *Diario,* IV, 246, 349, IV, 93.

49 Metodio Da Nembro, *La Mission dei Minori Cappuccini in Eritrea* (Rome, 1953), 120-22.

IV

The settlement policy which, as we have seen, had been canvassed with growing support since 1889, led in due course to legislative action. Decrees were drawn up in the spirit of the 1891 report to make vast areas of the plateau available to Italian colonisation.[50] An initial decree establishing the principle of State lands in Eritrea was signed by King Umberto of Italy on January 19, 1893,[51] and a few months later on June 6 a Cadastral office was set up.[52] On August 26 Baratieri issued a decree forbidding anyone to occupy abandoned land without authority from the Government. The decree defined such land as territory whose inhabitants were no longer in the area whether they had left it in order to emigrate, had been driven away by calamities, or had suffered expropriations at the hand of former kings.[53]

The policy of the Italian authorities at this time may be seen from two important documents produced in April 1894: a report by Franchetti on his hopes and achievements, and a directive from Prime Minister Crispi to General Baratieri on the significance of Italian settlement. Franchetti's attitude was well summed up in the report which he produced on April 2. Observing that Italy faced a shortage of capital side by side with a surplus of labour he reiterated that the best solution for his country's difficulties was to encourage working class emigration by making land available in Italian Africa. In this way proletarian Italians could be turned into land-owning farmers without unduly burdening either the State finances or the capital resources of Italy. Experience to date, he claimed, had shown that settlers could live on a small loan from the Government and would be in a position to repay it after a short period of time. The financial responsibility of the Italian Government need not therefore be considerable, and was insignificant in comparison with the Colony's military expenses, which later would come to an end as soon as sufficient settlement had been achieved.[54] The presence of Italian farmers was essential, he

50 Omodeo, *Eritrea,* 15; Virgilii, *Emigrazione,* 188.

51 Mori, *Manuale,* II, 639-46.

52 *Ibid.,* II, 721.

53 *Ibid.,* II, 745-47.

54 Franchetti, *Mezzogiorno,* 312-15.

argued, because efficient colonisation could only begin with the production and supply of foodstuffs. Once these were available trade would develop, conditions would become favourable for capitalists to settle, and in due course artisans would move in to meet the demand for their type of skill. The process of colonisation would then be complete.[55]

Franchetti's remarks revealed that a considerable change in the situation had occurred since the report of 1891. At that time the Commissioners had been urging that "abandoned" lands should be declared State property, and, as we have seen, this had in fact been decreed on January 19, 1893. Franchetti was now at pains to ensure that the "natives," who had now largely recovered from the famine and were benefiting from the absence of hostilities, should be prevented from "arbitrarily" returning to the "vast fertile plains" which had been "reserved for Italian colonisation" by being decreed state property. "It is indispensable," he declared, "that native cultivation should be forbidden in the areas destined for Italian colonists. I know that at first sight it seems painful to place obstacles to the cultivation of the land. But this impression disappears when one realises that the obstacle to cultivation is only apparent because the natives have not only the power to carry their labour long distances to the uncultivated land at their disposal, but are encouraged to do so." He opposed even the temporary grant of State land to the "natives" on the ground that it would "create difficulties to future colonisation," and added that unless the "natives" were prevented from occupying such land it would be impossible to achieve "a large Italian agrarian colonisation of the plateau," without which Eritrea would remain a merely military Colony and a burden on the Italian State. Moreover he argued that unless the resettlement of "natives" was firmly stopped nothing would prevent them from pouring across the Ethiopian frontier, in which case the docile population would become insubordinate, even the native troops might be affected, and there would be a danger of insurrection.[56]

Franchetti's assertion that Ethiopians might cross the frontier

---

[55] *Ibid.*, 320.

[56] *Ibid.*, 330-33.

to settle on "unoccupied land" requires comment. A significant migration was undoubtedly at this time underway, prompted partly by the great famine and partly by employment opportunities under Italian rule.[57] Wylde states that the Italians, who were short of labour, encouraged settlers from across the frontier, while Powell-Cotton claims that under Italian rule there was greater security and lighter taxes. At all events there was, as Wylde says, a "steady influx" of immigrants into the colony. Though the greater number came from nearby Tigre, others, Bent says, were from Gondar, Shoa and the Galla lands. This is confirmed by Martini, as well as by the Duchesne-Fournet mission which encountered Eritreabound migrants near Lake Tana.[58] Efforts by the Ethiopian authorities to prevent this movement seem to have been largely unsuccessful, though Ras Makonnen then ruler of Tigre, was reported in March 1889 to have ordered the arrest of Amharas and Tigres found endeavouring to cross the frontier. The Ras is said also to have issued a decree that people leaving, the country to become Italian *askari*, or soldiers, would be liable to severe punishment, including the loss of their land (*resti* and *gulti*).[59] The influx of these land-hungry migrants was naturally a source of alarm to persons like Franchetti who wished to see all "unoccupied land" reserved for European settlement. The Società Italiana was nonetheless correct in arguing that under the traditional system of tenure immigrants from other parts of Ethiopia would never have been allowed to obtain land at the expense of the local people.[60]

Explaining his settlement policy in greater detail, Franchetti stated that each Italian family should be given 15 to 20 hectares of land free on condition that it cultivated them with its own hands for a minimum of five consecutive years. The purpose of this latter

---

57 Pankhurst, "Status," 47.

58 Wylde, *Abyssinia*, 143, 263; Powell-Cotton, *Sporting Trip*, 520; Bent, *Sacred City*, 20; Martini, *Nell'Africa Italiana* (Milan, 1896), 108-10; F. Lemmi, *Lettere e Diari d'Africa* (Rome, 1937), 155; Paoli, *Eritrea*, 78; Franchetti, *L'Italia*, 35; Bartolemmei-Gioli, *Colonizzazione*, 32; *L'Africa Italiana*, 794-95, 821.

59 Martini, *Diario*, I, 599, 608, II, 107, 117-18; F.O. 403/177, Barnham, April 25, 1892.

60 Omodeo, *Eritrea*, 55.

provision was to guarantee the settlers' seriousness of purpose and ensure that the land was actually cultivated. Since most of the farmers would be unable to provide for their transport or installation in Africa they should receive loans. An idea of the requirement of an average household could be seen from the case of a typical family, that of a Signor Gornati, which was composed of 4 adults and 3 children between the ages of 4 and 12. Its expenditure for the first year, including transport from Italy was slightly over 4,000 lire, made up as follows:

Transport	978.73 lire
Agricultural equipment	141.19 lire
Cattle	1,147.50 lire
Provisions	1,275.36 lire
Seeds	100.00 lire
Housing	600.00 lire
	4,242.78 lire

The Gornati family's expenses for transport and cattle being somewhat on the liberal side Franchetti argued that 4,000 lire should be taken as the average requirement for a family.[61]

The cost of installing the settlers, he assumed, would tend to fall as time went on. In the early stages the Italian administration would be obliged to build housing for the colonists, but later immigrants would be able to find temporary accommodation with those already established. Housing, moreover, was not a major problem as simple dwellings could be constructed in 15 to 20 days and tents could be used temporarily except during the rainy season. The climate was such that no sheds were required for cattle.[62]

Emphasising the importance of settler agriculture he argued that the "natives" could only produce small quantities of provisions and even these would be of poor quality. The Italian farmers would therefore have to produce their own supplies and also those required by settlers awaiting their first harvest. Once agricultural production was effectively underway immigration could rise in geometrical proportion.

---

61 Franchetti, *Mezzogiorno*, 315-16; *L'Africa Italiana*, 324.

62 Franchetti, *Mezzogiorno*, 322.

An increasing rate of production was, he considered, easily possible. A single family using one plough could cultivate at least 5 hectares the first year. Experiments had shown that the average yield per hectare was substantially more than 10 quintals, but even on the basis of this figure the family could be assured a production of 50 quintals or well above that required for food and seed for the year ahead. In the second year the family could be expected to bring a further 5 hectares under cultivation so that production would rise to some 100 quintals, or at least twice the family's needs. Production could be expected to go on rising until the entire farm had been brought under cultivation.[63]

Franchetti calculated that after the second harvest settlers would be able to devote their produce to the repayment of debts. Because of the difficulty of selling their crops the farmers might be expected to prefer making payment in kind, but should be allowed to pay in cash if they so wished. He proposed that 3% interest should be charged on State loans, but was confident that the rate could later be raised to 5%. Such conditions, he felt, should prove attractive to philanthropic bodies, such as cooperative and other saving banks.[64]

Elaborating on this theme in the Italian Parliament on May 3, 1894, he declared that "the plateau with its fertile soil and abundance of water can allow of, and amply reward, the labour of Italian farmers. The simplest and most economical method [of settlement] seems to be that of colonisation with farmers who must become proprietors of the land accorded to them and who will have the ability to pay back by installments the expenses incurred by the State in establishing them."[65]

Crispi, who returned to power as Prime Minister in December 1893, gave these ideas his full support, and was well aware that they could only be carried out effectively by subordinating Eritrean to Italian interests. This is evident from a letter which he wrote to Baratieri on April 28, 1894, which reveals that the principle of emigration and settlement was far more a matter of State policy

---

63 *Ibid.*, 321-23, 403.

64 *Ibid.*, 319-20.

65 Matteoda, "Pionieri," 237; *L'Africa Italiana*, 324, 334, 358-59.

than it was, for example, in British East Africa. Crispi observed that the General "knew better than anyone else" that one of the foremost aims of Italian colonial expansion was "to prepare a vast field suitable for emigration," a population movement which had been "closed to other countries," but was nonetheless useful for "our commerce." The letter went on: "The studies thus far made and the efforts of the good Franchetti are sufficient to demonstrate that this aim is both logical and practical. To attain it two things only are required: time and patience." Coming to the heart of the question, he gave his backing to a ruthless solution of the land problem in a series of sentences which combined a complete disregard for Eritrean land rights with a scrupulous insistence on Italian budgetary orthodoxy. He declared:

> in order that the objective is not compromised we must be on guard that native colonisation does not debar our own road and that we are not swayed by an exaggerated scrupulosity when taking over lands which must be in great measure considered *res nullius* and available to the first occupier. Since it is not doubted that these are also your ideas, I am certain that you will do everything to translate them into action, assisting, that is to say, the establishment and development of Italian colonies on the plateau, always, be it understood, within the limits of the budget, and, on the other hand, restraining native colonisation until it has been possible to direct into those regions a spontaneous and vigorous current of national [i.e., Italian] emigration.
>
> The advantages which the security of Eritrea will derive from a strong Italian population established at Asmara, Keren and other convenient localities, well armed and well trained in the use of weapons, a population which will have every interest in defending the lands it cultivates and owns, will surely not escape you for whom the political and military history of the different colonial powers has no secret.[66]

Baratieri was from the outset totally convinced of the desirability of settlement. He accepted the thesis that "the land belonged to the State," his only reservation being that the authorities in alienating land should take precautions to avoid producing an "atmosphere of hostility among the natives."[67] Even before the

[66] F. Crispi, *La Prima Guerra d'Africa* (Rome, 1914), 272-73.

[67] O. Baratieri, *Mémoires d'Afrique* (Paris, n.d.), 167.

receipt of Crispi's letter he had begun issuing a series of decrees specifying areas of the Colony as State lands "reserved for colonisation." The first such area was announced on May 11, 1893, and lay between the villages of Adi Bari, Godofelassi, Zabonena and Adi Mongunti in Serae.[68] Later in the same year, similar decrees were issued on September 18 in respect of the Mensa area,[69] and on December 2 for the Sambel area, as well as the territory of Gheggiret village and the area of the military camp at Fort Baldissera.[70]

Decrees establishing State land and expressly reserving it for colonisation were issued throughout 1894: an area near Himberti in Hamasien on January 19,[71] the allegedly abandoned territories of Adi Are, Chileule, old Azerna, an area cultivated by the families of the Mai Tsada bordering Adilai, the already State owned area of Godofellassi, and four other places: new Azerna, Enda Maliel, Adi Vlai and Amba Zerib on June 6;[72] a stretch of country, partly belonging to the Bizen convent, between the rivers Laba, Wad Gaba and Aidereso on June 12;[73] an area between the Massawa-Saati road and the Iangus and Aidereso rivers on August 24;[74] a piece of land near Modacca and Scinnara on September 19;[75] the allegedly depopulated villages of Chinevale, Adi Ghedella, Adi Zerentai Segherdale, Adi Baridi, Bet Mariam, Mefaliso, Adi Godo, and Adi Secche Assaarti, as well as "redundant land" belonging to the villages of Daro Anto, Adi Adda, Zeban Ona, Adi Colon, Mai Libus, Adi Casciai, Enti, Adi Godati, Ghesa Vasa, Ghesa Gobo, Adi Gobo, Adi Sadi, Mai Armaz and Decmane on November 9,[76] "abandoned lands" in the Barca valley on November 26,[77] and the "depopulated" village of Adi Consub and "redundant land" belong-

---

68 Mori, *Manuale*, II, 716.
69 *Ibid.*, II, 854.
70 *Ibid.*, 832-83, III, 323-24.
71 *Ibid.*, II, 854.
72 *Ibid.*, III, 200.
73 *Ibid.*, 215-17.
74 *Ibid.*, 260-61.
75 *Ibid.*, 266.
76 *Ibid.*, 285-86.
77 *Ibid.*, 316-17.

ing to the villages of Gomoro and Adi Scimindui on December 11.[78]

Decrees establishing further State lands continued to be made throughout the first half of 1895. On February 28 Baratieri signed a decree listing 18 areas of State lands: Zazega, Wolkitba, Adi Conci, Asega Sada Christian in Hamasien, the Scillele lands at Asmara, Medri Zien and the Ad Zaul lands in Carnescim, the lands of Dega Gabru, Demba Ghermet, Maldi Tsada, Wara, Deca Gebru, Decamare, and Cheferes in Dembesan, the lands of Assaldait in Loggo Cina, Resti Saada, Tamesghi and Emesese in Taccala, a part of Serae, Resti Wod Eutabe in Adi Mawa and the lands of Lamsai, both in Dubub, and the Ad Unnio lands in Akel Guzai.[79] Lands belonging to rebels were declared the possession of the State by a decree on March 20,[80] while the area of the Gura agricultural station was classified as State land reserved for colonisation on July 12.[81]

V

The Italian policy of expropriation inevitably had political implications. As Margery Perham notes one of the first effects of the occupation was that the upper structure of provincial administration was swept away except in so far as the new administration allowed favoured chiefs to hold their own estates.[82] The province of Hamasien for example, had been ruled by its famous governor, Ras Aloula, who, as commander of the Ethiopian armies of the extreme north, subsequently won great distinction in resisting Italian penetration. Wylde, who saw Aloula's administration at work in 1883, was greatly impressed: he records that taxes were collected regularly every six months[83] and that "a good house and a full farmyard with clean clothes and general prosperity did not entail an increased taxation."[84] Like other provincial governors, the chief had been given lands in the province the tenure of which was dependent on his service. Thus Wylde mentions a "large farm," as well as "several

78 *Ibid.*, 327, 288-89.
79 *Ibid.*, 351-52.
80 *Ibid.*, 364.
81 *Ibid.*, 453, 361-63.
82 Perham, *Ethiopia*, 292; Martini, *Diario*, II, 237; Nadel, "Tenure," 20.
83 Wylde, *Soudan*, II, 336.
84 Wylde, *Abyssinia*, 264 et passim.

villages" which Aloula held for his soldiers.[85] After their occupation the Italians seized Aloula's house at Asmara and the whole of his estates. Wylde, who visited the area again in 1896, reports that "for nearly five years Ras Aloula had been anxious to get hold of General Baratieri, who had taken his houses, lands and property, not only in the Hamasien but in Tigre as well; the only house that had been spared was that in Axum. Because of the sacred nature of the town, the Italians did not dare to plunder it, as they would have lost the confidence of the entire Abyssinian people which they wished partly to retain."[86]

The Italian land policy led to widespread discontent among the Eritreans. Wylde cites the *shum*, or chief, of one of the largest villages in the Godofelassi region—an area selected, as we have seen, for early settlement—as complaining bitterly. The chief's argument was that if Italy claimed the land by right of conquest it might be said that

> all private titles to landed property are invalid and no native has a right to anything; but what the choum complained of to me was that neither he nor the majority of the land-owners fought against the Italians; on the contrary, they aided them under the idea that they would be treated fairly and that their property would be respected.

Wylde, travelling through the area, comments:

> . . . I passed through the new Italian agricultural settlement and I saw that they had the pick of the ground, and this was given to the settlers from Italy, dispossessing those that had cultivated the land formerly, and whose ancestors might have worked on it for centuries. I have only given one isolated case in one district, but this had been done in other parts as well.

Turning to the political, philosophical or moral aspects of the problem, Wylde asked:

> What confidence could the native be expected to have in a government that started business on such a basis? . . . There is land in the Hamasien sufficient for all, and had the government taken what they required for fortifications and government offices nothing would

[85] *Ibid.*, 145.

[86] *Ibid.*, 220; Conti Rossini, *Italia*, 28; Bent, *Sacred City*, 18.

> have been said; and had they issued a proclamation that all the natives should be allowed to retain their cultivated property on having their claims registered, and also allowed grazing rights on the mountains, no difficulty would have arisen, and the government would have found that they had more territory than they knew what to do with. Abyssinia, in spite of all it has gone through, still has a very large population, and the people show a great vitality and have large families, so it is impossible to wipe them out like the Australian natives or New Zealanders. There is no reason that I can see at present why the Christian population should diminish; on the contrary, there is every prospect of their increasing in number under a settled government; so the land question is one of the greatest importance, and as long as the Abyssinians are treated in a fair and equitable manner they will be found to make good and peaceful subjects, and the reverse if treated badly. I think when the English public learns the facts of our dealing with the land belonging to the natives in Africa that they will be thoroughly disgusted, and I think that the wholesale seizure of land that has taken place in some parts is little removed if any from theft. I am sorry to use such a harsh term, but nothing milder will meet the case; these lands are given away to the first settler that comes along. . . . I do not think the Italian government are so much to blame, as they had a precedent for it from what hitherto has been done by us in Africa; but I consider it was dishonest and ill-advised and I am afraid that there is a good deal of property held by people in Africa that the title-deeds would not bear looking into.[87]

The expropriation of monastery land had particularly serious implications, the significance of which becomes apparent when one remembers the highly religious character of the Ethiopian people. The most serious evictions occurred at the famous convent of Debra Bizen in Hamasien. Though Article IV of the Treaty of Uccialli, which was signed on May 2, 1889, specified that the possessions of the convent should remain the property of Ethiopia, the monks were not spared.[88] Bent, travelling in 1893, noted that they had been deprived of most of their lands "in return for a sum of money which does not satisfy them." The result, he adds, was that "in the whole of their Red Sea colony the Italians have no more vehement opponent than the monks."[89]

---

[87] Wylde, *Abyssinia*, 129-31.

[88] C. Rossetti, *Storia Diplomatica dell'Etiopia* (Turin, 1910), 42; Martini, *Nell'Africa Italiana*, 83.

[89] Bent, *Sacred City*, 44.

The various acts of expropriation had a profound influence on the Eritrean people. As a report of the Italian Società per il Progresso delle Scienze noted, they "provoked the discontent of the native population," and induced an atmosphere of rebellion which led in due course to war between the Italians and Ethiopians.[90] The fact that many of the Eritreans possessed rifles and had the support of well armed forces across the Ethiopian frontier made the "land question" far more explosive at this time in Eritrea than in the corresponding stage of settlement in a colonial territory such as British East Africa.

The most striking manifestation of this discontent was the rebellion of Dejazmach Batha Hagos, the chief of Akele Guzai, on December 15, 1894. This event came as a considerable shock to the Italians who regarded Batha Hagos as one of their most loyal chief. So far from having a record of service to the Ethiopian cause, he had fought against the Emperor Yohannes and Ras Alula and had on one occasion sacked the town of Adowa. Italian surprise at the revolt was intensified by the fact that its leader had been converted to Roman Catholicism, the State religion of Italy, and might therefore have been presumed more "loyal" than other Eritreans. Italian writers, seizing on his conversion, which had been effected by French Lazarists, argued at the time that the disaffection had been spread by missionaries jealous of Italian influence.[91] No concrete evidence, however, was provided for this assertion which was ridiculed by the French writer De la Jonquière.[92]

The significance of the land question is apparent from the local traditions as recorded by Kolmodin who relates that when Batha saw the Italians gradually appropriate the land of Akele Guzai he said to his brother Sengal, "let us rebel!" Sengal asked, "What reason can we invoke for a rebellion against Italy?", whereupon Batha replied:

> O my brother Sengal, do not be so stupid.

---

90 Omodeo, *Eritrea*, 15.

91 Martini, *Diario*, II, 188.

92 De la Jonquière, *Italiens*, passim.

When the white serpent has once bitten you
You will search in vain for a remedy against its bite.[93]

In the proclamation issued at the time of his rebellion, Batha Hagos is quoted by Mantegazza as saying, "We curse the Italians; they are taking our land." These words apparently made a considerable appeal to the populace. They were taken up by the soldiers of Ras Mangasha of Tigre, who, seizing upon Batha's epigram, sung about the danger to be feared from the Italians: "From the bite of the black servant one recovers; the bite of the white serpent is fatal."[94]

The rebellion was the signal for extensive fighting between the Italians and Ethiopians which culminated over a year later in the Italian defeat at Adowa. The Società Italiana per il Progresso delle Scienze, which put the blame for starting hostilities squarely on Italian policy, claimed that Crispi's guilt was not that he had lost a battle but that he had provoked a war.[95]

Some years later, settlement policy and resultant expropriations were held by Italians to have contributed to the failure of Italian expansion. At a congress organised by the Italian Colonial Institute in 1911, Agnese, Director of Colonial Affairs in the Italian Ministry of Foreign Affairs, observed that the "land question" was the most delicate one affecting the colonial people, and drew attention to Baldissera's proclamation of 1889, which had promised the protection of traditional rights. Though Agnese agreed with the 1891 Commissioners' thesis that State ownership of land was a "fundamental and basic principle" of Ethiopian tenure, he declared that this did not justify seizure of land from people who cultivated it on the basis of either acquired rights or traditional occupation. He also attacked the old conception of "abandoned land," arguing, more or less along the lines followed in this paper, that surplus or aban-

[93] J. Kolmodin, *Traditions de Tsazzega et Hazzega* (Upsala, 1915), 201.

[94] V. Mantegazza, *La Guerra in Africa* (Florence, 1896), 262, 267-69, 282; Melli, *Eritrea*, 91; G. F. H. Berkeley, *The Campaign of Adowa and the Rise of Menelik* (London, 1935), 62-64; Conti Rossini, *Italia*, 111; Crispi, *Prima Guerra*, 291-5; De la Jonquière, *Italiens*, 198-202; R. Perini, *Di Qua dal Mareb* (Florence, 1905), 247-50; Baratieri, *Mémoires*, 105-10; G. Canuti, *L'Italia in Africa e le Guerre con l'Abissinia* (Florence, 1897), 106-12.

[95] Omodeo, *Eritrea*, 47.

doned lands had existed during the period of war, cholera and famine, but that "on the return of peace the villages were reoccupied and the lands were no longer surplus." Looking at the question from a purely Italian point of view, he stated that the 1893 decree establishing State land and the subsequent acts of expropriation had led to the "gravest inconveniences," and cited the observations of an Ethiopian who, while admitting serious defects in the administration of his country, nevertheless expressed wholehearted preference for Ethiopian as against Italian rule, on the grounds that the latter endangered the rights of ownership. "In Ethiopia," he declared, "we are maltreated, burdened with taxes and without good justice; but we have the land and no one takes it from us. . . . The Italian Government in Eritrea is taking the land from the inhabitants. We therefore prefer to remain here."[96]

Others at the congress supported Agnese: Martini, speaking as a former Governor of Eritrea, bluntly observed that populations subject to Italian rule had rebelled, rallying to Menelik's cause because they had been robbed of the land. He cited the case of the convent of Debra Mercurios near Adi Quala where 150 monks had been rendered destitute and converted into "a real nest of dangerous malcontents" and told the possibly apochryphal story of a conversation between Menelik and Ras Tessema in which the latter remarked that the people of the Ethiopian province of Tigre would be hostile to Italy "because they know very well that the Italians take the land."[97] Finally, C. Rossetti, another Italian expert on colonial affairs, remarked that Eritrean residents in Khartoum had complained to him that the Italian government has seized the land.[98]

VI

From 1895 on, there was much discord among officials and later armed conflict with the Ethiopians. On February 21, 1895, Franchetti resigned as controller of settlement,[99] the result of a pro-

---

[96] Istituto Coloniale Italiano, *Atti del Secondo Congresso degli Italiani all'Estero* (1911), II, part 1, 482-83; Omodeo, *Eritrea,* 16-17n, 48-49.

[97] *Secondo Congresso,* II, part 1, 486; Omodeo, *Eritrea,* 16-17n.

[98] *Secondo Congresso,* II, part 1, 487.

[99] Franchetti, *Mezzogiorno,* 403; Matteoda, "Pionieri," 338; Mori, *Manuale,* III, 349.

longed dispute with Baratieri, who thereupon assumed responsibility for settlement policy. On April 25 he issued a notice that State lands would continue to be made available to Italian settlers, but on different terms than before. Each family was to receive 8 to 25 hectares according to its size, the fertility of the soil, and the type of cultivation. Such land, normally in temperate areas between 1,000 and 2,500 metres in altitude, would still be given on a temporary basis for 20 years, tenure being rendered permanent as soon as the holders had worked the land continuously for five years with their own labour and had paid an acquisition fee of from 10 to 50 lire per hectare, payable at any time within the 20 year period. Colonists were to be encouraged by a ten year exemption from taxation. Would-be settlers were advised to arrive between October and December, and were informed that the cost of establishing an average family would be from 2,500 to 3,500 lire. No more assistance, however, would be given in raising the money. On the other hand, the Government promised to provide temporary lodging, but expected colonists to shoulder certain responsibilities, including, significantly enough, defence in time of emergency.[100]

The statement all in all could hardly have been expected to encourage many settlers. A family of prospective colonists was invited to spend 2,500 or more lire, but was offered little in return. As an anonymous Italian critic later observed: "What farmer in Italy possessing such a sum would decide to emigrate? And if he did would he wish to risk his life and savings in a country where the results of European farming were still unknown? Would he not prefer to go elsewhere?"[101]

Meanwhile in Eritrea itself the settlers became increasingly anxious as the threat of hostilities between Italy and Ethiopia became more serious. There was some panic after the revolt of Batha Hagos in December, 1894, and the fighting with Ras Mangasha which followed it.[102] Any chances of success which the scheme might have had were destroyed when Menelik mobilised for war in September, 1895. The Italian withdrawal from Makale in December caused panic among the colonists. The Ethiopian victory

---

[100] *Ibid.*, 411-14, 447-48; *I Nostri Errori*, 178-79.

[101] *Ibid.*, 178.

[102] *Ibid.*, 171.

at Adowa on March 1, 1891, transformed the situation, for as Wylde says, "nearly all the Italian cultivators immediately ran away to the coast."[103] Commenting on the settlement at Godofelassi as he saw it immediately after the battle, he suggested that the Italians had in fact achieved little to cause them to cling to the land. "The agricultural settlement," he says, "was a very poor affair, and the houses built for the settlers were simply a copy of the ordinary Abyssinian round-shaped, with the addition of a fireplace and a chimney. They were neither clean nor sanitary, and their fittings were ill-arranged. . . . I looked in vain for good barns, storehouses and cattlesheds. No vestige of gardens had been planted. The agricultural implements were also mostly very poor, but I saw a fair specimen of a light iron plough for two oxen which was a great improvement on that used by the natives, and brought up the ground quicker and better."[104]

A minor but abortive attempt at settlement was made by a Venetian Catholic society with the help of Father Michele, the Apostolic Vicar of Eritrea, but the handful of would-be colonists who arrived found that no preparations had been made for them. There were no houses near the lands they had been allocated, no agricultural implements, no cattle, no provisions, no armed escort. The emigrants, who were unaccustomed to the conditions in the Colony, were greatly depressed by the previous failures, and decided to return home.[105]

Italian settlement had in fact suffered a severe blow from which it could not easily recover. This was underlined by an Italian publication of 1898 which explained that the fields had been abandoned and allowed to deteriorate; the cattle, agricultural implements and crops were either lost or stolen; the settlers, many of whom had fled in panic and spent many months in the heat of Massawa, were completely demoralised.[106] Though the end of hostilities removed the immediate danger to security, the humiliation of the Italian defeat maintained the despondency of the settlers. Morale was low

---

103 Wylde, *Abyssinia,* 131; Mantegazza, *La Guerra,* 284; de Lauribar, *Abyssinie,* 52.

104 Wylde, *Abyssinia,* 131.

105 *I Nostri Errori,* 173.

106 *Ibid.,* 171; Bartolommei-Gioli, *Colonizzazione,* 54-59.

even though strict precautions were taken. As Powell-Cotton notes, "no native, unless a soldier, was allowed to carry arms."[107]

From the economic point of view, too, things were far from hopeful. As Bartolommei-Gioli noted, the end of the war was followed by a contraction in the market for agricultural produce. The settlers also suffered from the fact that as the country gradually recovered from the great famine the Eritreans began marketing increased quantities of provisions at substantially lower prices than those demanded by the Italian farmers with their higher standard of living.[108] Little seems to have come of Bartolommei-Gioli's own idea of raising the land tax in order to reduce the profits of the "native" and thereby to oblige him to restrict his holdings in areas suitable for European cultivation and to move to lower and less healthy areas.[109]

The idea of settlement, though not officially repudiated, ceased to dominate government policy as before. The officials entrusted with the continuation of the scheme proved moreover less enterprising than Franchetti: they were bureaucratic in their methods, ignorant alike of agricultural needs and local conditions, and were too frequently changed. They made no attempt to ascertain which areas were most suitable for colonisation in part, it is said, because any comprehensive survey would have revived and intensified the fears of the Eritrean population.[110]

Above all the policy of land expropriation which had evoked such bitter discontent was for the time being at least suspended. The issue of decrees establishing State lands and reserving them for colonisation had, significantly enough, been terminated at the outbreak of fighting in the latter part of 1895. No expropriation orders were made between July 1895 and May 1899; the only decree relating to land in this period was one of March 31, 1897, which provided compensation for the people of Bet Gabru who had earlier been deprived of their lands in Scinnara,[111] Decrees creating or defining State land began to be issued again in May 1899, but no

---

107 Powell-Cotton, *Sporting Trip,* 435.

108 Bartolommei-Gioli, *Colonizzazione,* 56.

109 *Ibid.,* 43.

110 *I Nostri Errori,* 173, 177-78.

111 Mori, *Manuale,* III, 604.

longer made reference to the reservation of land for colonisation. The post-war Governor, Martini, who took office on December 16, 1897, was, as we have seen, totally opposed to the land policy of his predecessor and had no desire of reinstating it. In his diary, which is a revealing document, Martini, noted as early as March and April, 1898, that the seizure of monastery lands at Debra Bizen had been "unjust" and the "greatest possible error."[112] In later entries he ridiculed Franchetti's ignorance of customary land tenure and described the Bizen expropriation as a "foolish error," the effects of which had been "very injurious for us." He added that the confiscation of land belonging to the Debra Mercorios monks was "unjust and unjustifiable" as well as stupid and damaging to Italy.[113]

The degree to which the colonisation plan had failed can be judged from a report written on June 15, 1901, by the British envoy in Addis Ababa, Thomas Hohler, in which he remarked that the Italian colonists had left after the battle of Adowa but that "none had since come to take their place."[114] Later he observed in his memoirs that the Italians "seemed to be making no progress whatever" in Eritrea where there were "really no colonists and only a few shopkeepers." He added "The colony was not popular and the officers only came to it attracted by the higher pay they received. Again the officers are not popular: at one moment they will be genial and familiar with their men, at another abusive, coarse and tyrannical."[115]

The low calibre of Italian personnel was in part due to the fact that the Government of metropolitan Italy had largely lost interest in the Colony. Theoretical approval for a policy of settlement was voiced by the Foreign Minister, Tommaso Tittoni, on May 16, 1907, but the need for "great caution" was also stressed—a clear recognition that the lesson of Baratieri's mistakes had been learnt. The speech argued that the "best pieces of land," if really unoccupied, should be reserved for immigrants, but added: "if upon the expiration of the leases which the natives at present hold we should send

---

112 Martini, *Dario*, I, 106, 119.

113 *Ibid.*, II, 29, 99, 226, 301, 407, III, 32.

114 F.O. 403/313, Hohler, June 15, 1901.

115 T. Hohler, *Diplomatic Petrel* (London, 1942), 59.

them away from the land they now occupy, then the question would become very serious and would assume a political character . . . it is clear that any provision too lightly decided upon might start a dangerous unrest in the Colony."[116]

Two years later the question of land allocation was regulated by the Italian Land Statute of 1909 (revised in 1926) which transformed further land into Crown property or *terre demaniali* (domanial lands). The application of this statue affected a large variety of lands:—lands which were decreed Crown property for military or economic reasons, or for reasons of public utility (e.g., building-land, roads, rivercourses, land needed for fortifications or aerodromes, mines, quarries and forests); lands the old titles to which were repealed for political reasons; and land to which no clear native title existed.[117] The new statute represented a compromise between the desire of encouraging settlement and the fear of provoking discontent as Baratieri had done a decade or so earlier. Though the law did not envisage the extensive interference with traditional rights proposed by the 1891 commission its application tended once again to serve the interests of settlement. "The regard for the Italian colonists," writes Nadel, "often overruled all other considerations, so that the expropriations exceeded the terms of the Statute and became indistinguishable from expropriations *ad hoc*. The banks of rivers are a typical instance: here it became the established practice to regard as domanial, not only the rivercourses themselves, but also the land on the banks to a depth of 20–30 yards—land, that is, which is specially adapted for the European type of cultivation."[118]

The urge to settle, however, had, as we have seen by now largely evaporated. An Italian writer summing up the position in 1911 declared, "Italian colonial expansion is slow," and added, "the civil bureaucracy of Italy still blocks the way to those economic and commercial reforms which are . . . desirable."[119]

---

[116] T. Tittoni, *Italy's Foreign and Colonial Policy* (London, 1914), 281.

[117] Nadel, "Tenure," 18-19.

[118] *Ibid.*, 19n.

[119] A. Baldacci, "Italian Colonial Expansion," *United Empire* (1911), 498.

VII

The failure of the settlement scheme, which had done so much to arouse opposition to the Italians, may be illustrated by official figures. These reveal that Italian emigration to all parts of the world rose steadily between 1890 and 1905 as shown in the following table:[120]

ITALIAN EMIGRATION, 1890–1905

Year	Number of Emigrants
1890	217,244
1891	293,631
1892	223,667
1893	246,751
1894	225,323
1895	293,181
1896	307,482
1897	299,855
1898	283,715
1899	308,339
1900	352,782
1901	533,245
1902	531,509
1903	507,976
1904	471,191
1905	726,331

Though Italian emigration between 1890 and 1905 thus totalled no less than 5,822,222 persons the number of Italians who had gone to Eritrea were infinitesimal and even fewer, as we have seen, had remained there. The Eritrean Census of 1905 showed that the total European population amounted to only 3,949.[121]

No less remarkable was the fact that out of 1,617 adult male Europeans there were only 62 persons classified as agriculturalists as against 834 military, 349 in industry and 219 in commerce. The detailed occupational break-down was as follows:[122]

120 *L'Emigrazione Italiana dal 1910 al 1923,* 819.

121 *Relazione sulla Colonia Eritrea,* I, 46, 50.

122 *Ibid.,* 50; Omodeo, *Eritrea,* 46.

EUROPEAN OCCUPATIONAL PATTERN IN ERITREA, 1905

Occupation	Males	Females
Agriculture	62	—
Industry	349	18
Commerce	219	10
Domestic service	6	9
Public administration	86	1
Military	834	—
Teaching	1	4
Culture	11	19
Professions	49	1
Without profession	54	261

The number of settlers was in fact steadily declining. In 1902 there had been 126 colonists of whom only 36 cultivated more than 5 hectares, the total area under cultivation being only 1,524 hectares. By 1913 the number of settlers had fallen to 61 and the extent of cultivation to 1,146 hectares.[123]

The statistics of colonisation reveal that the idea of settlement, which had inspired Italian expansion and provoked substantial popular resistance by the local inhabitants, had been almost entirely unsuccessful. The failure of the policy of Franchetti and of those who followed in his footsteps was symbolized in 1904 when a commission of agricultural labourers was sent to Eritrea from Romagna to investigate possibilities of settlement. Ascending the slopes of Ghinda, one of the men indignantly exclaimed, "Romagna shall never come here."[124] Though the Italian Government never renounced its policy of settlement the practical difficulties of colonisation were such as to prevent its realisation on any significant scale. At the end of the first quarter of the twentieth century Eritrea was the home of only a handful of Europeans, a mere fraction of them engaged in agriculture, even though it had been the subject of attempts to create a colony of settlement from the 1880's onwards. It was left to Mussolini, in this respect a disciple of Franchetti, to attempt to solve the Italian population problem in Africa. Italian settlement in Eritrea was again attempted in the 1930's, but this movement also was of too short a duration to have an effect comparable to that of colonization in a settler country such as Kenya.

123 *Ibid.*, 58n.

124 F. Coletti, *Dell'Emigrazione Italiana* (Rome, 1911), II, 137.

VII.

The Church Missionary Society at Mombasa 1873-1894

by

NORMAN R. BENNETT

Assistant Professor of History, Boston University

THE BRITISH GOVERNMENT did not give full attention to the problem of the slave trade from East Africa until the years after the ending of this trade from West Africa.[1] In the early seventies the Government decided that a new treaty was necessary with the Sultan of Zanzibar, replacing the treaty of 1845 between Britain and Zanzibar, so as to forbid the exportation of slaves from his dominions on the African mainland. It had been shown that greater effort was necessary in policing the waters adjacent to the Sultan's territory.

This decision to end the sea-borne slave trade led to plans for the building of freed slave centers in the Sultan's dominions somewhat similar to those already existing in West Africa. It was hoped that such settlements would serve both to improve the lot of the rescued Africans and to work against the continuance of the slave trade. The subject of this paper is the progress of the Church Missionary Society (C.M.S.) establishment near Mombasa which was founded as the result of these hopes.

The Church Missionary Society had established the first Protestant mission station in East Africa, near Mombasa, in 1844.[2] Included among its early members were the well-known exploring missionaries, J. L. Krapf, J. Rebmann and James Erhardt. The C.M.S. efforts were not successful, however, and the mission in time was all but abandoned, Rebmann alone representing the Society for many years.

He was not able to cope with the difficulties of the situation. A

---

1 For British policy, see R. Coupland, *The Exploitation of East Africa, 1856–1890* (London, 1939), 152ff.

2 For the early years of the mission, see Eugene Stock, *The History of the Church Missionary Society* (London, 1899), II, 125ff; J. Lewis Krapf, *Travels, Researches, and Missionary Labours during an Eighteen Years' Residence in Eastern Africa* (London, 1860); R. C. Bridges, "Krapf and the Strategy of the Mission to East Africa, 1844-1855," *Makerere Journal*, V (1961), 37-50; Roland Oliver, *The Missionary Factor in East Africa* (London, 1952), 5-9.

British official visited Rebmann at Rabai, near Mombasa, in 1864; the missionary then had spent eighteen years on his station. The official found the mission in decay. Rebmann himself was in poor health and seemed to have lost his spirit from the long period of apparently fruitless missionary labor. It was reported that many years before he had decided it was "a moral impossibility" for the local Africans to accept Christianity, and thus he had given up trying to convert them. Rebmann's energies were then devoted to building, but his progress was so slow that his work decayed before it was finished.[3] The C.M.S. officials were aware of this situation and had an explanation for their allowing Rebmann to remain in East Africa: "The chief inducement with the Committee to continue the Mission is the hope that Mr. Rebmann's linguistic labours may lay the foundation of future evangelistic success. . . ."[4] These hopes were never fully realized.

This rather sad picture was to change in 1873 as a result of a British diplomatic mission to act against the slave trade carried on in the Sultan of Zanzibar's dominions. Sir Bartle Frere[5] was the leader of this mission. It was clear that if he were successful, slaves taken from illegal carriers would have to be landed somewhere. The C.M.S. considered that this situation provided for a revival of their position at Mombasa. Members of the mission held discussions with Frere before his departure for Zanzibar; they felt that he had intimated to them that their station would become a principal depot for the landing of captured slaves.[6] The mission was partly correct in this assumption. Frere had demonstrated interest in stations for freed slaves even before he was designated to negotiate with the Sultan of Zanzibar. Following a suggestion of Livingstone, he incorporated in a memorandum to the Foreign Office the idea that a settlement of freed Africans would be "a powerful agent in the . . .

[3] Playfair to Bombay Government, Apr. 9, 1864, Foreign Office (F.O.) 84/1224, Public Record Office, London; Rebmann to Hamerton, Nov. 27, 1854, Zanzibar Museum.

[4] Venn to Pelly, May 24, 1865, E-46, Zanzibar Archives. (Hereafter, Z.A.)

[5] For the background to this mission, R. J. Gavin, "The Bartle Frere Mission to Zanzibar, 1873," *The Historical Journal,* V (1962), 122-48.

[6] Hutchinson to Tozer, Jan. 16, 1873, Church Missionary Society (C.M.S.) Archives.

direction of commerce and of civilisation" for East Africa; Frere made no specific reference to missions, however.[7] The Foreign Office was receptive to this suggestion and instructed Frere to report on the probable disposal and custody of future freed slaves in East Africa.[8]

This decision was the apparent result of discussions going on in Britain concerning the previous policy of landing captured slaves at such places as the Seychelles and Mauritius. Protests against this policy, as somehow leading to the exploitation of these Africans, were rising in the late 1860's and led to some public meetings concerning the subject.[9] Thus the Foreign Office was ready for Frere to conduct a study to remove any stigma that Britain was using the former slaves for the benefit of her colonial settlements.

Frere arrived in East Africa in January 1873, where he soon visited most of the important centers on the African coast. He inspected the mission stations then in operation—the Roman Catholic Holy Ghost Mission,[10] the Universities' Mission to Central Africa, the C.M.S. and the United Methodist Free Churches Mission. The Roman Catholics, located in Zanzibar and Bagamoyo, received the highest praise for their work. The Protestants did not fare so well. Frere said of the C.M.S.: "It has been longer at work, with less apparent result, than any mission on this coast." Frere, however, still held that all the missions had a role to play; he thought that freed slave settlements could be founded in the Sultan's territory with no fear for their safety, and that they could support any number of slaves. An additional point in the favor of this plan was the fact that the missions would not require the direct support or

---

7 Frere memorandum dated Aug. 26, 1872, in F.O. 84/1386. For Livingstone's ideas, Sir Reginald Coupland, *Livingstone's Last Journey* (London, 1945), 223.

8 Granville to Frere, Nov. 9, 1872, F.O. 84/1385. The C.M.S. wrote Frere to press this point, while the Bishop of Winchester spoke publicly of an establishment of freed slaves in the area. See Hutchinson to Frere, Dec. 19, 1872, C.M.S. Archives, and the Bishop's speech as reported in *The New York Herald* of Nov. 17, 1872.

9 Stock, *History*, III, 74-76. See also reports of meetings in *The New York Herald* of Nov. 17, 1872 and May 23, 1873.

10 For the Holy Ghost Mission, see Norman R. Bennett, *Studies in East African History* (Boston, 1963), 54-75.

the supervision of the government.[11] In a preliminary plan, Frere instructed Kirk, British representative at Zanzibar, to send what slaves he could to the missions, particularly the Holy Ghost Fathers and the U.M.C.A., with a few for the C.M.S. and the Methodists. He also recommended that the government contribute a share of the cost of such a step as far as children were concerned.[12]

Frere incorporated his sentiments in a full report to the Foreign Office on the freed slave problem.[13] He thought that any settlement should meet six conditions: (1) security and freedom for the slaves landed; (2) possibility for the slaves to maintain themselves by their own labor without any permanent burden to Britain; (3) education of all slaves able to receive it; (4) proximity to a climate the slaves were accustomed to; (5) freedom for the slaves to aid in the formation of other "free, self-sustaining communities"; (6) all to be accomplished at "no inordinate expense to the English Treasury." With these conditions, Frere decided that any potential station had to be located near the area of the original capture of the slaves; he concluded that this eliminated all places but Zanzibar and the opposite coast. Thus Frere recommended the dominions of the Sultan where he had proved to his satisfaction that no hindrances would be placed before missionary societies engaging in such work.[14]

But the missions in Zanzibar itself did not meet all of Frere's conditions—for the rest, stations on the coast were necessary. He mentioned a series of possible posts from Somaliland to the Portuguese settlements, recommending the utilization of the four missions that already had stations established on that coast. He noted that most of them were planning future expansion; he suggested that a £5 subsidy for each slave given would be a great aid to this development. Of interest to the theme of this paper is the

---

[11] Frere to Granville, Mar. 25, 1873, F.O. 84/1389.

[12] Frere to Granville, Apr. 3, 1873, enclosing Frere to Kirk, Apr. 1, 1873, F.O. 84/1390.

[13] Included in Frere to Granville, May 7, 1873, F.O. 84/1391.

[14] The U.M.C.A. and Holy Ghost Fathers had already received limited numbers of slaves and had experienced no difficulties. See Gertrude Ward, *Letters of Bishop Tozer* (London, 1902), 81ff; U.M.C.A., Zanzibar Diary, 1864-1888 (in possession of the present Zanzibar U.M.C.A. Mission), entry of Sept. 16, 1864 and ff.

fact that only the local C.M.S. representative, of all the missionaries consulted, opposed Frere's plans. Rebmann, who now was against introducing "anything like an industrial or worldly element into the teaching or action of the mission," had no interest in the scheme. Events had passed Rebmann by, however, and his days in East Africa were almost over. To Frere, there was little reason to pay attention to him since his way of life had robbed him of all influence in the area. Frere said: his "holy life of ascetic self denial and indifference to all worldly enjoyments and employments . . . have had the usual effect of exciting admiration, without securing the imitation, of the people around him."[15]

John Kirk in Zanzibar gave full support to Frere's ideas. Previously, in 1871, he had reported to the Foreign Office the need for a new location, perhaps "somewhere on the coast, possibly not an English possession but certainly under our administration," as a place from which to control the busy land slave trade. He admitted that the British would have problems in securing the right place for this establishment, but he recommended freed slaves be landed, since the "depositing [of] them at Aden or Seychelles to be treated worse than slaves" was no proper method of disposal.[16]

The C.M.S., therefore, at the end of 1873 decided to send reinforcements to Mombasa to revive their mission and to prepare it for the reception of freed slaves—even though the Foreign Office had made no commitment to land any there. Two missionaries, J. Sparshott and W. Chancellor, and their families, arrived in November 1873 to take up this work. They found Rebmann nearly blind and arranged, after some difficulty, for his return to Europe. Sparshott, the leader of the new group, found little to encourage him in the attitude of the British officials in Zanzibar. Kirk said only that "he will think of us if any [slaves] come in his way."[17] Kirk then returned temporarily to Europe; his replacement, Prideaux, was a little more favourable to the C.M.S., but he made any possible

---

[15] See the enclosures in the despatch listed in footnote 13 for mission views on freed slaves.

[16] Kirk to F.O., Mar. 20, 1871 and July 19, 1871, E-61, Z.A.

[17] Sparshott to C.M.S., Dec. 12, 1873, C.M.S. Archives. Kirk's attitude came from a visit to the station in November 1873; he was unimpressed with its development.

disposition of slaves conditional on the ability of the mission to prove that they could support them.[18]

The missionaries prepared for slaves in spite of this initial discouragement. They soon began to experience problems common to other mission stations in Africa resulting from their assuming jurisdiction over Africans, sometimes as the result of a failure of local government officials to act, but often for little other reason than their own short tempers. As a consequence, the first of a long series of difficulties for the mission, the British officials, and the administration of Zanzibar occurred. Sparshott assaulted a native who refused to stop what the missionary considered an unjustifiable disturbance. Immediately afterward a group of soldiers came from the Sultan's governor at Mombasa to surround his residence. All ended well in this instance with the payment of a small sum to the injured African. More important, however, was the fact that Sparshott saw nothing reprehensible in his actions; he wrote home that he often acted in this manner, and that "on one or two occasions caught a fellow a good stripe with a stick."[19] This attitude of disregarding the Sultan's officials would bear bitter fruit for the C.M.S. in the future.

Sparshott and his associates soon demonstrated another tendency that characterized the C.M.S. in East Africa—the inability of fellow missionaries to work together in peace. Sparshott, and others later, apparently were willing to meet and to overcome any handicap to spread their religion but that of controlling their own impulses in relation to each other. Rebmann was the first problem; he delayed leaving and soon had the two new missionaries taking opposite sides as to his future. While he remained, Rebmann opposed all the new plans of the C.M.S. He had decided that conversion of the Africans was impossible for the present, at least until "the natives have been taught the whole of Old Testament his-

---

18 Prideaux to C.M.S., Feb. 10, 1874, E-64, Z.A.

19 Sparshott to C.M.S., Jan. 8, 1874, C.M.S. Archives. Sparshott did not neglect to mention that such difficulties with the governor boded against the future success of the C.M.S. plans for freed slaves. See H. B. Thomas, "The Death of Dr. Livingstone: Carus Farrar's Narrative," *The Uganda Journal*, XIV (1950), 120, for another notice of Sparshott's ill-treatment.

tory."[20] While Rebmann remained, all forward progress of the mission came to an end.[21]

The arrival of an experienced missionary to take command at Mombasa stopped this bickering for a time. W. Salter Price, who had served at the C.M.S. center at Nassick, in India, where former African slaves were trained, landed in East Africa in late 1874. He had instructions to build up a new mission station that would offer industrial training to Africans and to develop the old center of Rabai as a Christian village.[22] The death of Livingstone, with the effects this had in Britain, apparently was a main stimulus to this sending of Price with money raised through the renewed interest in missions.[23]

Price was appalled at the state of the mission, describing it as "at the lowest ebb whilst outwardly everything had an air of dirt and dilapidation." He also noted that the British officials in Zanzibar remained little interested in sending any slaves to the mission.[24] Prideaux in Zanzibar in fact wrote home to oppose the entire idea of a freed slave station in East Africa. He praised the Seychelles, and, referring to slaves previously given to missions, said, "it is impossible to deny that so far as the amelioration of the freed African is concerned, those institutions have been practically failures." Therefore, since he had no specific instructions concerning his behavior to Price, he merely introduced him to the Sultan and then left him on his own until word came from Britain.[25]

Price went directly to work to improve this situation. His first task was to secure land outside of the city limits of Mombasa for the creation of a settlement for the freed slaves yet to come.[26]

---

[20] Sparshott to C.M.S., May 21, 1874, C.M.S. Archive; Kirk to F.O., Nov. 6, 1873, E-63C, Z.A.

[21] Chancellor to C.M.S., Aug. 6, 1874 and Sept. 29, 1874, C.M.S. Archives.

[22] Stock, *History*, III, 83. Interestingly enough, Frere in his depatch of May 7, 1873, given above had noted that an East African mission for freed slaves needed a man like Price of Nassick.

[23] E. C. Dawson, *James Hannington* (London, 1887), 308.

[24] Price to Hutchinson, Nov. 19, 1874, C.M.S. Archives. Price and Sparshott soon quarrelled and the latter was recalled. See Price to Hutchinson, Jan. 4, 1875; Price to Wright, received Feb. 22, 1875: *ibid.*

[25] Prideaux to F.O., Jan. 2, 1875, E-71, Z.A.

[26] The C.M.S. had wished new land from the start and had instructed

Good land was found in possession of an Arab willing to sell, but it became apparent that the owner feared persecution from the Wali, or governor, of Mombasa for dealing with a Christian. Price had anticipated such problems, applying to the Sultan at an early date for permission to buy land. He reported, "I am most anxious to do nothing calculated to give offense to the authorities, however unreasonable and annoying their requirements may be."[27] This was a rare attitude among C.M.S. missionaries.

The sale was delayed by local fears and the absence of John Kirk in Britain.[28] When he did return, the Sultan gave full approval and assurances when Kirk pointed out the British-Zanzibar Treaty of 1845 permitted establishments by British subjects.[29] Kirk was prepared to help the C.M.S. more actively because of talks he had had with their officials while in London; the C.M.S. officials felt that this visit presaged more active government aid in the future.[30] This assumption was correct since Kirk on his return promised to send slaves, asking Price how many he could handle.[31]

With this approval, and with the purchase of the necessary land, the C.M.S. was ready to go forward.[32] Price asserted they could accept 250 slaves at once, plus any number of slaves in the follow-

---

Sparshott to secure it. There is no report of any action by Sparshott, See Hutchinson to Kirk, Dec. 22, 1874, C.M.S. Archives.

[27] Price to Kirk, Feb. 23, 1875, E-69, Z.A.; Price to Hutchinson, June 14, 1875, C.M.S. Archives.

[28] Prideaux did not get along with the Sultan and advised Price to await Kirk. From Price's "Journal," entry of Feb. 13, 1875, *ibid.*

[29] Kirk to Price, Mar. 22, 1875 and Apr. 28, 1875, *ibid.* The Sultan later made this statement with reference to land-holding on the coast: "His Highness . . . said that he denied all right of native tribes within his power to hold property in land, that the land was crown land, and the native had no right to sell. That he would give the land you [some Methodist missionaries] had bargained for and reserve to himself the right of compelling the people to refund the money that had been taken under what he called false pretences by parties that had no power to sell." Kirk to Wakefield, Mar. 5, 1877, E-73, Z.A.

[30] Hutchinson to Price, Feb. 12, 1875, C.M.S. Archives.

[31] Kirk to Price, Mar. 17, 1875, *ibid.*

[32] For the final details of the land question, Price to Kirk, Apr. 7, 1875, *ibid.*; Price to Kirk, May 13, 1875, E-69, Z.A.

ing year. He noted that he preferred children, but would take all ages for the moment.[33]

Slaves were soon sent to the mission. Over 250 slaves, about 180 of them children, arrived: the C.M.S. work had finally begun.[34] The missionaries quickly learned, however, that great problems would arise from their efforts to deal with Africans that had little previous contact with western civilization. Price noted that they could work with the children satisfactorily, but that the adults were "a lot of idle savages, and until they can be made to understand their position and our kind feelings towards them we shall have something to do to keep order." He sent an immediate request for more Europeans for work on the station.[35]

In addition, the inevitable problem of jurisdiction over Africans located on the mission arose. The missionaries had to deal with "several cases of crime and evil conduct": they decided to enforce their own concept of the law. They faced cases involving murder and the enticing of mission people away by local Swahilis. But Price realized that he might be breaking the law, since the area of the mission was in the territory of Zanzibar. He wrote Kirk for advice.[36] Kirk replied at once that Price had to go through the local judicial system. There was an approved practice, Kirk stated, whereby a mission could act to regulate its internal affairs, but this was all. Any case involving corporal punishment had either to be sent to the Sultan's court or to receive the advance approval of the Consul.[37] Price accepted this decision, releasing the few individuals he then held in prison.[38] No serious harm had been done; if the mission had continued to act in this way, much future friction would have been avoided.

The landing of the former slaves at Mombasa also raised the

---

[33] Price to Euan Smith, Aug. 16, 1875, C.M.S. Archives; Price to Holmwood, undated 1875, E-69, Z.A.

[34] Price to Hutchinson, Sept. 22, 1875, C.M.S. Archives; Euan Smith to Price, Aug. 30, 1875 and Sept. 18, 1875, E-70, Z.A.; Euan Smith to F.O., Sept. 20, 1875, E-72, *ibid.*

[35] Price to Wright, Oct. 5, 1875, C.M.S. Archives.

[36] Forster to Wright, Oct. 5, 1875, *ibid.*; Price to Kirk, Oct. 9, 1875, E-70, Z.A.

[37] Kirk to Price, Oct. 18, 1875, *ibid.*

[38] Price to Kirk, Nov. 21, 1875, *ibid.*

question of their exact status. In early 1875, Sparshott appeared to have the impression that they were British subjects.[39] This matter had been raised in East Africa at least as early as 1870 when the Consul at Zanzibar had requested a decision from the Bombay Government since Kirk and Seward, both then officials in Zanzibar, regarded freed slaves as subjects.[40] Later references indicate that the reply was negative; Kirk answered the C.M.S. in 1875 that he could not give former slaves his full protection since they would then be on a par with British subjects.[41] Thus the mission appeared to have no course but to follow the Muslim rules of law for regulating their major problems.

To resolve the problem of Muslim jurisdiction, the C.M.S. had worked from the beginning of its renewed interest in East Africa to secure the appointment of a British Vice-Consul for Mombasa. They hoped he would be a member of their mission, even proposing he work without cost to the government.[42] In 1876 the mission pushed firmly for what they considered a legitimate claim, with Price suggesting an additional step:

> The recognition of our colony as British soil under the protection of the British flag would no doubt be a great step towards the suppression of slavery in East Africa. As it is the existence of our colony is now widely known, and the number of poor slaves who come to us for our protection from many quarters . . . is increasing. The decision as to one's duty in these various cases is often painfully embarrassing; the dictates of humanity say one thing, the miserable laws of the country say another. We try with God's help to do the best we can under the circumstances, perhaps stretching a point or two in favour of the poor slave. . . .[43]

The C.M.S. decided on positive action before the Foreign Office had made any decision, hoping to influence it to act. Captain W.

---

39 Sparshott to Prideaux, Jan. 16, 1875, E-69, *ibid.* In the 1850's a recent writer notes that inhabitants of Sierra Leone were regarded practically as protected subjects. See C. W. Newbury, *The Western Slave Coast and Its Rulers* (Oxford, 1961), 56.

40 Churchill to Bombay Government, Sept. 13, 1870, F.O. 84/1325.

41 Kirk to F.O., Dec. 25, 1875, E-72, Z.A.

42 Price to Euan Smith, July 16, 1875, E-72, Z.A.; Euan Smith wrote to F.O., July 26, 1875, *ibid.*, favoring this plan.

43 Price to Hutchinson, Mar. 1, 1876, C.M.S. Archives. The problems of slaves fleeing to the mission will be discussed below.

Russell, a former naval officer, was appointed independent lay superintendent of the mission in April 1876; his instructions openly stated the hope he would soon be Vice-Consul.[44] Once the appointment was made, the C.M.S. wrote to the Foreign Office to request that Russell be designated a Vice-Consul; his salary was to be £400 a year, the Society requesting the Government to pay about one-half of it.[45] The outlook appeared favorable for this step since, at the same time, Kirk sent home a report backing the plan, although he pointed out that any C.M.S. official would have a delicate task in resolving the problems of a Christian community on Muslim soil.[46] No immediate action was taken, however, in spite of continued C.M.S. urging; they even offered to release Russell from their service so that he might be a full-time official.[47]

All these importunities came at the time of a minor crisis in Mombasa. A new decree against the slave trade by the Sultan had created some unrest;[48] the activities of the mission added to it. The threat to the C.M.S. came from their harboring slaves fleeing from nearby owners. When the owners came after their property, they were seized. The result was a petition sent to the Sultan blaming Price, "for where as he formerly turned away any slave that took refuge with him from his master, now he harbours him and when they [the African Christians] find a slave in irons they release him." The Sultan's governor, who had tried unsuccessfully to settle this, came out particularly hard against the mission: "these negroes are arrogant, finding themselves supported by the Missionaries and reckless as to consequences." The intervention of Kirk ended the difficulty; he was hopeful all had learned a lesson for the future.[49]

---

44 Instructions . . . to Captain W.F.A.H. Russell, Apr. 25, 1876; Wright to Price, June 1, 1876; *ibid.* For details on Russell, *Register of Missionaries . . . and Native Clergy from 1804 to 1904, ibid.*

45 Lister to Kirk, May 4, 1876, enclosing Hutchinson to Derby, Apr. ?, 1876, Q-15, Z.A.

46 Kirk to Derby, May 5, 1876, F.O. 84/1452.

47 Hutchinson to Kirk, Aug. 21, 1876, C.M.S. Archives. Oliver, *Missionary Factor*, 82-83, points out that the C.M.S. must have expected greater governmental aid than they were to receive.

48 See Coupland, *Exploitation of East Africa*, 224-29.

49 Kirk to Derby, June 7, 1876, with enclosures, F.O. 84/1453. The Nassick

These events caused Kirk to reflect on the projected plan for a C.M.S. member as Vice-Consul. He noted that such an official would have to preside over his own mission people if similar disputes recurred. Kirk then came out openly against the scheme. He said he would favor it only if the British government lacked funds for alternative action, "but in that case the Consul will be a small advantage to any but the Society whose servant he is."[50]

The Foreign Office also reacted strongly to this affair. One official, Wylde, noted that legal moves against Price could be avoided, but he had to be informed of "the necessity of behaving in as conciliatory a manner as possible towards the authorities and people by whom they are surrounded." Lord Derby agreed, and then demonstrated his general attitude to the C.M.S. Wylde had recommended that the Government counsel the mission to stop all interference with domestic slavery. Derby replied that Wylde was right, but that they should not mention this since "we cannot trust these people not to use any such advice against us if they see their way to gain popularity by it." He added, "And they are sure not to take the advice."[51] Thus no Vice-Consul was appointed and Zanzibar law continued to apply to the mission residents.

While the C.M.S. attempted to get a Vice-Consul for Mombasa, it also worked to receive a subsidy from the Government, as Frere had recommended, for the care of freed slaves.[52] Kirk favored a subsidy for all missions in East Africa, and recommended £5 a slave. In return, each mission would be expected to accept slaves at the shortest notice.[53]

Christians, brought from India, were long a problem to the mission. Price, with prior experience, usually worked well with them, but others took an uncharitable view. Sparshott called them "the very dregs of society, a shame any dishonour to Christianity." See Sparshott to Wright, May 21, 1874, C.M.S. Archives. See also a later letter from some of these Africans stating their side of the problem—David, Semler and others to C.M.S., Feb. 28, 1881, *ibid.*

[50] Kirk to Derby, June 21, 1876, F.O. 84/1453.

[51] Notes on Kirk to Derby, June 7, 1876, *ibid.* See also Notes on Kirk to Derby, June 27, 1876, *ibid.*

[52] Derby to Kirk, May 4, 1876, F.O. 84/1451; Hutchinson to Kirk, Apr. 7, 1876, C.M.S. Archives.

[53] Kirk to Derby, May 5, 1876 and June 20, 1876, F.O. 84/1453. Kirk also recommended an advance of £500 to the C.M.S. for building, etc.

Foreign Office officials were divided on this. Wylde, as he had previously, gave his support to the proposal. Lister concurred; he was worried over the remarks made about sending freed slaves to British colonies as laborers. Pauncefote also agreed. Derby, however, was not convinced. He said: "I do not like what is in effect subsidising these Missions. It is a thing we have never done." Pauncefote met this by observing: "Is it not rather paying them for services performed and reimbursing them for expenses incurred." Lister in spite of his general agreement did not wish to forward the matter to the Treasury at that time; Derby accepted this evasion, and there the problem remained for some time.[54]

Kirk therefore had no alternative. He considered the missions could receive no more slaves without a subsidy; he thus sent many new slaves to Natal where there was a great demand, and where there were proper regulations for their care. He continued to write the Foreign Office, however, that the Zanzibar area was the best location for these slaves.[55]

Price returned to England during this period; he there stressed the problem of caring for slaves without support from the Government. He reported that there were 380 freed slaves at Frere Town, about 250 of them adults. The estimated cost of putting an adult slave in a condition to support himself was £5; this did not take into account the cost of operating Frere Town. The children cost £3 a month until the age of fifteen. Thus Price felt that the Government should be asked to contribute £2,420.[56] Russell continued to press similar demands on Kirk, but the British official could do nothing more.[57] The mission then appears to have dropped the matter for a time.

Frere Town, therefore, had to carry on its early development

---

[54] Notes on Kirk to Derby, May 5, 1876 and June 20, 1876, *ibid.*

[55] Kirk to Derby, Sept. 21, 1876, F.O. 84/1454. For disposal of slaves in 1877, see Kirk to Derby, Sept. 14, 1877, F.O. 84/1486. Wylde noted on this despatch that a subsidy of £5 a slave was cheap compared to the Sierra Leone costs of £5,000 a year.

[56] Price to C.M.S., Jan. 25, 1877, C.M.S. Archives. For a slightly different estimate of the numbers at Frere Town, Kirk to Derby, Jan. 10, 1877, enclosing Russell to Kirk, Jan. 4, 1877, F.O. 84/1484.

[57] Russell to Kirk, Jan. 4, 1877; Kirk to Russell, Jan. 10, 1877, E-73, Z.A. Kirk to Russell, Jan. 20, 1877, C.M.S. Archives.

with no British official present and with no financial support from the government. Captain Russell tried to cope with this difficult situation. He saw that subjecting the young slaves to religious teaching alone was not producing the desired result. He tried to have them do physical work for part of each day and he planned to move the surplus population from Frere Town to develop the older center of Rabai. After initial help, it was hoped that those sent would become self-supporting.[58]

Two problems blocked Russell's attempts at efficient organization of the mission—friction among the C.M.S. representatives and lack of discipline in the Nassick Christians. Russell found the Africans unruly and decided to found a prison to check the disorder resulting from cases of adultery, wife beating and other episodes. This perhaps necessary effort to maintain order caused trouble with an ordained member of the mission. He seemed to desire that the station be run on the lines of a police state: anyone guilty of a so-called immoral act was to be imprisoned at once, even if proof were lacking. Russell would not submit to this interpretation, always insisting on an investigation.[59] Russell also relied heavily on the Nassick Christians; he called them the "backbone of the colony" and treated them almost as he would Europeans. Another member of the mission refused all contact with Russell over an incident arising from Russell's viewpoint.[60]

All concerned were probably somewhat in the wrong on the above issues. Russell tried to be fair to all, but the African Christians were clearly out of hand. Kirk visited the mission in March, 1877, after the missionaries reported the local population was about to attack them. The rumor was untrue; Kirk became very annoyed at the unnecessary trip. He observed the disorder at the station and commented very adversely against it: "I learned to my dismay that there existed a want of discipline and subordination among

---

[58] Russell to Hutchinson, Jan. 1, 1877; Russell to Wright, Oct. 9, 1877, C.M.S. Archives. The Rabai scheme did not succeed, partly due to the early return of Russell to England. See Russell to Wright, Dec. 23, 1877; Handford to Wright, Feb. 20, 1878, *ibid.*

[59] Russell to Wright, Jan. 1, 1877, *ibid.*

[60] Russell to Wright, June 21, 1877; Praeger to Wright, Mar. 29, 1877 and Apr. 21, 1877, *ibid.*

the leading Christianised negroes far more dangerous than an Arab attack would have been to the welfare of the settlement." All in all, Kirk considered the mission had gone into decline since the departure of Price.[61]

Before any improvement could be attempted, Russell was forced to return to Britain. The problem was left to the new lay superintendant, J. Streeter, who was to lead the C.M.S. into difficulties nearly fatal to its position in Mombasa. He found the lack of discipline very irritating and took direct action to end it. After trying to make a group be quiet one evening (they answered that they were discussing the Bible!) he had an African "tied to a cocoanut tree and given two doz. with a hide whip." Streeter appeared delighted that this method had the desired effect.[62] No reaction followed from London or Zanzibar, so Streeter continued in his approach to Christian discipline.

At the same time, the problem of local slaves fleeing to the mission for protection became acute. One aspect of the problem was the presence of a settlement of runaway slaves near Mombasa.[63] Members of this African group wanted to build on mission grounds. Streeter formally refused permission, but this order clearly was not his real desire.[64] Immediately the former slaves started to enter the mission settlement in small groups. Streeter decided to take no action, and to make no report to Zanzibar, but he wrote home that difficulties were inevitable.[65] The missionaries were not really worried, however. One African evangelist, Jones, stated expressly that all slaves fleeing to them came on the understanding they would not be protected if their masters came after them. He noted that no masters had yet come.[66]

---

[61] Kirk to F.O., Mar. 3, 1877, Q-18, Z.A.; Russell to Hutchinson, Mar. 29, 1877, C.M.S. Archives.

[62] Streeter to Wright, May 22, 1878, *ibid.*

[63] Such instances were not isolated. In 1873 the Sultan's forces attacked, but failed to dislodge, a similar settlement near Pangani. Kirk to F.O., Dec. 8, 1873, E-55, Z.A.

[64] Streeter to Wright, Aug. 10, 1878, C.M.S. Archives.

[65] Streeter to Wright, Nov. 7, 1878, *ibid.*

[66] Jones to Wright, Oct. 10, 1878, *ibid.* Jones played an important role at the Mombasa mission; see the brief biographical details in Jones to C.M.S., June 30, 1893, *ibid.*

Troubles were not long delayed. About 100 slaves fled from their nearby Giriama masters; the owners became "rather incensed," and several came to demand their return, or at least a cash settlement. The slaves had integrated themselves into the Rabai community; the missionary there, Binns, refused to let force be used to secure their return. He was told that the Giriama would come in force and he began to fortify his settlement.[67] Streeter saw the danger, and admonished Binns, but he took no real action. Inevitably there was a crisis. A group of Giriama came to reclaim their slaves by force when Streeter was absent; they had aid from the Wali of Mombasa. Only the danger of a Masai raid drew the group away in time to keep the peace.[68]

These episodes caused the Wali to protest to Kirk and the Sultan. Kirk wrote to Streeter to obey local law, but the missionary was ready to defy him, albeit discreetly. He wrote to his superiors that he would do as little as possible to prevent any refugees from entering, declaring that he would surrender none of them.[69] Kirk was aware of the potential dangers of this course of action, but he could not compel the C.M.S. men to act. He pointed out that the Sultan had force to compel them to follow the laws of the land, and that he (Kirk) would do nothing to protect their station. Kirk considered that he could only advise them to remove all the slaves before any armed force arrived.[70] The mission merely reported his decision home with no comments.[71]

The matter seemed to pass satisfactorily from a danger point. Kirk arranged a discussion between the Wali and Streeter, with apparently good results. Kirk was satisfied.[72] Streeter was also pleased, reporting that the Wali and he were "good friends." But his attitude was unchanged: he claimed that he had done no

---

67 Binns to Wright, Oct. 5, 1879, *ibid.*

68 Streeter to Wright, Oct. 1, 1879, *ibid.*

69 *Ibid.*

70 Kirk to F.O., Jan. 9, 1880, Q-24, Z.A. Kirk had a similar problem in Zanzibar with slaves fleeing to him. He never gave them shelter, though he often delayed their owners while they fled. See William P. Johnson, *My African Reminiscences* (London, 1898), 38.

71 Binns to Wright, Feb. 3, 1880, C.M.S. Archives.

72 Kirk to F.O., Nov. 12, 1879, Q-22; Kirk to F.O., Feb. 7, 1880, Q-24, Z.A.

wrong, and even though he had violated local laws, that "what this country wants is a lawbreaker—then a law maker."[73]

This attitude of civil disobedience brought the mission into difficulties again in 1880. In June there was fear of a general slave outbreak in Mombasa. A large number of the "better class of slaves" left the city to hold a three-day meeting nearby. The owners, apparently, did not know what had been discussed and feared future developments; the missionaries agreed. One said, "It looks to us like the dawning of an insurrection among the more intelligent slaves."[74] The mission stood to be in the center of any disturbance since it was reported to the station that all the slaves of Mombasa would go there if troubles began. The townspeople also heard this rumor, and in the opinion of the missionaries, began looking for an excuse to attack the station before any general outbreak occurred.[75]

In time, news of this unrest reached Zanzibar through letters to the Sultan, though Kirk had received no reports from the missionaries on their position. But he had learned from English visitors to Mombasa that the missionaries carried arms and spent every night in fear of attack. These reporters said that only the authorities of the Sultan had kept the local population in check. Kirk also heard that the apparent cause of the renewed feeling against the missions was the killing of an Arab's servant by Africans living on mission grounds. All this information was somewhat unclear, so Kirk decided to investigate.[76]

When the Consul's party reached Mombasa, they found that the missionaries feared an attack by the town and that the town feared the incitement of their slaves by the missionaries. The presence of the party was calming, allowing Kirk to conduct a thorough investigation.[77] He explained to the Foreign Office that in the past the fugitive problem had been less acute since these slaves were owned by tribal Africans, not by inhabitants of Mom-

73 Streeter to C.M.S., Jan. 30, 1880, C.M.S. Archives.

74 Menzies to Wright, June 18, 1880, *ibid.*

75 Menzies to Wright, Sept. 22, 1880, *ibid.*

76 Kirk to F.O., Sept. 22, 1880, Q-24, Z.A.

77 Kirk to F.O., Oct. 19, 1880, *ibid.* The following paragraphs are taken from this despatch.

basa. He recalled that he had helped Streeter and the African leaders to agree to let those already in the mission remain, but to accept no more. The missionaries had violated that agreement; in addition they began to give refuge to Mombasa slaves. The missionaries never denied the right of an owner to recover a slave, but they would give no aid. Since at Rabai, the main place of refuge, there were 200 armed Africans subject to no controls, the background for Arab grievances was obvious.

So tensions began to increase between Arab and missionary. The Wali often said he was ready to defend the station, but the distance of the missionaries from Mombasa made for scanty protection from a surprise attack. While affairs were thus delicately balanced, Streeter took a step that could have precipitated war. When he heard of a possible slave rising he decided not to ask for aid from Zanzibar. Rather, he made a large white flag bearing the word "freedom" (in Swahili) and kept it in open view in his residence. Then he let reports spread that if the insurrection started, he would raise it as a sign for all the rebels to gather at the station.[78]

This was the situation when an incident took place. At Rabai, armed groups were patrolling the area to keep a watch for Arab owners. They murdered an unarmed Arab and some of his party for plunder; the Arab was known as a peaceful trader. No report was made to the Wali by the missionaries, although they learned of the affair and buried the Arab. Eventually the Africans implicated in the murder were surrendered to the authorities for trial. The townspeople, however, held that the Europeans were fully responsible. An armed attack on a group of fugitive slaves living outside Mombasa in a Methodist center followed. It appeared that the C.M.S. would be next.

At this time Kirk's party arrived. Their investigations proved that the murder had occurred as described above. They learned that runaway slaves had been received "wholesale" and had been allowed to integrate themselves entirely with the mission Africans. Streeter freely admitted that he hoped for a slave rising. Kirk could take only one decision. He told the mission that if they participated

---

[78] The flag was still on display during Kirk's visit. See note 79.

in a rebellion, they would not find a Mombasa mob against them, but rather the forces of the Sultan. Britain would not oppose the Sultan. Kirk then advised the mission to warn the Africans to flee before the owners came, concluded other disputes, and left Mombasa.

Kirk was satisfied with the results of his work. He wrote to the C.M.S. in Britain explaining his condemnation of the mission as the only alternative to war and ruin. He did not neglect to mention the fact that the missionaries accused each other of having caused these difficulties.[79]

The C.M.S. authorities came to the defense of their Mombasa settlements. Basing their viewpoint on information received from the missionaries in East Africa, they felt compelled to answer Kirk's charges that the mission knowingly harbored fugitive slaves in violation of local law. The C.M.S. commented on the difficult task it had assumed as an aid against the slave trade, mentioning the little support they received from the Government. This latter point included a charge against Kirk: he was said to neglect his duty by not paying frequent visits to troubled Mombasa. Thus, the mission directors asserted, it was no wonder that its missionaries, left virtually alone, took measures for their own protection—including Streeter's flag. The defense closed with the words of one of the missionaries at Mombasa as an explanation of their action: "We are Englishmen as well as Christian missionaries and cannot consent to fold our hands and see poor miserable wretches ill-used and put to death for no other crime than running away from savage masters."[80]

The Zanzibar officials reacted strongly to the Society's charges. But they were willing to let them pass and accept the new C.M.S. resolve to avoid difficulties in the future.[81] The Foreign Office

---

79 Kirk to Hutchinson, Dec. 13, 1880, C.M.S. Archives; Kirk to F.O., Nov. 14, 1880, Q-24, Z.A.

80 Lister to Kirk, Feb. 8, 1881, enclosing Hutchinson to Granville, Jan. 14, 1881, N-24, *ibid.* For one of the Mombasa missionaries' views, Binns to C.M.S., Jan. 18, 1881, Précis Book, C.M.S., Archives.

81 See notes on Lister to Kirk, Feb. 8, 1881, cited in footnote 80; Kirk to F.O., Mar. 28, 1881, enclosing Kirk to Sultan of Zanzibar, Mar. 19, 1881; Kirk to F.O., Apr. 4, 1881: Q-25, Z.A.

reacted similarly, advising Kirk that the Sultan's authority should be so strengthened . . . that British Missionaries should not be tempted by motives of humanity to interfere in matters with which they should have no concern."[82] Stability and order, not wholesale and rapid emancipation of slaves, were the objects of policy.

With the above problems settled, it might have appeared that this most troublesome mission would give the harassed officials some peace. This was not the case. News that could have resulted in a major scandal for the mission reached Zanzibar. A British official, Holmwood, had to be sent to investigate charges of the Wali of Mombasa that Streeter had chained and "brutally beaten" an African, and had imprisoned an Arab.[83] There was no question of guilt, since a letter from Streeter followed the charges, admitting the action. The missionary reported giving the African five strokes—"which is my well known rule"—to make him confess. The treatment of the Arab was also admitted.[84]

Although it was evident that Streeter had "totally mistaken his position and grossly exceeded his powers," the investigation had to go on. Holmwood visited the African concerned, and with the Wali's aid, compiled a list of all those beaten or imprisoned in the past three years. This action was necessary since the Wali and the African had drawn up formal charges against Streeter. While Holmwood conducted this investigation, he received a petition from the inhabitants of Frere Town protesting against specific instances of Streeter's enforcement of "law." He learned that Streeter had stripped a woman to the waist, giving her about twenty-five stripes; he saw a man, flogged a year previously, who still presented "a frightful appearance" from sixty strokes administered by three men. The missionaries tried, but failed, to block these discoveries by intimidating mission Africans who wanted to testify.

Not unnaturally, Holmwood and his aide, Byles, a naval officer, were shocked. According to one missionary, when Holmwood

---

[82] Lister to Kirk, May 31, 1881, N-24, *ibid.* The Foreign Office arranged with the Admiralty for frequent visits by the Navy to Mombasa; Pauncefote to Kirk, Mar. 1, 1881, *ibid.*

[83] Kirk to Holmwood, June 30, 1881, N-24, *ibid.*

[84] Streeter to Kirk, June 18, 1881, C.M.S. Archives.

viewed the scars of whippings, "he broke out and sternly rebuked Mr. Streeter in a most unbecoming manner before all the people." To Kirk, Holmwood stated, "persons inflicting such injuries are unfit to be entrusted with the charge of human lives." Byles summed it up in his report as "a disgrace to the honour of Englishmen."

Holmwood, however, despite his personal feelings, acted to save the name of the mission—and of England. He told Streeter he could no longer act in this manner, but did not make any formal charges; he merely sent the evidence to Kirk for final decision. The attitude of the missionaries to these events is best expressed by this comment on the investigation and Holmwood's course of action: "there was nothing in the conduct of the Mission we desired to hide or hush up." Streeter added: "I don't deny that I am at fault but all here agree with my proceedings and it has had the best effect on our community."[85]

Kirk reacted as Holmwood had done. He instructed Holmwood to settle the affair out of court to "save the Mission the scandal of a serious criminal trial." Otherwise, Streeter might have been tried under the Indian penal code which had stringent rules on mistreatment. Holmwood thus secured a letter from Streeter allegedly admitting his guilt (Holmwood interpreted a Streeter letter in this fashion although Streeter did not really admit his faults), plus apologies and compensation to the Africans injured. Holmwood needed to apply pressure for this type of settlement, but once concluded it was accepted by the Sultan, with the expectation that Streeter would be recalled.[86]

All the implications of this affair for a Christian mission, plus the political dangers involved, were not grasped by the missionaries. One described Holmwood's labors as "a one-sided investigation most unfairly conducted." Another added that the Africans were

---

85 Menzies to Stock, July 12, 1881, *ibid.*; Kirk to F.O., July 1, 1881, July 20, 1881 and July 21, 1881, both with enclosures; Kirk to F.O., July 25, 1881, enclosing Streeter to Kirk, July 12, 1881 and Streeter to Holmwood, July 12, 1881, Q-25, Z.A. For an outside report of another instance of beating mission Africans, G. A. Fischer, *Mehr Licht im dunkeln Welttheil* (Hamburg, 1885), 59.

86 Kirk to Brownrigg, July 11, 1881, N-27, Z.A. See Kirk to F.O., July 20, 1881, Q-25, *ibid.* for his charitable explanations of Streeter's deeds.

as children, requiring some form of punishment.[87] Streeter reacted in the same way, trying to justify all of his actions to the Society.[88]

The C.M.S. leaders in Britain were pushed to action by the Government. Granville described the incidents as "unjustifiable and unwarrantable" and stated that the Mombasa mission should have an entirely new staff. He added that the Government could not continue to lend support to an organization that mistreated the subjects of a friendly power.[89] The Foreign Office, however, accepted Kirk's ruling and took no action against the Society. When the missionaries at Mombasa learned that the Society planned to accept the Government's advice, including the removal of Streeter, they demonstrated their continuing lack of awareness of the problems involved, blaming all on a supposed anti-missionary bias on the part of Holmwood.[90]

Kirk returned to Britain at this time, where he joined in discussions by the C.M.S. concerning the future of the mission. He recommended the sending of a special agent to Mombasa to repair the damages caused by Streeter.[91] The C.M.S. agreed, appointing W. Salter Price to return to his former post. He was given the Foreign Office recommendation that all the staff should be sent home. He planned to confront them with the Foreign Office statement and let them make their own decision.[92] When he reached Mombasa, Price was appalled at what he discovered; he described two or three of the cases of mistreatment as "too bad almost to think about."[93] When he discussed the complicity of the other missionaries in Streeter's excesses, he found they denied all knowledge of them (one called them a "surprising revelation"); Price,

---

[87] Menzies to Stock, July 12, 1881; Taylor to Stock, July 12, 1881, C.M.S. Archives.

[88] Streeter to Stock, July 12, 1881, *ibid.*

[89] Lister to C.M.S., Oct 21, 1881, Précis Book, *ibid.*

[90] Menzies to Wigram, Dec. 6, 1881, *ibid.* News of the affair did reach the press; see the account in *L'Afrique Explorée et Civilisée,* IIIme année (1881-1882), 130, for example.

[91] Kirk to F.O., Nov. 5, 1881, F.O. 84/1601. Kirk noted on this meeting: "You can hardly conceive how ignorant these people are on matters that deeply concern their own officials."

[92] Price to Wigram, Dec. 14, 1881, C.M.S. Archives.

[93] Price to Miles, Jan. 24, 1882, *ibid.*

on learning of Streeter's imperious character, accepted their claims.[94] Price told his superiors that he regarded the affair as concluded, and proceeded with the ordinary work of the mission.[95] He appeared to act with his usual efficiency, since the British Consul soon noted that all was going well at Mombasa.[96]

This happy situation did not last. In April, 1882, the Wali of Mombasa found it necessary to complain to the Sultan against the conduct of Price and his people. He charged that "they never cease to injure poor people residing in this town and seduce their slaves and entice them. . . ." He said he had requested that they follow the agreements worked out by the British officials, but to no avail. The Wali became so aroused that he threatened to use troops against them.[97] Price reported at the same time that the mission was almost in a "state of siege" since the Wali had blockaded the settlement, threatening to fire on anyone attempting to enter.[98]

The then British Consul, Miles (Kirk was in Britain), was very surprised at this new episode. He at once called the Wali and Price to Zanzibar to settle the dispute. The Sultan, as usual under British influence, took a lenient view of the affair, allowing it to drop when Price agreed to take measures against receiving fugitive slaves.[99]

Another problem dealt with at this time was the fugitive slave settlement at Fulladoyo, near Mombasa. This village had been founded due to the efforts of an African educated by the Methodist mission. He became an independent evangelist, eventually forming a settlement in Giriama country. These former slaves, at one time estimated as numbering from 600 to 700, had constant relations with the C.M.S., with some coming to the mission to settle. Price

---

94 *Ibid.*; Menzies to Wigram, Jan. 2, 1882; Taylor to Wigram, Jan. 3, 1882, *ibid.*

95 Price to Hutchinson, undated, *ibid.*

96 Miles to Granville, Feb. 10, 1882, F.O. 84/1620; Miles to Granville, Apr. 6, 1882, with encolsures, F.O. 84/1621.

97 Muhammad ibn Suliman to Sultan of Zanzibar, May 21, 1882 and May 22, 1882, N-14, Z.A.

98 Price to Miles, May 20, 1882, *ibid.*

99 Miles to Granville, May 31, 1882; with enclosures, and June 24, 1882. F.O. 84/1621. Granville noted: "The Sultan has shown great forbearance and good temper in this case."

told the Sultan how difficult it was to stop this, but informed him the mission would in no way recognize any responsibility for protecting them. This disclaimer was accepted. The Arabs destroyed Fulladoyo in 1883, which solved the problem temporarily, but the fugitives later regrouped to cause new trouble for the British.[100]

Price proved no more able or willing than other missionaries to stop the flow of fugitive slaves onto mission grounds. The trouble broke out anew at the end of 1882. Consul Miles had to visit Mombasa to conclude a temporary agreement.[101] As previously, the agreement was not upheld.

At this point in the history of the Mombasa mission, a general evaluation of progress was undertaken by the C.M.S. It was not difficult to see that the mission had not worked out as planned. A primary aim of the founders of the settlement had been to make it self-sufficient. A missionary now reported: "Frere Town has been proved beyond a doubt to be incapable of becoming self-supporting." This caused great problems since the Africans in the mission had to secure a living. There seemed no prospect of this. The solution recommended was, if all efforts to provide local work failed, to move the Africans elsewhere.[102] Rabai was the obvious place available for these Africans. The C.M.S. officials in London recognized this, but were unwilling to act. They maintained that the Society had undertaken special responsibility for the freed slave center at Frere Town; at Rabai they had only the usual duty to spread Christianity. Thus, although they might prefer to move to the superior location of Rabai, they considered they could not abandon Frere Town.[103]

Kirk also took part in this discussion. He informed the C.M.S. that it was time to appoint an important church official to the mission and to retire the office of lay superintendent, since the recent appointment of a Vice-Consul for Mombasa made this post

---

100 Price to Miles, Jan. 23, 1882, Parker to Lang, Dec. 21. 1886, C.M.S. Archives; Miles to Granville, May 31, 1882 and June 24, 1882, F.O. 84/1621.

101 Miles to F.O., Mar. 30, 1883, E-78, Z.A.; Kirk to Granville, Apr. 27, 1884, F.O. 84/1644.

102 Handford to Lang, Jan. 23, 1884; Shaw to Lang, Nov. 22, 1884, C.M.S. Archives.

103 Lang to Shaw, Feb. 29, 1884, *ibid.*

unnecessary.[104] Kirk harshly said: "The fact is that Frere Town now ought to become a mission, it has ceased for years to receive fresh slaves and there is no prospect of any captures." The C.M.S. agreed, and in June, 1884, announced that a bishop was to be appointed to head the mission in East Africa.[105]

But as this discussion went on, the problem of fugitive slaves erupted again. The C.M.S. in London asked a missionary, Shaw, to explain a sentence in one of his letters: "The owners know that if they are cruel the slaves will run away to us and get protection."[106] Shaw answered merely that the missionaries did not encourage slave action and that they did refer all known cases to the Wali. He added that since land adjacent to the mission was open to all, the problem could not be avoided. The Vice-Consul, he continued, knew of it and had made no complaints as long as official channels were utilized for disputes.[107]

The missionaries claimed that Kirk was aware of their actions, but his reports show he considered the mission harbored slaves in spite of their denials.[108] He made it quite clear to the C.M.S. directors that he did not approve of their actions. In August, 1884, he told the Society that Rabai was "made up chiefly of runaway slaves and notwithstanding all the missionaries there say to the contrary, many of these are from Mombasa town itself."[109]

Despite this attitude, the British officials began to send captured slaves to the mission again: in November, 1884, over 160 were landed.[110] More came in December. Kirk's seeming reversal was explained by his statement that he wanted the C.M.S. to accept them or "he shall be compelled to hand them over to the French mission and that both on religious and political grounds he preferred handing them over to our English Mission." The religious factor had never prevented Kirk from giving slaves to the French

104 Kirk to F.O., Jan. 26, 1884, E-83, Z.A., for the sending of Vice-Consul Gissing.

105 Kirk to Cust, Mar. 16, 1884; Lang to Lane, June 13, 1884, C.M.S. Archives.

106 Lang to Shaw, Feb. 29, 1884, *ibid.*

107 Shaw to Lang, Apr. 14, 1884, *ibid.*

108 Kirk to F.O., May 31, 1884, E-83, Z.A.

109 Kirk to C.M.S., Aug. 4, 1884, C.M.S. Archives.

110 Handford to Lang, Nov. 26, 1884, *ibid.*

before; a political decision resulting from the friction between France and England in Africa was obvious here.[111]

The first C.M.S. Bishop, James Hannington, arrived to meet this situation. He was upset at some aspects of the mission, calling the missionary living quarters luxurious, while the station hospital was "about equal to a pigstye," but, in general, praising the accomplishments of the missionaries.[112] But the C.M.S. did not have the new Bishop's leadership for long. He soon set out on his famous trip to Buganda, where he was killed by order of the Kabaka, Mwanga.[113]

Another blow to the C.M.S. followed the death of Hannington, when Handford, lay director of the mission, was arrested in Zanzibar after attempting to disappear into the African quarter with an African woman. As an African missionary noted, this was the crime for which Handford had driven many African Christians from the station.[114] Aside from the moral effect, this episode deprived the station of one of its effective leaders during a time of need.

At this late date an old problem was resolved. The renewed landing of slaves caused the C.M.S. to press again for financial aid from the Government. They asked for £5 each for slaves. Kirk supported the request; the Foreign Office complied. In July, 1886, a grant of £1,545 was given for the 309 slaves received between 1 January, 1884, and 1 April, 1886.[115] The other British Protestant missions received similar grants; the French Catholics did not.[116]

A new Bishop, Parker, came out to succeed Hannington in mid-1886. He had instructions to improve one major fault of the mission: the schools were not turning out trained teachers for mission work in spite of the many years of trial.[117] Before he began working to

111 Handford to Lang, Dec. 1, 1884, *ibid.* See Bennett, *Studies*, 68.

112 Hannington to Wigram, Feb. 9, 1885, *ibid.*; Dawson, *Hannington*, 325.

113 Oliver, *Missionary Factor*, 104.

114 Jones to Lang, Oct. ?, 1886; Lang to Shaw, Apr. 19, 1886, C.M.S. Archives. Kirk to F.O., Apr. 8, 1886, F.O. 84/1777.

115 Kirk to F.O., Jan. 8, 1886 and June 30, 1886, E-93, Z.A.; Lister to Kirk, Nov. 26, 1885, with enclosures, E-86, *ibid.*; Hutchinson to Lister, Nov. 20, 1885, F.O. 84/1744; Lister to Kirk, Mar. 24, 1886, E-91, Z.A.

116 Bennett, *Studies*, 68.

117 Lang to Parker, June 29, 1886, C.M.S. Archives. In 1885, a missionary reported 189 pupils. See English to Lang, Aug. 1, 1885, *ibid.*

improve this, Parker voiced his strong disapproval of another aspect of the mission. His main concern was evangelization, so he said: "It cannot be right for us to create a community of paupers and then support them all with money subscribed for the conversion of the heathen." The problem was that the small Christian African community depended entirely on mission funds for survival, since the Christians could not support themselves while living in Frere Town.[118] A previous despatch from London anticipated this complaint: the directors said it was the duty of the C.M.S. to continue receiving slaves as in the past, and to support them when necessary.[119] Parker did not play a significant role in removing the above faults since he too soon went inland to die on the shores of Lake Victoria.[120]

While attempts at reform were blocked by the deaths of the Bishops, the problem of fugitive slaves continued to cause trouble. In June, 1887, consular officials found it necessary to investigate C.M.S. fears of an attack. The fears were groundless, but Arab resentment caused by the fugitive question was evident. A new agreement was concluded: Arabs wishing to search the mission for slaves required a pass from the Wali.[121] It was no doubt hoped that he would keep tempers on both sides down by cautious action.

Perhaps this continuing difficulty, with the others above mentioned, caused the missionary, Shaw, to say at the end of 1887: "There is a deadly atmosphere here (spiritually) and I can assure you that I have very little hope of our people here, the more I know of the place and the people the more sick at heart I feel." Shaw blamed much of this on the so-called bad influences that surrounded the mission, but his view gave no hope for change.[122]

---

118 Parker to Lang, Dec. 21, 1886; Shaw to Lang, Dec. 9, 1886, *ibid.*

119 Lang and Fenn to Shaw, Nov. 4, 1886, *ibid.*

120 See Stock, *History*, III, 420.

121 Holmwood to Lang, June 13, 1887, with an addenda of June 18, 1887, C.M.S. Archives; Berkeley to Holmwood, June 24, 1887, in Holmwood to F.O., July 10, 1887; Macdonald to F.O., Nov. 16, 1887, E-99, Z.A. For a missionary view, Shaw to Lang, June 30, 1887 and Aug. 19, 1887, C.M.S. Archives.

122 Shaw to Lang, Dec. 24, 1887, C.M.S. Archives. A statistical note for the end of 1887, "Statistics of the Eastern Equatorial African Mission," listed 446 African Christians at Frere Town and 1817 and Rabai. In *ibid.*

And the problems did not cease. One slave owner visited Rabai under terms of the pass agreement. He was met at the outskirts and advised to return. No other owner then dared to try. The consul, MacDonald, inquired aout this; Binns, the missionary in charge, admitted that he had no power to compel obedience. He reported that Rabai was practically independent, with its own armed groups. MacDonald then visited Rabai without warning. He talked to W. Jones, the African missionary,[123] and in general was very impressed with the organization of the place. The Africans lived together by tribes and ran most of their own affairs. There was obviously no way to prevent them from harboring fugitive slaves without a large regulatory force. Thus the Consul accepted the mission promise to do all possible to discourage the violation of local law.[124]

In an attempt to resolve all problems, the C.M.S. decided to send W. Salter Price again to Mombasa. The consul, Euan Smith, had just visited C.M.S. headquarters in London, where he dwelt upon the fugitive problem: orders to stop this "mistaken kindness" were an important part of Price's instructions.[125] Price arrived in East Africa in March, 1888; he went at once to the Wali to assure him the mission would cooperate on fugitives.[126] If the C.M.S. was really determined to resolve the fugitive problem, Price might have been their best choice, but one has to remember that he himself had been unable, or unwilling, to end this source of unrest during his earlier period of office. There soon were complaints against him from Arab owners.[127]

The solution of this problem now took on particular significance. The Imperial British East African Company assumed administration of the coastal area from Wanga to Kipini for the Sultan in 1888. Then a period followed when the IBEA had to be very careful not to excite a general rising of the local population, especially

---

[123] Hannington had praised him for working "exactly as an experienced European." See Hannington to Wigram, Mar. 2, 1885, *ibid.*

[124] MacDonald to F.O., Feb. 13, 1888, E-107; see also Churchill to Euan Smith, May 25, 1888, E-104, Z.A.

[125] Lang and Gray to Price, Feb. 21, 1888, C.M.S. Archives.

[126] W. Salter Price, *My Third Campaign in East Africa* (London, 1890), 125.

[127] *Ibid.*, 85, 105.

since an outbreak against the similar German takeover of the Tanganyika coast had occurred in August.[128] Price seemed fully aware of the problems of the new situation; he pointed out to Euan Smith that he would have to keep the mission clear of all ties to the political activities of the IBEA since the mission would be the first place to be attacked if a rising occurred.[129]

This reserve did not of course mean that the IBEA and the mission would not cooperate. The Company soon invited the mission to establish stations on its route to the interior and the invitation was accepted.[130] This cooperation had definite limits, however. The missionaries appreciated the order that a successful company would bring to East Africa, but they also feared the effect that the Company would have on their African Christians by employing them away from missionary controls. Arrangements were made to regulate recruiting for the Company, but the problem was never satisfactory settled since the Christianity of the African Christmas seemed too fragile to survive separation from the station.[131]

The IBEA avoided all local troubles, by "paving their way with dollars,"[132] and by paying close attention to local wishes. This meant that the old sore of fugitive slaves had to be solved. Mackenzie, director of the Company in Mombasa, considered that fugitives were accepted on the mission stations on the "most frivolous pretext," and consequently the successful operation of his policies was endangered. He reported that a meeting of the Arab community had been held before his arrival. The Arabs had decided to ask Mackenzie to abolish the mission. They justly could not understand why the mission should hold fugitive slaves, their former

---

[128] For these events, see Fritz Ferdinand Müller, *Deutschland-Zanzibar-Ostafrika* (Berlin, 1959), 357 ff.

[129] Price to Lang, Sept. 5, 1888, Sept. 15, 1888, Nov. 28, 1888; Price to Euan Smith, Sept. 15, 1888, C.M.S. Archives.

[130] Mackenzie to Price, Nov. 13, 1888; Price to Lang, Nov. 20, 1888 and Dec. 19, 1888, *ibid.*

[131] Shaw to Lang, Sept. 25, 1889, *ibid.*; Price, *Third Campaign*, 152, 167. For a revealing episode on outside labor for African Christians, see John C. Willoughby, *East Africa and its Big Game* (London, 1889), 33. Willoughby found the former slaves so regulated by the mission that he concluded they "had only left one form of servitude to embark in another."

[132] Price to Lang, Dec. 10, 1888, C.M.S. Archives.

property, while the British spoke against slavery. Mackenzie was able to get this resolution quashed before it was made public, but he had to take action to meet Arab protests. With General Mathews (the Sultan's representative),[133] and Arab officials he visited Price to state their case. Price considered the Arabs had "absolutely no cause for complaint"; he agreed, however, to allow a commission to investigate Rabai, promising to give up any fugitives located there. Price also consented to an IBEA official being appointed to watch over Rabai in the future.[134]

This move had the full support of the Consul, Euan Smith.[135] Price, although he consented to the investigation, was unhappy at the decision, particularly over the inclusion of Mathews. He held him to be "hostile to missions and missionaries." Euan Smith met these hesitations by stating that the Arabs appeared to have just cause for complaint, and that if no solution by cooperation could be achieved once and for all, the mission had to prepare for the imposition of rules "of an exceedingly drastic and stringent character."[136]

Price had no choice; the investigation began. He did his best to ensure a report favorable to the mission, writing to Jones "to make a clean sweep of the settlement" before the commission arrived. A crisis occurred. Jones reported there were more fugitives present than he had estimated, that many were Christians who refused to leave, and that they were preparing, with the aid of their friends, to defend themselves. Jones concluded that he had lost all control of them.[137] To Price, this was a "revelation"; he now estimated there were several hundred slaves there instead of the thirty

---

133 For his career, Robert Nunez Lyne, *An Apostle of Empire* (London, 1936).

134 Mackenzie to Euan Smith, Oct. 18, 1888, with addenda, in Euan Smith to Salisbury, Oct. 22, 1888, F.O. 84/1910; Price, *Third Campaign*, 182 ff. For the official account of the investigation, P. L. McDermott, *British East Africa or IBEA* (London, 1893), 22 ff.

135 Euan Smith to Price, Oct. 14, 1888, C.M.S. Archives.

136 Price to Euan Smith, Oct. 16, 1888 and Euan Smith to Price, Oct. 17, 1888, *ibid.* Price was not convinced. He noted on this despatch, "Col. E.S. does not know him [Mathews]. He writes of us as 'those d—d missionaries'."

137 Price to Lang, Oct. 24, 1888, *ibid.*

or forty he originally thought to find.[138] Price warned Mackenzie of this dangerous situation and the IBEA official met the new problem with great skill. He asked the Arabs, who were unaware of the exact numbers there, to adopt a new solution, suggesting that he (Mackenzie) arrange for the redemption of the slaves. The Arabs agreed. Mackenzie did this on Price's revised estimate of the number of fugitives; the commission was to determine the exact number for the settlement.[139]

The commission found Price's estimate to be incorrect; 933 fugitives were reported at Rabai (plus 488 at the other Protestant stations in the area). Euan Smith, on learning this, placed full responsibility on the mission, and supported all of Mackenzie's efforts to satisfy the former Arab owners. The fact that 480 of the fugitives had been on C.M.S. property less than two years, and 623 less than three years, demonstrated exactly the amount of regulation imposed by the mission in spite of all promises. Price was crushed; he could only repeat that this was "nothing less than a revelation" and that his orders had not been carried out as strictly as he intended![140]

Effective regulations, so long avoided by the C.M.S., now went into effect against fugitives. The director at Rabai appointed African officials to supervise entry of outsiders and notices expelling unauthorized persons were posted.[141] Price still did not face the facts of C.M.S. responsibility; he complained to Mackenzie that his reports gave the impression that the mission had knowingly broken the law and now acted to redress it only under compulsion![142]

---

[138] "Memo of Runaway Slaves at Rabai," Nov. 3, 1888, *ibid.* Price unfairly placed the blame on Jones, claiming he had always given him strict orders against fugitives.

[139] Price, *Third Campaign,* 194-97.

[140] *Ibid.,* 220; Euan Smith to Salisbury, Nov. 20, 1888, enclosing Mackenzie to Euan Smith, Oct. 26, 1888, Nov. 9, 1888, Nov. 15, 1888, Price's Memo of Nov. 3, 1888, Price to Euan Smith, Nov. 15, 1888, Price to Mackenzie, Nov. 14, 1888, F.O. 84/1910.

[141] Price to Barness, Dec. 26, 1888; Price to Euan Smith, Jan. 14, 1889, C.M.S. Archives.

[142] Price to Mackenzie, Jan. 14, 1889, *ibid.* Price's fears were of course true. H. P. Anderson noted on a despatch from Euan Smith that the trouble was due "to the duplicity of the missionary agents about the runaway slaves. They

The problem of the discovered fugitives was ended when Mackenzie arranged for the Company to obtain "freedom certificates," at a fixed rate, for the slaves. On January 1, 1889, 1422 fugitives were freed from all the Mombasa area; 900[143] were from Rabai. The total cost was £1,372.16.5. Mackenzie, however, considered that he had acted beyond his powers in arranging this costly solution; he requested that the C.M.S. or its friends bear part of the cost. The directors of the Company agreed and suggested that the Government, the missions, and the Company each pay one-third.[144] Although Price protested against C.M.S. involvement in paying a share of costs,[145] a joint agreement was eventually reached: the Government paid £800; T. F. Buxton and other friends of the various missions, £1,200; the Company paid the balance—£1,372.16.5.[146]

The old problem seemed settled. The slaves were officially free and were allowed to remain on mission grounds. With this came a strict instruction from the Foreign Office: the missions were to refuse more fugitives "without making any exception." If the missions violated this rule, it was "done at the risk of the person giving the shelter."[147] Even this directive did not succeed in obtaining cooperation from the C.M.S. Mackenzie learned that two new slaves had found refuge at Frere Town; he had to go there with their owner to free them before any additional trouble occurred.[148]

---

acted in direct disobedience to the Society's order." Note on Euan Smith to Salisbury, Nov. 19, 1888, F.O. 84/1910.

143 Price claimed only 643 were the responsibility of the C.M.S. See Price's "Memo No. 2 on the Runaway Slave Question at Rabai," Jan. 29, 1889, C.M.S. Archives.

144 Buxton to C.M.S., Dec. 21, 1888; Mackenzie to C.M.S., Dec. 21, 1888, Précis Book, *ibid.* Mackinnon to Salisbury, Feb. 18, 1889, F.O. 541/29.

145 Price's "Memo"—citation in footnote 143.

146 Report of the Directors of the Imperial British East Africa Company (I.B.E.A.), June 1, 1889, in Sanderson to Portal, Aug. 20, 1889, E-115, Z.A.; for slightly different figures, McDermott, *IBEA*, 30. For a criticism of this solution, Margery Perham (ed.), *The Diaries of Lord Lugard* (London, 1959), I, 56.

147 Lister to Euan Smith, Feb. 1, 1889, E-114, Z.A.

148 Mackenzie to Euan Smith, Mar. 13, 1889, in Euan Smith to Salisbury, Mar. 20, 1889, F.O. 84/1977. For Price's views of this action, Price to Lang, Mar. 13, 1889, C.M.S. Archives; Price, *Third Campaign*, 311.

Thus the basic source of difficulty for the mission over the years with the local population was at last settled.[149] The C.M.S., after denying for years responsibility for causing the unrest, was found culpably negligent in the matter. The IBEA and Mackenzie demonstrated "wisdom and judgement" and in doing so possibly saved the C.M.S. from the consequences of its disregard for local law and sentiments.[150]

Price left East Africa for the last time in March 1889. He was replaced by Bishop Alfred Tucker who was to give real direction to the C.M.S. mission in East Africa.[151] Even though the fugitive problem appeared finished, the new leader had many long-standing problems to solve. The mission teachers found it impossible to keep their boys in order;[152] the African Christians from Bombay remained a source of disorder;[153] and all plans for industrial training had failed.[154] In sum, the educational aspect of the mission was almost a complete failure.[155]

Plans for improvement were formulated even before Bishop Tucker arrived. The successor to Price at Frere Town, Dr. Stephen Pruen, an experienced East African missionary,[156] presided over a meeting of the resident missionaries in May, 1889, to decide what course to follow. They recommended expansion of the industrial training offered to mission Africans and increased training of teachers.[157] A decision was made to start these improvements with

---

[149] The fugitive problem at Fulladoyo (see above) was settled also. See Euan Smith to Salisbury, Feb. 24, 1890, enclosing Mackenzie to Euan Smith, Feb. 12, 1890; Euan Smith to Salisbury, June 14, 1890, enclosing Lugard to Euan Smith, June 9, 1890, F.O. 84/2059. Also, Perham, *Lugard Diaries,* I, 61 ff.

[150] Euan Smith to Salisbury, Feb. 7, 1889, F.O. 84/1976.

[151] This story is recounted in Alfred R. Tucker, *Eighteen Years in Uganda and East Africa* (London, 1908).

[152] England to Lang, May 11, 1886 and June 9, 1886, C.M.S. Archives.

[153] Shaw to Lang, Feb. 11, 1886, *ibid.*

[154] Binns to Lang, Dec. 19, 1887; Price to Lang, Apr. 10, 1888; Price, "Information and hints for Dr. Pruen," Aug. 25, 1888, *ibid.*

[155] See Price's bitter letter to Lang of Sept. 5, 1888, *ibid.* In 1889-1890 there were only about seven African teachers at work. See Pruen to Lang, Aug. 9, 1889; Binns to Wigram, Sept. 17, 1890, *ibid.*

[156] His experiences in the interior are in part recounted in his, *The Arab and the African* (London, 1891).

[157] Pruen to Lang, May 17, 1889, C.M.S. Archives.

resources collected at the mission; 1,000 rupees were raised from the resident Africans.[158]

These steps did not stop dissatisfaction at Frere Town's progress in matters of training by the time of Tucker's arrival.[159] Before he could attempt a solution, however, he learned of three fugitives settling at Rabai in spite of all that had gone before. Tucker questioned Jones closely about this and found that there were actually over one hundred new fugitives living there. To avoid a major upset the Bishop made a public declaration of this and took steps to have them earn their freedom by work. Then Jones was informed that any other discoveries of this kind would result in his expulsion from the mission.[160] The incident passed without repercussion.

Tucker then, after dealing with C.M.S. affairs in the interior, began a serious evaluation of the Mombasa mission. He first decided that Frere Town would surely decline when the government stopped delivering slaves since it had no good agricultural land. He suggested that the mission refuse to accept any but five- and six-year-old slaves. To them would be added young Africans from interior stations so that Frere Town would develop into an educational center. Tucker considered this the only feasible step since few slaves of any kind were now received from the Government.[161]

Next the Bishop made a more thorough report of all aspects of the mission. It was a devastating study.[162] He reported that eighty-three boys were housed in the mission dormitories. They had practically no supervision when out of school. The fact that twenty boys slept in an area fourteen feet by six feet accounted for the many acts of immorality he discovered. The seventy girls in their dormitory were in a similar condition. He summed up his attitude on the dormitories with this statement: "In their present condition

---

158 Pruen to Lang, May 24, 1889, *ibid.* An African elder said of this: "But when you [Pruen] go a new secretary will come, and will stop all we are trying to do." Pruen admitted this statement to be just.

159 See Binns to Lang, Dec. 7, 1890 and Feb. 27, 1891, *ibid.*

160 Tucker to Gould, July 9, 1890, Fitch to Tucker, July 4, 1890, *ibid.* For Lugard's comments, Perham, *Lugard Diaries*, I, 233.

161 Tucker to Lang, Apr. 5, 1892 and May 16, 1892, C.M.S. Archives.

162 Tucker to Wigram, June 3, 1892, *ibid.*

they are not merely a disgrace to the Church Missionary Society but to Christianity itself." He added that one missionary, Binns, described the girls' dormitory as little more than "a feeder for the ranks of prostitutes." Tucker's evaluation of the 485 adult Christian Africans was in a similar vein.

The Bishop concluded that the C.M.S. at Frere Town had been largely a failure, and that major changes were required. His recommendations were in line with those made earlier—to make Frere Town an educational training center for children (after a thorough overhaul of the dormitory system).

The resident missionaries supported their bishop. They noted their "regrets that Bishop Tucker's report is in the main correct"; they asked that no more slaves be landed by the Government.[163] They later added: "With these facts before them your Cte can but report that they consider Frere Town to have failed to attain any of the objects for which it was established.[164]

Bishop Tucker's anger subsided somewhat. In 1892 he changed his description of the dormitories from "a disgrace to Christianity" to "far from creditable to the C.M.S.,"[165] but he did not change his views. Tucker, in fact, became very upset when he saw that the London officials of the C.M.S. did not seem to share his views of the lamentable state of affairs at Frere Town.[166] Tucker's plans for a training center were put into operation in 1894,[167] and the period of Frere Town as a center for freed slaves was over.[168]

The record is clear. The hopes of the C.M.S. and its supporters for a settlement similar to those founded on the West African coast for freed slaves never materialized. The C.M.S. had a difficult task, their center being established in an area outside of direct British control, but the same conditions were met more successfully by the Holy Ghost missionaries at Bagamoyo. The C.M.S. was never

[163] Finance Committee (Mombasa) Report, Nov. 2, 1892, *ibid.* For one missionary's dissenting view, Binns to Wigram, Nov. 7, 1892, *ibid.*

[164] Finance Committee's Report on the State of Frere Town, Nov. 19, 1893, *ibid.*

[165] Tucker to Lang, Aug. 14, 1892, *ibid.*

[166] Tucker to Lang, Aug. 31, 1893; Tucker to Baylis, Sept. 26, 1893, *ibid.*

[167] Tucker to Stock, Aug. 21, 1894; Tucker to Baylis, Sept. 26, 1894, *ibid.*

[168] For an incomplete estimate of slaves received between 1875-90, Smith to Baylis, Apr. 18, 1893, *ibid.* The figure given is 921.

able to meet the problems involved and to live in harmony with the legal rulers of the land. The responsibility for this discord appears to rest almost entirely with the mission. Though they hoped for more support from the British government than they received, this lack of support was apparent at an early date, giving the missionaries full opportunity to adapt to local regulations. Under the law of Zanzibar, civil and religious obligations were clear, but the missionaries, who recognized the authority of the Sultan in some things (i.e., as on the power to regulate land sales), refused to accept the regulations relating to slavery. Their task in Mombasa was to educate and Christianize liberated slaves, not to give aid and succor to fleeing slaves. But they decided to give this assistance, even if they lacked the physical power to make it effective. In so doing they went against local British policy and against that of their parent body in England. With their European ideas of slavery, and of African life in general, the result was understandable, but their actions still must be judged as conduct unworthy of visitors on foreign soil by permission of the ruling government.

VIII.

Missionaries as Chiefs and Entrepreneurs: Northern Rhodesia, 1882-1924

by

ROBERT I. ROTBERG

Assistant Professor of History and Research Associate, the Center for International Affairs, Harvard University, Cambridge, Massachusetts

IN MANY AREAS OF AFRICA, Christian missionaries were the vanguard of the West. Not unexpectedly, they organized themselves and their activities in peculiarly Western ways. They brought new techniques of material advance and social control and thereby introduced Africans to other Western ideas and practices in addition to the doctrine of Christianity. As gradual as it may have been, this process of transferring Western skills and knowledge also brought about a reorganization of indigenous society and polity. Trade goods encouraged new material demands; roads and bridges made communication and labor migration more common. And sadly for those who wished to preserve traditional life, more rapid change became a continuing and sequential process. Once missionaries established themselves, built stations, and ensured their ties to the outside world, there could be no cessation. Missionaries became major agents of change and, for a time, holders of considerable authority; moreover, they became more and more enmeshed in a temporal and secular network of their own creation.[1]

This involvement took place in two major ways. First, they became concerned intimately with the ordering of the lives of Africans. In addition to those campaigns of exhortation against "sinful" customs which they carried directly to the rural villagers, missionaries gathered Africans at central stations and exerted considerable control over daily behavior. Unlike most of the early freed-slave villages in East Africa, however, missionary centers in Northern Rhodesia were less often models of Western development. Whatever the intentions of their founders, they appear to have served more simply as centers in which Western ways could be demonstrated and, in many cases, they provided for missionaries a

[1] This essay, and the larger study of which it forms a part, is based on research which was generously supported by the Rockefeller Foundation, the Rhodes Trust, the Beit Fund, and the Colonial Social Science Research Council.

reliable corps of tribesmen to whom the menial, but necessary, tasks of any Western community could be devolved.

Missionaries spent long hours engaged in those secular activities which, albeit without forethought, contributed so crucially to eventual African participation in the Western economy. They opened stores and traded widely. They kept accounts, ran postal services, and participated in that myriad of pursuits necessary to Western life in a remote and isolated part of the world. The "natives" were introduced to the ways of the white man—to his evangelical predilection for thrift and hard work and to his penchant for clothes, particularly the bright calicos. Africans discovered that they were rewarded for copying the white man's speech, habits, and economic thought. Whereas preferment and status had previously come by exploit, by magic or mysticism, or simply by ascribed rights of lineal succession, the new order conferred prestige on the basis of special modes of achievement.

The following missionary bodies were active in Northern Rhodesia between 1882 and 1924: London Missionary Society (LMS), Paris Missionary Society (PMS), Primitive Methodist Missionary Society (PMMS), Wesleyan Methodist Missionary Society (WMMS), United Free Church of Scotland (CS), White Fathers (WF), Society of Jesus (SJ), Dutch Reformed Church of the Orange Free State (DRC), South Africa General Mission (SAGM), Plymouth Brethren (PB), Brethren-in-Christ (BC), Church-of-Christ (CC), and Seventh-day Adventists (SDA). Each kindly gave me full cooperation and access to relevant materials.[2]

I

Wherever missionaries went in Central Africa, they soon appreciated the difficulty of transmitting Christian dogma by exhortation alone, and they therefore devised measures to increase their daily influence. They started schools and hospitals. They also organized villages dependent upon the missionary and responsible

[2] The material available is great in quantity, rich in quality, and virtually unused. The treatment in this paper is, however, necessarily selective. References to "Diary," "Letters," "Logbook" and "Notebook" are preceded by the name of the mission station concerned.

to him. The missionary became a temporal governor.[3] He ruled and directed numerous Africans who had seen fit to renounce traditional authority and to adhere to the new order. For a time his power was absolute and unchecked. Consequently, the system developed its own abuses, and only with the assumption of settled territorial administration by a secular government did it fall into disuse. During its active life, however, it was perhaps the most important institution making for substantive change.

All missions in Northern Rhodesia were involved, at some time, in direct government. At Luanza, Johnston Falls, Kaleba, and Chitokoloki the Plymouth Brethren administered villages; at Kaleñe Hill they even controlled a series of Lunda, Lovale, and Ovimbundu settlements within five miles of the mission station.[4] Near Magwero the Dutch Reformed Church early gathered Africans around the mission and governed them strictly.[5] White Fathers, Jesuits, and Seventh-day Adventists all did the same in their own fashion.[6] The Paris Missionary Society and the Primitive Methodists were, however, unable to induce other than school boys to stay permanently with them.[7] At Chisalala, Musonweji, and Kaba Hill, the South African General Mission was similarly unable to exert that control to which it aspired.[8]

---

[3] For a comparative analysis, see Ruth Slade, *English-Speaking Missions in the Congo Independent State 1878–1908* (Bruxelles, 1959), 164 ff. See also Roland Oliver, *The Misisonary Factor in East Africa* (London, 1952), 51.

[4] Personal interviews: Chief Kanganja (Lumingu Village, June 24, 1959); Ffolliot Fisher (Hillwood Farm, June 25, 1959); William Lammond (Johnston Falls, Sept. 16-17, 1959); Mrs. George Suckling (Chitokoloki, June 30, 1959). See also Stanley R. Coad, Dec. 20, 1922, in *Echoes of Service* (Mar., 1922), 63-64; Daniel Crawford, *Thinking Black* (London, 1913), 324-27, 445-47. But see Slade, *Missions*, 127.

[5] Personal interview: Ella Botes (Magwero, Apr. 13, 1959).

[6] Czarlinski to Parry, Nov. 15, 1920; Chikuni Letters, 1911-1925; Campion Papers, Campion House, Salisbury; Torrend, diary, Diocesan Office, Lusaka, Nov. 8, 1918, Jan. 24, 1919. Personal interview: L. Etienne (Chilubula, Sept. 2, 1959); M. A. Prokoph, "Chikuni 1905-55," *The Catholic Teacher,* IV (Sept. 15, 1955), 8-18.

[7] Minutes of Synod Meeting, Aug. 22, 1904, at Kanchindu Mission; Pickering to Lea, Apr. 30, 1901, Lea Papers (MMS) archives, London. Personal interview: John R. Shaw (Lusaka, Jan. 22, 1959).

[8] Melland to Wilson, Apr. 4, 1919; Harris to Middlemiss, Oct. 9, 1917;

The Universities' Mission to Central Africa (UMCA), particularly at Chipili, developed villages on the East African pattern immediately it commenced activity in Northern Rhodesia.[9] The mission drew its labor from these villages and ruled them paternally. As late as 1917, capitãos were enjoined to settle all disagreements, to investigate all applicants for residence in the villages and to report them to the priest, and to guard particularly "against people who have chucked or been chucked by other missions."[10] The UMCA, like other societies, extended its rule to the countryside as often as possible; it set about rationalizing Christian communities and other centers. William Deerr frequently intervened to settle conflicts between warring villages and to impose peace "for the good of all."[11] Punishment for failure to conform to mission regulations or doctrine usually took the form of corporal punishment, tempered at Msoro with humor, or dismissal.

> [Two villagers] the previous night having missed roll-call, orgied at Manokola and arrived with the milk, were condemned to serve on the road gang under Manoel, for a week. As a merciful concession they were not chained.[12]

But the UMCA system of government, like that of other missions, finally broke down under the weight of its own bureaucracy and upon a realization that Christian influence was not being furthered to any appreciable extent by minor theocracies. At Chipili this divestment came only in 1922, when Charles Leeke ordered villagers to disperse themselves as best they could to the surrounding

---

Harris' report in Middlemiss to Faithfull, July 1, 1916, all in South Africa General Mission (SAGM) papers, Wimbledon; Musonweji Diary, July 11, 1923; Harris to General Missionary Committee, May 20, 1913: ". . . it appears the Government do not recognize Dr. Watney as headman [of the village near Kaba Hill]." Hamilton, report of a deputation, 1926, SAGM papers.

[9] See Monica Wilson, *Communal Rituals of the Nyakyusa* (London, 1959), 166; Oliver, *Missionary Factor,* 58-65, 73.

[10] Chipili Diary, i, May 31, 1917.

[11] Chipili Diary, i, May 8, 1913, May 10-12, 1917; see Mapanza Diary, Feb. 9-10, 1914, 160; *Central Africa,* 1914, 247-49; Henry Faulkner, June 2, 1922, *Echoes,* Sept., 1920, 208-9; See May to Laura, May 5, 1919, May Papers, London (privately held).

[12] Ranger, Msoro Logbook, ii, Feb. 2, 1924. See also Fort Jameson Diary, Feb. 6, 1912.

countryside. He retained a small compound for servants and schoolboys, and was clearly relieved to remove the mission from details of daily administration.[13]

Only the London Missionary Society (LMS) carried the village system, organized so tentatively elsewhere, to its logical conclusion. Unique circumstances forced it to begin governing Africans; once established, this government simply grew. In 1887, David Jones realized that his ministry, to be successful, must be a settled one. Local Mambwe and Lungu, long fearful of Bemba and Arab raiding parties, were accustomed, moreover, to live in well-protected stockades.[14] They had welcomed the LMS as protectors, but they had refused to live with their new rulers until the mission built proper fortifications and demonstrated a capacity to resist incursions.[15] Stockades were therefore constructed by the mission at Kawimbe and Niamkolo in 1890, and this tardy and piecemeal approach increasingly meant a growth in the mission's exercise of temporal control over the lives of Africans.

The LMS at first did not appreciate all the advantages inherent in a system of village government. Gradually, however, its members transformed a means for protection into a means for rigid and uncompromising control. Such control permitted the mission to consolidate its local influence and to ensure a steady attendance of children and adults at school and service. Villagers were compelled to attend church at specified times and to send their children regularly to school. When Jones moved to Kawimbe, for example, he insisted upon the obligation of Africans to attend Sunday services faithfully, and to work "cheerfully" on behalf of the mission.[16] Those everywhere who did not comply were punished by

---

13 Chipili Diary, ii, 9-25, Jan. 31, 1922; *Central Africa,* 1922, 270-72. Gerrard Todd Pulley, personal interview (Oxford, Apr. 25, 1960).

14 William Watson, *Tribal Cohesion in a Money Economy* (Manchester, 1958), 13, 72 ff.; Lionel Decle, *Three Years in Savage Africa* (London, 1898), 296.

15 Swann to Thompson, Feb. 26, 1890, Central Africa (CA) viii/1/a; Jones to Thompson, Apr. 15, 1891, CA viii/3/c; Aug. 30, Sept. 19, 1890; CA viii/2/a,b; archives, London; Sharpe to H. H. Johnston (H.M. Commissioner and Consul-General in British Central Africa), Dec. 17, 1892, FO 2/54, PRO.

16 Jones to Thompson, Sept. 16, 1891, CA viii/4/b; Hemans to Thompson, Apr. 13, 1904; both in LMS archives.

the missionary. Paid employment was restricted to Africans who were members of the special towns. Indeed, after the threat of Bemba invasions was eliminated, employment seems to have become the primary incentive for the continued residence of Africans within mission-run villages.[17]

Missionaries of the LMS defended the system at length:

> . . . we cannot depend on gathering the people together for the purpose of telling them our message or of getting the children into our schools. If we lose control of our villages we may lose our people and the work of years would be undone.[18]

Another missionary wrote:

> Without full control of the villages the children would not come to school; the people would not attend Sunday services; the villages would be thoroughly corrupted; missionaries would often be, as in the early days [before villages], without servants; if called upon hurriedly to go on a journey it would be impossible to get men [as carriers]; in cases of emergency . . . it would be impossible to get them [to help]. . . .[19]

The missionaries concluded that they could only hope to make an initial impression within their villages. Not until such villages flourished could they expect a spread of evangelical influence to the rural areas.

The LMS made stringent laws to regulate their domain. Villages were to be kept clean; no villagers were to use the village enclosure, or his own hut, or the huts of others, for "improper purposes." No loaded guns were permitted. Guns were not to be fired within the

---

[17] When there were still fears of Bemba invasions missionaries armed villagers so "as to inspire them with confidence, without in the least disturbing the prevalent impression respecting us that we will fight only in self-defence. . . ." Jones to Thompson, July 23, Aug. 27, 1892, CA viii/6/a; LMS archives.

[18] May to Thompson, Nov. 9, 1898, CA x/2/a; see Minutes of Tanganyika District Committee meeting, Oct. 12-23, 1898, CA x/2/a; LMS archives.

[19] Hemans to Thompson, Nov. 2, 1898, CA x/2/b; LMS archives. For example, "The Bishop had left behind an invalid whose life he had saved, and at his request a messenger arrived to take him to hospital at Fort Jameson. As no Ansenga could be found to carry him, I filled my water-bottle and went to Kapunula to help carry him myself. The dogs! Ran into the bush, lied, and everything else." Ranger, Msoro Logbook, i, May 8, 1918.

villages. All children were enjoined to go to school. Villagers were compelled to attend church on Sunday and holidays.[20] Infractions were punishable by flogging, by road work without pay, or by the forfeit of hoes and spears. Drunkenness, adultery, stealing, blackmail, ordeal by poison, attempted murder or murder—were punishable by whippings or heavy fines.[21] Where there was no standard penalty, or where the accused did not readily admit his misdeed, the missionary heard the cases as prosecutor, defense attorney, judge, and jury together. After decision was rendered and sentence pronounced, he became gaoler and welfare society director. Missionaries simply assumed all the functions of government.[22]

Like Deerr at Chipili and most others throughout the country, the LMS missionaries came to be regarded as chiefs. The village system destroyed the authority of the indigenous leaders and induced them, even before the imposition of a secular administration, to regard the white man as superior and all-powerful.[23] African teachers arrogated positions as sub-chiefs and imposed missionary "law" as thoroughly as possible in the countryside.[24] When indigenous chiefs realized that their own rule was being undermined, and consequently attempted to retaliate, missionaries acted forcibly to restrain them. Tafuna was defeated and imprisoned when he opposed the mission in 1891. Near Kambole two minor chiefs tried to persuade their former subjects to quit the mission by confiscating the people's supply of grain. Percy Jones of the LMS sent several men to retrieve

---

[20] Minutes of Tanganyika District Committee meeting, Oct. 12-22, 1898, CA x/2/a; LMS archives.

[21] See Jones to Thompson, Dec. 4, 1898, viii/2/c; LMS archives.

[22] "Many a little Protestant Pope in the lonely bush is forced by his self-imposed isolation to be prophet, priest, and king rolled into one—really a very big duck, he, in his own private pond." Crawford, *Thinking Black*, 324-25.

[23] "The native chiefs are today powerless and can demand no obedience from their people. . . ." Hemans to Thompson, Nov. 2, 1898, CA viii/2/b; Deerr made his villages promise to hold him as chief. *Central Africa*, 1916, 149-50; 1920, 63; 1913, 115, 141-45; Personal interviews: Lammond (Johnston Falls, Sept. 16, 1959); Mrs. Buckley (Motherwell, Oct. 29, 1958); Mabel Shaw (London, Nov. 17, 1958); Doke (Kafulafuta, July 8, 1959); Mwinilunga District Notebook, 163; Slade, *Missions*, 125.

[24] Leonard Kamungu, during his two years at Msoro, was always regarded as a chief: Msoro Logbook, Jan., 1911, and Mar. 13, 1913. Thompson to Thomas, Sept. 22, 1894, CA xxv, 500; LMS archives.

it but "the chief's gate was shut in their faces and they were defied." Therefore, W. Harwood Nutt armed his men and "got the goods away" after punishing the recalcitrant chiefs.[25] Very few of the missionaries ever concerned themselves about such diminution of indigenous authority. Those who did, either applauded it, or believed the risks attendant upon lessening chiefly power were adequately compensated by the importance of the labors carried on for and by the mission within the special station villages: ". . . work carried on in native villages is not to be compared with the work prosecuted in our own."[26]

Before the directors of the LMS in London had any reason to suspect such a consolidation of power, their missionaries were unquestioned rulers of a large part of Northern Rhodesia. Even after the establishment of a settled administration at Abercorn, the LMS continued to rule many African men, women, and children. Individual missionaries suspended the teleological ethic and moved swiftly to excesses endemic in any such system of control unmitigated by firm control over policy. Just as the village system, and its attendant assumption of rule, elsewhere in Africa did inevitably result in an imposed and personalized code of law and the rigid means of enforcing it, so in Northeast Rhodesia did the LMS find it necessary and right to run its mission stations and villages, and even the surrounding areas, with as sure and hard a hand as a medieval lord his demesne. When it gathered Africans within a stockade, conflicts arose which ordinarily would have been settled within the indigenous system. Hence the mission found it had to impose its own rule, to ensure care and maintenance of essential works, to appoint new subordinate authorities, and generally to rationalize the entire locale in such a way as to have it function as a happy and integrated whole. Minor baronies had existed in Africa, but the LMS developed a mode of secular rule in Northern Rhodesia which went beyond any which were experienced elsewhere.

The system made extensive use of force and corporal punishment. Missionaries themselves administered whippings with a *citoki*

---

25 Nutt to Thompson, July 25, 1895, CA ix/3/c; LMS archives.
26 *Ibid.*

made from cured hippopotamus hide. "In one of our stations at this moment there are half a dozen long strips of thick hippo-hide hanging from a tree, with heavy weights, being cured for the abominable practice in the hands of the missionaries of the LMS, of horsewhipping the natives, in accordance with the necessity of their positions. . . ."[27] Beatings, thrashings, and innumerable minor punishments were all part of the mission's method of keeping order to attain spiritual goals.[28] They were not alone, of course, in furthering their position among Africans by rendering corporal punishment. Traders, travelers, and administrators were hardly ashamed of administering the *citoki* when chiefs, servants, or passersby misbehaved or showed them less than the expected deference.[29] Missionaries were simply acting as white men throughout Africa have often behaved when confronted with "outright disobedience," "simple malfeasance," or "irresponsibility" on the part of weaker and essentially "subject" people.[30] Missionaries, however, also punished as Christians, in furtherance of spiritual callings, and they did not confine punishment simply to children or servants.

The prevalent system and its excesses were rarely questioned before they were challenged by James Mackay, an older missionary

---

27 Purves, in Mackay to Thompson, Aug. 6, 1898, CA x/2/c; LMS archives.

28 Even before there were villages, missionaries saw little reason not to beat Africans for theft or other disreputable actions. David Jones believed: ". . . any one that understands the African's character knows he must be well looked after or he will take all sorts of advantages . . . ," Jones to Thompson, Feb. 22, 1888, CA vii/3/b, LMS archives. See also Coillard to Jessie, Nov. 4, 1891, Coillard Papers, folios 1878-1891, National Archives, Salisbury; A. J. Hanna, *The Beginnings of Nyasaland and North-Eastern Rhodesia* (Oxford, 1956), 27-37; Oliver, *Missionary Factor,* 59-60.

29 Val Gielgud, a district officer, was able to give only ten cuts to an African who misbehaved because of the "ill-timed appearance" and disapproval of Colin Harding, the Administrator of Barotseland. "In punishing him I was not acting as a government official, but simply as a white man who had to establish and sustain the prestige of his race among a wild community. . . ." Gielgud to Codrington, Nov. 21, 1900, A/3/8/1, North-East Rhodesia (NER) archives, Lusaka.

30 This is not meant to constitute a value judgment. Missionaries had no natural right to *expect* obedience or to compel patterns of Western behavior. They did so, however, and excesses ensued.

who had previously served the LMS in Madagascar.[31] His own accusations, and the angry admissions and explanations in mitigation offered by his colleagues, serve to summarize the unexpected predicament in which the LMS and other missions in Northern Rhodesia found themselves. It was accepted by all concerned that mission villages had been responsible for road making, good schools, a large congregation, and a certain degree of prosperity. On the other hand, the system took time and energy which should have been devoted directly to evangelical objects. It tended to prevent a "right understanding on the part of the natives of the real nature" of the missionary endeavor.

> The frequent administration of corporal punishment by the missionary often exercise[d] a most baneful influence upon his personal character and tend[ed] largely to prevent the spiritual progress of the mission.[32]

Dr. Mackay's indictment continued:

> First, the missionary as chief appears to us a mistake because of the moral influence of the position of the man himself; secondly, it creates friction between members on a station, and thirdly the fact of having a merely nominal head or chief makes it difficult or even impossible for the natives to understand that the companions of the missionary in charge, whoever he may be, are other than his headman. . . .
>
> The fact of having as a missionary society to take magisterial charge of a station, is . . . not conducive to a right understanding on the part of the natives of our real intentions regarding them, if they are at all able to understand these beneficient intentions, or are taught them, they are in this mission at any rate able to be immediately nullified by the necessity of our having to inflict punishment. In fact instead of being regarded as the white men who carry to them the good tidings of God's love . . . we are known and feared. . . .

---

[31] Mackay, a senior member of the LMS' Madagascar medical staff, had been refused permission to return there by the French government unless he agreed to obtain a French medical diploma.

[32] Minutes of Tanganyika District Committee Meeting, Oct. 12-22, 1898, CA x/2/z; Purves early thought missionaries should not become chiefs, but he was overruled by others. "I . . . therefore have disputed the right of Dr. Mather to act as Law Maker and Judge without appeal. . . ." Purves to Thompson, Oct. 2, 1894, CA ix/2/e; LMS archives.

> . . . the spiritual side of the work seems almost necessarily quite subordinate to the material.[33]

Missionaries were prepared to justify the punishments that they had meted out. John May pleaded that he had only seen Charles Benjamin Mather use the whip once, when watchmen had been caught smoking. "For such flagrant disobedience they received a well-deserved punishment and never tried the same thing again." After Mather's death, May averred that he himself had only used the whip twice. On the day of Mather's funeral May had given orders that no guns were to be fired. The orders "expressly given" were "expressly disobeyed" and May had the various offenders thrashed. On another occasion a suspected murderer was whipped severely before being sent on to Abercorn, where the British South Africa Company administration placed the suspect in chains for a month.[34]

Percy Jones claimed that he had only administered the *citoki* six times—all in necessary circumstances—during his months at Kambole. For a case of suspected adultery he beat both parties. He also used the whip for drunkenness, on a man who broke a boy's arm during an argument, on one for using another's hut as a lavatory, to punish a man for firing a gun with intent to wound, and for one case of "repeated disobedience."[35] Later, when Jones was at Niamkolo for a year, his whippings included those for drunkenness, use of poison ordeals, adultery, theft, a "bad case of blackmail," and again for "repeated disobedience."[36] Another missionary was accused of forcing boys who could not swim into the water, of beating a man who would not sell him a gun, and of using a cricket bat to punish a man who displeased him in a game.[37]

---

33 Mackay to Thompson, Aug. 6, 1898, CA x/2/c; LMS archives.

34 May to Thompson, Nov. 9, 1898, CA x/4/c; LMS archives.

35 Percy Jones to Thompson, Oct. 27, 1898, CA x/4/c; LMS archives. The problem of excreta seemed to be common. At Kafulafuta the South African Baptist missionaries were always worried about improper use of huts. See the Kafulafuta notebooks 1912-20, at Kafulafuta Mission.

36 Jones to Thompson, Oct. 27, 1898, CA x/4/c; LMS archives.

37 Hemans to Thompson, June 5, 1899; Mackay to Thompson, July 6, 1899, CA x/3/d; LMS archives.

The society's directors condemned these abuses of excessive authority when they were at last brought to their attention. "The Society's missionaries," they said, "are not in future to take any responsibility in passing sentences or administering punishment."[38] The directors presumed that the Company's administration was ready to govern fully and thus to obviate the need for further mission control.

> As soon as there is a fixed and responsible authority in the government of country, the religious teachers ought not to have anything further to do with the administration of justice.[39]

In fact, the local representatives of the LMS in Northeast Rhodesia had for some time simply acquiesced in the continued exercise of temporal authority by missions. They had expected a certain amount of cooperation and a division of responsibility between the two spheres.[40] After the board's pronouncement, however, and following its own growing personal disillusionment with certain of the missionaries, the administration began to demand that missionaries cease the exercise of physical punishment. As indicated by Percy Jones' flagrant insistence upon beating adulterers himself despite the administration's wishes and those of his own board, the LMS missionaries relinquished their prerogatives only with reluctance.[41] Robert Laws reported as late as 1905 that missionaries were still exercising authority by means of the whip, and urged the LMS board to direct this energy into more desirable channels.[42] The Board cautioned its missionaries once again:

---

[38] Thompson to May, Dec. 24, 1898, CA xxvii, 102-04; LMS archives.

[39] Thompson to Mackay, Feb. 17, 1899; CA xxviii, 168; LMS archives.

[40] Thompson to Carson, Mar. 29, 1895, CA xxvi, 116-18; LMS archives.

[41] Jones, in extenuation, pleaded: "In a country . . . where so called magistrates can carry out any course which seems to suit their nature, it behooves the missionaries, as the only friends the hapless native has, [*sic*] to stand up against cruelty, adultery, injustice, and murder.": Jones to Thompson, May 28, 1899, CA x/3/b; LMS archives.

[42] Laws said none of the missionaries had professed knowledge of the Board's directive of 1898 curtailing missionaries' temporal powers. Laws to Thompson, May 29, 1905; Hanna, *Beginnings*, 50, seems to conclude that it ceased then, but such could hardly have been so. See also "I have flogged my own houseboy, but this is my own business." Wareham to Thompson, Jan. 4, 1905, LMS archives.

> . . . under no circumstances is flogging to be resorted to by the Society's missionaries as punishment of *adult* natives, and . . . it is not advisable that a missionary should, in any case, take the law into his own hands by inflicting penalties. . . .[43]

Slowly the LMS relaxed its control over mission villages. Excesses tended to be more infrequent, and younger missionaries were loath to continue practices which had been condemned so roundly by a visiting deputation and by their own directors.[44] The administration was also more zealous in protecting its own rights, but the most important reason for the cessation of missionary punitive powers was a real diminution in the demand for stockades and protected villages.[45] The mission could hardly demand unquestioned fealty once mobility had increased and it no longer remained the sole source of protection, employment, or advancement.

II

The increase in temporal control coincided with a rapid growth in missionary economic involvement. Exercise of considerable mission entrepreneurial initiative came inexorably, yet at the same time in ways unintended. Deviation from single-minded religious efforts resulted from a double-barreled missionary economic problem: "financial support from home was often somewhat precarious and slow in arriving, while, on the other hand, they were continuingly conscious of the pathetic conditions of the native populations. . . ."[46] Christianity, as introduced by the missions, resulted in the stimulation of new wants, the inculcation of a desire to work and the introduction of new agricultural skills, crops, and equipment. As the system worked in many parts of Rhodesia, the theory of salvation almost appeared to be: If you wished to qualify for an Evangelical heaven,

---

[43] Thompson to McFarlane, Apr. 7, 1906, [my italics], CA xxxiii, 486, LMS archives. Oliver accepts W. P. Livingstone's date of 1904 for this statement, but the records are contradictory. Oliver, *Missionary Factor*, 59.

[44] Wilfred McFarlane, in a letter to the author, Apr. 21, 1960.

[45] At first there was a devolution of temporal powers to appointed headmen and other functionaries, but even this arrangement was later dropped. Robertson *et al.* to Thompson, Aug. 11, 1904; LMS archives.

[46] Arthur H. Cole, "The Relations of Missionary Activity to Economic Development," *Economic Development and Cultural Change*, IX (Jan., 1961), 124.

you covered your nakedness, possessed your own goods (often purchased from the missionary), and labored energetically in the Lord's earthly vineyard.

The transmission of Western entrepreneurial ideas proceeded indirectly, but nevertheless effectively, from the examples of missionary economic endeavor in Northern Rhodesia. Missionaries were zealous and industrious; they inculcated those Western social attitudes which were conducive to thrift and hard work and they introduced technological advances which contributed to higher output and dependence upon Western markets. Higher consumption of Western material goods was regularly encouraged. "Progress" and "uplift" were concepts implicitly introduced into the fabric of indigenous society together with the otherwise solely spiritual content of Christianity. By so doing, missionaries accustomed Africans to Western ways of life and prepared them gradually for a more total participation in the European economic and social framework.[47]

In Northern Rhodesia economic activities went hand-in-hand with evangelism. From the first, Africans associated missions with trade goods as much as with the gospel. Mission stores stocked calico and ornaments and later sold every conceivable commodity from dresses and shoes to soap and candy. With increasingly more widespread use of coin, station shops burgeoned. Trading led to large-scale production of direct benefit to the local standard of living. Missions developed agricultural, wood-working, or processing schemes dependent upon free or inexpensive mission labor and upon the heavy exercise of mission influence.

Trading on the part of missions began before there were any well-organized supply routes to Northern Rhodesia. Missionaries themselves ordered supplies in bulk from abroad and shipped them by a tortuous combination of sea and land transport and, ultimately, by human porterage. When local payments could only be remitted with trade goods, missionaries had to make provision for such sub-

---

[47] For an instructive discussion, see Godfrey Wilson, *An Essay on the Economics of Detribalisation in Northern Rhodesia*, i & ii (Livingstone, 1941 & 1942). For missionary contributions to the development of markets in Northern Rhodesia, see my "Rural Rhodesian Markets," in Paul J. Bohannan and George Dalton (eds.), *Markets in Africa* (Evanston, 1962), 581-600.

stitute money by conveying it from overseas along essentials. Africans also tired of calico alone and soo an opportunity to obtain Western clothes and accouter all kinds. The transition to a fully developed economic pro was therefore easy once demand had been whetted. By about 190 missions even ceased to require stocks of cloth as pay-rolls, and instead issued wages in silver.[48] Yet their obligation to provide goods readily did not, they felt, diminish, for Africans still expected them to cater to a demand for those Western products which the missions themselves had encouraged.

Missionaries soon realized that proceeds from stores and similar commercial activities could constitute important profits and thus could reduce dependence upon overseas funds and could mollify those directors who were concerned about high expenditures and small returns (in the form of souls saved). For those missionaries who depended for sustenance upon irregular contributions more than upon funds from an organized society, the temptation and the need to maximize profits was of course great. In other cases, men who found their taste for missionary life jaded could cheerfully rationalize being preoccupied with trade, accounts, or particular functions as shopkeeper and entrepreneur. George Suckling, at Chitokoloki (PB), was unduly preoccupied from the beginning with various ways to make money for himself and his mission.[49] Julius Torrend, at Kasisi (SJ), spent nearly every week worrying about his profits from potatoes or pigs. His diary contains daily entries on these subjects.[50] W. Govan Robertson, at Kawimbe, made himself into a super-accountant and self-styled treasurer for the LMS missions.[51] His careful balancing of ledgers was appreciated by his directors, although they indicated that no other missionary anywhere in the world had the time to forward such detailed reports of expenditure and profit. The general secretary of the LMS wrote:

---

48 Shortage of gold often caused mission crises. See Robertson to Douglas Buchanan, May 17, 1912; Robertson to Hawkins, Sept. 17, 1912; LMS archives.

49 Fisher to Darling, July 2, 1920, Fisher Papers National Archives, Salisbury; Suckling, *Echoes*, 1920, 230-31; see Slade, *Missions*, 234.

50 Torrend, diary, 1914-1921, *passim*, especially Aug. 11, 1914.

51 Robertson to Directors, July 30, 1902; LMS archives. Robertson to Bradford, Mar. 7, 1912, Abel Papers. McFarlane, in a letter to the author, Apr. 21, 1960.

in a very small mission like the
sary for the treasurer to give so
tion of . . . a report. . . . [It] is
than any similar [financial] report
ons, most of which are very much
a mission and the accounts of which
cated. My anxiety is that an undue
ot be spent by the treasurer on purely
work.[52]

ssion stations there were stores run by mis-
imports of trade goods exceeded 15 tons:
Kawim... was stocked with 1,600 fezzes, 4,300 fancy scarves, 1,850 ... of soap, 5,400 yards of red calico, 39,000 yards of sheeting and other calico, 2,000 pounds of beads, and large amounts of cheap jewelry, watches, umbrellas, salt, and chains.[53] Kaleñe Hill (PB), on an important caravan route, kept a wide variety of colorful goods.[54] Kasisi (SJ) would probably have been deserted had it not had a store.[55] The UMCA, Brethren-in-Christ, Wesleyan Methodist Missionary Society, South African Baptist Missionary Society, Primitive Methodist Missionary Society, SAGM and Dutch Reformed Church all ran profitable enterprises on their stations.[56] Home boards rarely objected to such trading activities because usually they, as well as their missionaries, welcomed any method of defraying expenses. The LMS only objected to Robertson's activities after other missionaries had complained about the amount of time he spent trading, and because of the sizeable capital immobilized by his schemes.

> We do not want the LMS to be anything but blemish free on the question of trading. . . . Every missionary should observe most carefully the rule that barter goods are to be used only for necessary purposes and that the mission is to discourage . . . those who are

---

[52] Thompson to Robertson, Apr. 25, 1914, CA xi, 466; LMS archives.

[53] Wright to Thompson, Jan. 23, 1903; Johnson to Thompson, Nov. 7, 1903; LMS archives.

[54] See Fisher to Darling, July 31, 1914, Fisher Papers.

[55] "Take the store away and we shall very likely be left alone in the middle of white people." Torrend diary, May 2, 1919.

[56] "Our store will soon rival the Mandala for the variety and amount of stock in hand." Msoro Logbook, ii, July 9, 1923; Chapman to Pickett, Nov. 14, 1903, Chapman Papers, MMS archives.

in its own employment from expecting the missionary to have a stock of goods which they can purchase from him. We have no right to come into competition with the regular trader, even for . . . our own workers.[57]

Government also disliked trading by missionaries because it believed such activity constituted unfair competition for the African Lakes Corporation and individual shopkeepers. In 1915, it insisted that missions should take out trading licenses and refrain from locating their stores on lands originally conveyed to the mission by the British South Africa Company, on payment of only nominal fees. One Jesuit missionary wrote:

> I have taken a £5 trading license for ½ year. Without it there is too much danger of going to gaol, because cash alone here will not do to pay servants, much less to buy grain for our own consumption. Yet, if I use goods for any of these purposes I am in constant danger of being sent to gaol, as happened 2½ years ago. . . . It was for paying three or four servants partly with such things as a singlet, an old worn coat, and I do not remember what else, that I was sent to gaol. Again with cash alone last year I was not able to buy as much as one-half the grain I needed for our own consumption. . . . Judge Beaufort . . . insisted . . . that for a man in my position the only practical thing was to take a trading license and have done with all difficulties.[58]

Missions attempted to increase profits in innumerable other ways. Gardens, worked by inexpensive labor, produced large quantities of agricultural produce marketable wherever there were Europeans. The LMS in 1900 also retailed 16,000 pounds of various indigenous crops to Africans. Export of beeswax and honey became a monopoly of the western Brethren.[59] The Brethren, Jesuits, UMCA, Brethren-in-Christ, and Seventh-day Adventists early had large scale, and profitable, developments in animal husbandry.[60] The

---

57 Thompson to Johnson, June 20, 1903, CA xxxi, 282-83. Wright to Thompson, Nov. 20, 1902, LMS archives. See also Harold Wareham, "The Central African Mission in 1902," unpublished typescript (n.d., c. 1944), Wareham Papers, Hayling Island, England. (Privately held.)

58 Torrend, diary, Aug. 29, 1918 and Oct. 18, 1918.

59 Personal interviews, Charles Geddes (Loloma, June 27, 1959); Ffolliot Fisher (Hillwood Farm, June 24, 1959).

60 Fisher to Darling, July 31, 1914, Fisher Papers; Mapanza Diary, Nov. 9, 1913, July 11, 1917, Feb. 28, 1918; Brethren-in-Christ, Minutes of General

sale of furniture and other industrial projects became, for a time, a very lucrative mission endeavor. Indeed, Suckling plunged himself into debt in expectation of amassing large profits from a furniture factory at Chitokoloki (PB), and other missions were worried regularly about the quality of their woodwork and about obtaining markets for it.[61] Suckling went to the trouble of building boats specifically to transport furniture made by Africans, under his supervision, down the Zambezi River to markets in Livingstone.[62]

III

The major ways in which missions exerted considerable secular influenced have been discussed. Missionaries also contributed to Northern Rhodesia's development in the course of many daily routine activities. They had to build their own roads; often they were the first to connect isolated parts of Northern Rhodesia to main centers. Stanley Buckley (PMMS) cut the first motor road from the Zambezi Valley to the railway line. Others maintained or cleared paths or roads from administrative bomas to tribal settlements or to their own stations. Methodists, the Paris Mission, and those of the UMCA, South African General Mission, or the Brethren, all ran their own postal systems until the government was prepared to provide runners and post offices. Others distributed grain during periods of seasonal hunger or acted as quarantine officers during smallpox or influenza epidemics. They built bridges, inoculated cattle, and generally behaved in such a way as to mediate between indigenous culture and an encroaching Western civilization.

European missionaries could not betray their own social context and behave other than as Western men. In responding to their

Conference, 1907, copies at superintendent's residence, Bulawayo; Moreau to Parry, Mar. 12, 1922; Moreau to Brown, Jan. 10, 1924, Campion Papers; Magoye District Notebook, 277-79.

61 Fisher to Darling, Apr. 4, 1921, Jan. 31, Mar. 18, 1922, Fisher Papers; Suckling, *Echoes*, 1920, 230; Sept. 30, 1921, *Echoes*, Jan., 1922, 13-15; Robertson to Thompson, Aug. 14, 1904; Robertson *et al.* to Thompson, Aug. 11, 1904; Robertson to Thompson, n.d. Apr., 1904; Wright to Thompson, Nov. 20, 1902; LMS archives. Czarlinski to Parry, Nov. 15, 1920, Campion Papers, Salisbury. Resident Magistrate's Notebook, Mongu, i, 33.

62 Suckling, Sept. 30, 1918, *Echoes*, Feb., 1919, 64-65. Fisher to Darling, Jan, 31, 1922, Mar. 12, 1923, Fisher Papers.

evangelical environment they had to assume innumerable tasks which were not necessarily germane to their spiritual pursuit. In order to survive, missionaries became transporters, brickbuilders, hunters, and herdsmen. They became educators, shopkeepers, and rural magistrates. In all these different roles the missionaries performed important tasks to ease their own physical lot and the lot of their charges. Significantly, they also introduced Africans to the Western way of life in nearly all of its manifestations.

IX.

The Economic Background to the Revival of Afrikaner Nationalism

by

LAURENCE SALOMON

New York City

IT WAS THOUGHT IN THE EARLY 1930's that Afrikaner nationalism[1] was disappearing as a divisive force between the Afrikaans- and English-speaking sections of the South African white population. The historian W. M. Macmillan, considered that "there need be little mention," in his *Complex South Africa* (1930), "of the dead or dying feuds of the two white peoples." An American historian in a 1945 study of nationalism grouped South Africa with the U.S.S.R. and Switzerland as examples of "successful multi-national states." On the basis of studies published in the previous decade, he wrote: "Already Boers read English books avidly, and their own literature is remarkably free of anti-British bias."[2]

This point of view accurately reflected certain aspects of the contemporary scene. Several of the issues that had led to the formation of the National Party by General Hertzog in 1912 had been or were being settled. With the unanimous consent of the mainly English-speaking Parliamentary Opposition, General Hertzog's administration had obtained recognition for Afrikaans as one of the country's two official languages in 1925; it had secured South Africa her own national flag, alongside the Union Jack, in 1928; and with the passage of the Statute of Westminster in 1931, had won Britain's full acknowledgement of South Africa's national sovereignty.

Moreover, since 1924, Afrikaner Nationalists and English-speaking South Africans had begun working together politically. The National Party had come to power that year in coalition with the Labour Party, an organ of mainly English-speaking white workers. Political co-operation between the two white language groups acquired an even broader foundation in 1933, when the depression

---

[1] This paper is based on research conducted in South Africa between 1958 and 1960 under a fellowship granted by the Ford Foundation.

[2] Oscar I. Janowsky, *Nationalities and National Minorities* (*with Special Reference to East-Central Europe*) (New York, 1945), 68.

led to a coalition of the National Party and its principal opponent, General Smuts' South African Party, which had long represented the interests of the wealthier English-speaking whites and non-nationalist Afrikaners. In the subsequent General Election of that year, the Coalition won 144 of the 150 House of Assembly seats. So harmonious and popular was the co-operation of Hertzog and Smuts that the two parties fused their individual identities to form a new entity in 1934, the United Party. Only a handful of the more "imperial-minded" of General Smuts' followers, and nineteen of General Hertzog's former parliamentary party colleagues, led by Dr. D. F. Malan, decided not to join the United Party. They established separate organizations on its wings, the Dominion Party and the Purified National Party. The former's appeal was virtually confined to one province, Natal, where pro-British sentiment was strongest, while the Purified Nationalists, in the light of Hertzog's achievements and continued attachment to Afrikaner interests, appeared to lack concrete issues which might be turned to political account: the constitution of the United Party allowed its members to make propaganda for turning South Africa into a republic; the Party undertook to apply bi-lingualism in practice; the country was free to secede from the Commonwealth and to remain neutral in time of war if Parliament so decided. To contemporary observers, the facts of the birth, parliamentary predominance and all-embracing policy of the United Party may well have signified the beginnings of a broad feeling of community between the two white groups, and a future that would see the memories of the Anglo-Boer War and other conflicts fade away.

We now know that this did not happen. The 1938 General Election, the first after the formation of the parties, saw the Purified Nationalists increase their parliamentary representation to twenty-seven, a small figure compared with the 111 members elected for the United Party, but one representing approximately half the Afrikaner electorate and only ten per cent short of the percentage of popular votes that would enable them to take office ten years and two elections later.[3] In the months following the 1938 General Election there was an astonishing revival of Nationalist

3 See Gwendolen M. Carter, *The Politics of Inequality: South Africa Since 1948* (London, 1958), Chart I, 448f.

feeling, stemming from the centenary celebrations of the Great Trek. Afrikaners by the thousands donned Voortrekker costume, grew beards and went to hail the ox-waggon trains that were sent plodding through countryside, hamlet and town to commemorate their ancestors' great journey into the interior. The Voortrekkers' tribulations at the hands of Briton and Bantu were recalled, and it was proclaimed at enormous festive rallies by such renowned orators as Dr. Malan that the Afrikaner's enemies were still the same.[4] As the waggons converged on their final destination, Pretoria, "an extraordinary spirit of fervid patriotism, bordering on adoration, swept over the country. Enthusiasm became nearly religious and sometimes hysterical, women bringing their babies to be baptised in the shadow of the waggons."[5]

South Africa had never seen such a celebration. The spirit of exclusive Afrikaner nationalism, thus renewed, did not fade with the passing of the centenary. It was fanned by the United Party's vote to take South Africa into the Second World War (a decision that caused General Hertzog and thirty-six of his followers to leave the Party); and it was reflected in succeeding years in the host of agencies that were established to duplicate for Nationalists the functions of organizations ranging from the Boy Scouts to the South African Automobile Association and the Red Cross. Cleavages between Boer and Briton multiplied rather than diminished, so that when Dr. Malan became Prime Minister in 1948, it was no longer surprising that for the first time in the history of the Union, a South African Cabinet was composed of members of only one of the white groups.

Why were the expectations of the early 1930's proved wrong? Why did the political split among the white people persist and widen?

An attempt to deal with these questions comprehensively is beyond the scope of this paper. I shall confine myself to a discussion of the role socio-economic factors played in the revival of Afrikaner nationalism. Certainly here a basis existed for the persistence of

---

[4] Dr. D. F. Malan, *Die Nuwe Groot Trek: Suid-Afrika se Noodroep: Dr. D. F. Malan se Rede op Bloedrivier 16 Desember 1938* (Kaapstad, n.d.), 5.

[5] D. W. Kruger, *The Age of the Generals: A Short Political History of the Union of South Africa, 1910-1948* (Dagbreek Book Store, 1958), 185.

sectional feelings among whites. Nothing that General Hertzog's administration had accomplished in the way of securing official equality of Afrikaans with English, or legal and symbolic equality between South Africa and Britain, had significantly narrowed the economic inequalities existing between the white language groups. Of every eight Afrikaner men in the country's nine biggest cities in 1939, one was an unskilled laborer, in contrast to one out of every eighty-five non-Afrikaner white men; on the other hand, only one out of every 213 Afrikaner men was a merchant, against one out of every nineteen non-Afrikaner white men.[6]

The origins of the Afrikaner's economic backwardness in relation to English-speaking whites (the details of which will be more fully described later on) can be traced to events that occurred long before the first arrival of Britons, to 1657, the year that saw the start of European (Dutch) colonization in South Africa, and also the beginning of slavery in the country. The use of imported slave labor for all occupations below that of its supervision helped establish a barrier to large-scale European immigration. Up until 1795, when British occupation of the Cape began, only 2,164 Dutch immigrants had found it profitable to enter the country.[7] Even after the abolition of slavery in 1833, the continued use of low-paid, indigenous, non-white labor for all manual work remained a factor restricting the growth of the white population mainly to that of its natural increase. In 1865, on the eve of the discovery of diamonds, the total white population is estimated to have been 350,000[8]—one per cent that of the contemporary United States.

Most of this small white population was thinly dispersed over huge stretches of country, eking out a modest livelihood through cattle and sheep farming. The economy of the white pastoralists was not strictly self-sufficient,[9] but their needs and those of their

---

[6] S. Pauw, *Die Beroepsarbeid van die Afrikaner in die Stad* (Stellenbosch, 1946), 235.

[7] Andre Pieter du Plessis, *Die Nederlandse Emigrasie Na Suid-Afrika: Sekere Aspekte Rakende Voorbereiding Tot Aanpassing* (Amsterdam, 1956), 17.

[8] L. T. Badenhorst, "The Future Growth of the Population of South Africa and its Probable Age Distribution," *Population Studies*, IV (Oct. 1951), 3 f.

[9] See S. Daniel Neumark, *Economic Influences on the South African Frontier, 1652-1836* (Stanford, 1957), 172-74.

low-paid non-white laborers, herdsmen and domestic servants were too limited to constitute a market sufficiently large to stimulate any appreciable specialization and manufacturing development. The advent of gold mining in the Transvaal in 1886 found that area a desert as regards industry, and the few rudimentary manufacturing enterprises in the country were almost entirely confined to the Cape Colony. Flour milling, baking, cart and waggon making, wine and brandy distilling, candle making, food preserving, blubber boiling, boat building and tanning more or less sum up South Africa's industrial development after two centuries of white settlement.[10]

The country and its people were caught almost wholly unprepared for the new economic activities which set in following the opening of the Kimberley diamond field in 1870 and the discovery of the Witwatersrand gold reef in 1886. Not only did the machinery and equipment for the mines and allied secondary industries have to be shipped in from overseas, but with local agriculture not geared to meet urban demands, even much of the food consumed by the mining populations had to be imported.[11] More significant was the absence of a local skilled labor force. No laboring class, skilled or unskilled, existed among the white population, and the Coloured artisans of the small Cape enterprises were neither numerous or available.[12] The exploitation of the discoveries necessarily became the work of immigrants.

Over 400,000 European—mostly British—immigrants entered South Africa between 1875 and 1904, a number greater than the entire white population in 1875.[13] Probably—the exact figure is unknown—more than half a million foreign Africans crossed the country's land borders during these years; and though these were ostensibly migrant mine workers, many did not return to their original homes.[14]

---

10 M. H. de Kock, *Economic History of South Africa* (Cape Town, 1924), 283.

11 See R. K. Cope, *Comrade Bill: The Life and Times of W. H. Andrews, Workers' Leader* (Cape Town, n.d.), 19.

12 Pauw, *Beroepsarbeid,* 31.

13 C. G. W. Schumann, *Die Ekonomiese Posisie van die Afrikaner* (Bloemfontein, 1940), 67 f.

14 See G. V. Doxey, *The Industrial Colour Bar in South Africa* (Cape

This sudden influx rapidly transformed an economically stagnant land into the world's largest gold and diamond producer and laid the foundations for sustained industrial growth. A year after its founding in the wild scrub country of the north east Cape Colony, Kimberley had 50,000 inhabitants—including more whites than had taken part in the Great Trek;[15] the population of Johannesburg passed the 100,000 mark ten years after the city's first appearance on the Witwatersrand hills.[16] Sixty-three miles of railroad on the eve of the diamond era were extended to 6,894 by 1909, as the mining cities were connected with five ports.[17] The total tonnage of ships berthing in South African harbors increased more than twenty-one-fold between 1862 and 1898;[18] the total value of imports rose almost tenfold and exports nineteenfold between 1865-69 and 1905-09.[19] Such was the turn of events that in 1882, the export of diamonds alone was worth more than South Africa's total exports in the year of the discovery of diamonds, and exceeded the value of the combined exports of the rest of sub-Saharan Africa.[20] By 1892, the private income of an immigrant, Cecil John Rhodes, who had arrived in South Africa with a few pounds in his pocket, was said to be thrice what the entire income of the Cape Colony had been twenty years earlier, and it was still growing.[21]

The element of continuity present during the industrializing experience of many other countries, in that indigenous populations direct or execute the new economic activities, was largely absent in South Africa's case, despite the fact that the latter was neither

---

Town, 1961), 15, and *Summary of the Report of the Commission for the Socio-Economic Development of the Bantu Areas within the Union of South Africa, Union Government* [hereafter U.G.], No. 61, 1955, 41.

15 C. W. de Kiewiet, *A History of South Africa: Social and Economic,* (London, 1941), 89.

16 du Plessis, *Emigrasie,* 30 n.

17 A. J. H. van der Walt, J. A. Wijd and A. L. Geyer, *Geskiedenis van Suid-Afrika* (Kaapstad, 1955), II, 240.

18 de Kock, *History,* 340.

19 *Ibid.,* 328.

20 S. Herbert Frankel, *Capital Investment in Africa: Its Course and Effects* (London, 1938), 54.

21 Sir James Tennant Molteno, *The Dominion of Afrikanerdom: Recollections Pleasant and Otherwise* (London, 1923), 25.

an empty or recently settled land. For many years participation of the older white and non-white population in the new industrial economy was inconsiderable. In 1910, forty years after the Kimberley fields were opened and 18 years after the beginning of deep level mining on the Witwatersrand, 72.8 per cent of the then 7,255 white, skilled mine employees were immigrants; not until 1921 did the number of white South African- exceed that of foreign-born miners.[22] The unskilled black laborers who did most of the manual work in the mining operations also came mainly from outside the country. In 1904, 76.5 per cent of the 77,000 African gold and coal miners working in the Transvaal came from foreign territories, chiefly Portuguese East Africa; and of the 323,000 black miners employed in the Transvaal at the outbreak of the Second World War, 51.99 per cent were peasant migrants from neighboring countries.[23]

The majority of the skilled and semi-skilled labor force for the railways, the building trades and other industries that sprung up in response to the markets created by mining and urban growth also was recruited mainly in Europe.[24] In the higher paid occupations, the predominance of the foreign-born was as pronounced and even more enduring. In 1921—thirty-five years after the discovery of the gold reef and half a century after the opening of the diamond fields—immigrants (chiefly English-speaking) controlled most South African industry and provided the bulk of its professional requirements, as the table below shows.

It will be seen that only in the lowest-paid professions, teaching and the civil service, were South African-born whites in the majority. (The top-salaried civil service positions were held pre-

---

22 de Kock, *History*, 442.

23 Sheila van der Horst, *Native Labour in South Africa* (Cape Town, 1942), 216 f.

24 *Report of the Unemployment Investigation Committee*, 1932 (U.G. 30-'32), para. 18; Cape of Good Hope, *Report of the Select Committee on the Poor White Question*, 1906 (S.C. 10-'06), para. 7; du Plessis, *Emigrasie*, 32; Carnegie Commission of Investigation on the Poor White Question in South Africa, *The Poor White Problem in South Africa: Report of the Carnegie Commission* (5 vols., Stellenbosch, 1932), I, 72. [Hereafter, *Carnegie Commission*.]

TABLE I

PERCENTAGE OF MALES BORN OVERSEAS, IN A NUMBER OF OCCUPATIONAL GROUPS IN SOUTH AFRICA, BASED ON 1921 CENSUS DATA[25]

	Occupational Group	Percentage Born Overseas
1.	Company Directors	76.0
2.	Merchants and Business Managers	68.8
3.	Doctors	62.3
4.	Architects	80.4
5.	Chartered Accountants	70.8
6.	Teachers	29.9
7.	Fitters and Turners	55.8
8.	Electricians	40.0
9.	Typesetters	59.8
10.	Carpenters	48.3
11.	Bricklayers	28.6
12.	Civil Servants	37.3
13.	Underground Goldminers	34.3
14.	Barbers	52.1
15.	Unskilled Laborers	10.0
16.	Farmers	5.8

dominantly by immigrants.[26]) In the trades, immigrants still comprised a considerable proportion of the personnel. The last two items in the table are noteworthy. They indicate what the local white inhabitants were doing when industrialism set foot in South Africa, and the occupation through which many of them first encountered the new economy.

This encounter was generally involuntary and unpleasant for many of the Afrikaans-speaking descendants of the original Dutch settlers. It was brought about by forces that made the countryside uninhabitable for more and more of the latter, forces which the newcomers helped speed in motion, but whose workings had begun manifesting themselves before the arrival of industrialism.

By 1870, the land frontier was coming to an end.[27] A hundred years of warfare with African tribes had left 90 per cent of the

25 Source: Pauw, *Beroepsarbeid,* Table VII, 122; the table relates to white people only.

26 *Ibid.,* Table III, 77.

27 van der Walt *et al., Geskiedenis,* II, 250.

country's land area under white, chiefly Boer, ownership.[28] It had also ensured that the field of agricultural labor would remain closed to whites, for Africans were taken on as tenants and laborers, in many cases on their former tribal lands, and set to work for a remuneration no white man would accept. After 1870, Boer sons generally could no longer hope to own new farms, and as there was no place for them as farm laborers the solution adopted by their prolific parents was to divide up the family farm equally among the children. For generation upon generation fragmentation of farms proceeded. Many of the once customary 6,000 acre farms over the years shrunk to tiny plots. In 1908, the Transvaal Indigency Commission reported a case where a single heir was entitled to 296,387,007/4,705,511,234,760 of a farm of 5,347 acres, i.e., less than half an acre.[29] Two decades later, the Carnegie Commission of Investigation on The Poor White Question in South Africa—the names of these commissions are indicative of what was happening—came upon an old man with 55 acres, ten children and more than 50 grandchildren, who informed the Commissioners that he intended dividing his property equally among his children so that each would at least have his own "*sitplekkie*" (sitting spot). Portions only of the 55 acres were arable in good seasons.[30] The onset of any natural disaster—drought, locusts, rinderpest being the most common—would be sufficient to dislodge these folk from their small holdings. They would then be compelled to sell out to more fortunate farmers and become *bywoners* (men living "on land belonging to another—usually a relative—without any clearly defined rights or duties"[31]) of whomever would have them. Field laborers or domestic servants they could not and would not become, because here they faced competition from landless Africans even poorer than themselves.

There was an early indication of the later "Poor White Problem"

---

28 The Natives (Land) Act of 1936 provided for a land purchase scheme to add land to the African Reserves. When the scheme is completed, Africans will have title to about 13 per cent of the country's land.

29 Transvaal Government, *Report of the Transvaal Indigency Commission, 1906-1908,* Transvaal Government [hereafter T.G.], No. 13, 1908, para. 117.

30 Carnegie Commission, I, 121.

31 *T.G.* 13-'08, para. 17.

in 1882, when the Boer Government in the Transvaal dispatched an expedition against the Mapoch chief, Niabel, ostensibly because of Niabel's refusal to deliver up to Republican justice an African who had murdered his step brother, the Sekukuni chief. The results of the expedition suggest that this was not its sole motive. To the surprise of none of the Boer commandos, the lands of the Mapoch were confiscated, surveyed and distributed in small holdings among their indigent comrades. The Mapoch themselves were ordered to be indentured as laborers and servants in Boer households and on farms throughout the Republic.[32]

The advent of mining only temporarily relieved the growing pressure of population in the rural areas. As there were no railways in the Transvaal in 1886, the whole of the mechanical equiment of the mines as well as food and supplies for the mining population had to be brought in by animal transport from the coast or from neighboring areas. Transport riding for a time furnished the Poor White countrymen with a socially acceptable occupation. Moreover, the arrival of a mining population created a market for agricultural produce which had never previously existed. Meat, forage and mealies were required, and these commodities the Transvaal farmer could most easily produce.

But the period of prosperity brought on by these developments was short-lived. The decline set in with the construction of the railways to Johannesburg. The Cape line reached the Rand in 1892, and by December 1895 the lines from Durban and Lourenco Marques had been completed. Those transport riders working on the major routes lost their jobs. Unfitted by previous education and training to seek skilled or semi-skilled employment on the railroads or in the mines,[33] they and others deprived of their living by the

---

[32] Francois Stephanus Cillie, "The Mapoch's Gronden: An Aspect of the Poor White Question" (unpublished M.A. Dissertation, University of Pretoria, 1934), 9 f.

[33] Although industrial and vocational schools had been established for Coloured and African pupils in the Cape as far back as 1854, it was not until forty years later that attempts were made to institute industrial education for whites—and then these efforts were aimed specifically as a remedy for the emergent Poor White problem. Even so, vocational education was associated for many years thereafter with mental deficiency and criminal tendencies, as

railways were forced back into the rural areas. Simultaneously, the farmers were hit. The forage and supplies for the thousands of animals engaged in transporting goods to the Rand were no longer required. Furthermore, the railways were bringing more cheaply from the coastal colonies and their ports supplies to the Witwatersrand population which had previously been purchased at high prices from local producers. Goods trains were unloading American maize at Park Station, Johannesburg, at a price almost equal to the cost of transport alone to the Afrikaner farmer riding his ox-waggon load into town from the Magatos Mountains, a few hundred miles away.[34] The immediate effect of railway construction, therefore, was to throw back onto the land large numbers of people previously engaged in transportation services, just at a time when the Transvaal farmer found his chief market threatened from the outside.[35]

No sooner had many of the transport riders returned to their precarious *bywoner* positions on the farms than they were swept away again, this time in many cases for good. In May, 1896, rinderpest spread through the Transvaal, killing more than two-thirds of the Republic's cattle population.[36] The *bywoners* could no longer plough and the impoverished farmers were unable to support them. As a result, many of the former transport riders trekked to the towns. From about this time dates the birth of white slum districts along the Witwatersrand, and on the outskirts of Pretoria.[37]

The Anglo-Boer War (1899-1902) was the next major economic disaster for Afrikaans-speaking whites. In order to secure their military victory, the British adopted a scorched earth strategy. Much of the Republics' countryside was burned to a wilderness. Agricultural implements, dams and an estimated 30,000 farm build-

---

well as with poverty. Carnegie Commission, Joint Findings and Recommendations, para. 18.

34 *T.G.*, 13-'08, Minutes of Evidence, Q. 5266.

35 *T.G.* 13-'08, paras. 19-21.

36 Adriaan Nicolaas Petrus Pelzer, "Die 'Arm-Blanke'-Verskynsel in die Suid-Afrikaanse Republiek Tussen die Jare 1882 en 1889: 'n Sosiaal-Historiese Studie" (unpublished M.A. Dissertation, University of Pretoria, 1937), 62.

37 *T.G.* 13-'08, para. 22.

ings were destroyed, Boer villages were razed to the ground, cattle and sheep were slaughtered or carried away.[38] In so devastating areas where Afrikaners lived, while leaving the cities of the English-speaking immigrants unscathed, the war increased the economic inequality between the two groups that has lasted to the present day.

It should be noted, however, that war damage was slight in rural areas of the Cape Colony, also farmed mainly by Afrikaners; and that some of these districts produced as many Poor Whites, the Carnegie Commission found, as the most impoverished regions of the Orange Free State and Transvaal.[39] But the link between the British anti-guerilla campaign and the Poor White problem proved to be more memorable.

In the winter months following the peace treaty, the ranks of the impoverished *bywoners* were swollen by destitute Boer landowners. Many of the latter returned from war to find their stock gone, their buildings demolished, the processes of rural life disorganized, requiring time, capital and morale before they could be set going again. Although the British government made a small grant and guaranteed a large loan to help repair war damage and promote economic development, the times were not propitious for complete recovery. From the beginning of January to the end of September 1903, only 8.09 inches of rain were registered in South Africa—a record drought.[40] That same year saw the start of a six-year trade depression.[41] The indigent white population of Pretoria trebled.[42] Ten thousand Afrikaners with nowhere to go stayed on in the British concentration camps for months after the war had ended.[43]

---

38 Cecil Headlam (ed.), *The Milner Papers: South Africa 1899–1905* (2 vols., London, 1933), II, 273; J. Ramsay Macdonald, *What I Saw In South Africa, September and October 1902* (London, 1902), 52; G. B. Beak, *The Aftermath of War: An Account of the Repatriation of Boers and Natives in the Orange River Colony 1902–1904* (London, 1906), 17; Pauw, *Beroepsarbeid,* 64.

39 Carnegie Commission, III, 217-20.

40 Beak, *Aftermath,* 119.

41 Schumann, *Posisie,* 78.

42 *Report of the Commission In Re Pretoria Indigents, para.* 15.

43 *T.G.* 13-'08, para. 24.

Most gates to employment were closed to them. Agricultural labor, it has been seen, had become the province of landless Africans and Coloureds. Skilled labor in the mines and in their satellite industries and services was provided by immigrant artisans with whom the uneducated Afrikaners were not qualified to compete. Unskilled labor in the mines, which offered the greatest scope outside agriculture for the employment of untrained workers, had become the domain of chiefly immigrant African migrant laborers, whose wages and working conditions, due to the industry's need to economize, were such that health and in many cases life itself, could not be maintained. It was estimated that in 1910, the death rate among the 180,000 African miners recruited from Portuguese East Africa was 82/1,000, or about 7,000 in all.[44] Even had Poor Whites been prepared to toil underground alongside Africans at the latters' rates of pay, it is doubtful whether the mine managers would have hired them. The trouble with white laborers, said Mr. P. R. Frames, the director of the country's biggest diamond mine, was that whatever they might be paid

> You could not search them and could not put them in a compound. You could not put them in detention houses at the end of the period of service, to see that they do not take any diamonds out. To be perfectly candid, you would have them on strike. You cannot have a big industry like that dependent upon labour that can any day go out.[45]

In these circumstances, the number of those classified as Poor White continued to rise: 106,000 in 1916; 120,000 in 1921; 300,000 in 1929-30.[46] This last figure represented 17.53 per cent of South Africa's white families, who were described by the Carnegie Commission as being "very poor"—so poor that they depended on charity for support, or subsisted in "dire poverty" on the farms. These "very poor," along with another 30.97 per cent of the Union's white families, classified simply as "poor"—"so poor that

---

44 *Assembly Debates,* I (1911), col. 1179.

45 *T.G.* 13-'08, Minutes of Evidence, Q. 6944.

46 *Verslag van Het Kerkelik Kongres Gehouden te Cradock op 22 en 23 November, 1916: Het Arme Blanken Vraagstuk* (Kaapstad, 1917), 9; *Second Interim Report of the Unemployment Commission,* 1921 (U.G. 34-'21), para. 2; Carnegie Commission, III, 217-22.

they cannot adequately feed and clothe their children," made up nearly half the white population of South Africa. At least nine out of ten of these impoverished families were said to be Afrikaans-speaking.[47]

Periodic droughts (1919, 1924-27) and depressions (1920-23, 1929-33) progressively drove more and more of these people off the land. Between 1911 and 1951, an estimated half million whites, mostly Afrikaners, left the countryside for the towns and cities.[48] Whereas before 1899 there were less than 10,000 Afrikaners in all South African towns, there were over a million by 1951, representing 69 per cent of the total Afrikaner population.[49]

Aside from the particular difficulties of finding work, the Afrikaner urban migrant encountered a situation unlike that experienced by his West European counterpart. The latter usually came among people of his own national group, speaking his own tongue. The Afrikaner entering the cities, like the African, did not. Misunderstanding, prejudice and hostility enjoyed greater play. The Commission In Re Pretoria Indigents—a title suggesting the business-like approach of its (English-speaking) members—considered the poor Afrikaner migrants in 1905 and damned them as an "undesirable influx":

> The poor white class is chiefly drawn from the original European settlers of South Africa whose function *should essentially be that of cultivators of the soil.*[50]

The Commission pointed out that Poor White children were "exposed to many temptations" in the towns; that the presence

---

[47] J. H. Coetzee, *Verarming en Oorheersing* (Bloemfontein, 1942), 36; Dr. N. Diederichs, *Ekonomiese Bewuswording: Kongresrede Gehou by Geleentheid van die Derde RDB.-Kongres in Bloemfontein op 3, 4 en 5 Julie 1945* (RDB. Voorligtingreeks No. 10), 9, claims that 98 per cent of Poor Whites were Afrikaners. See also Dr. H. F. Verwoerd, "Die Bestryding van Armoede en die Herorganisasie van Welvaartswerk," in *Verslag van die Volkskongres oor die Armblanke-Vraagstuk Gehou te Kimberley, 2 tot 5 Okt. 1934*, 28-30.

[48] Van der Walt *et al., Geskiedenis,* 279; *Pretoria News,* Mar. 23, 1955, in *Press Digest* 13/1955/134 f.

[49] *Vereeniging News,* Feb. 18, 1950 in *Press Digest* 8/1950/82; *Pretoria News,* Mar. 23, 1955, in *Press Digest* 13/1955/134 f.

[50] *Report of the Commission In Re Pretoria Indigents,* paras. 23, 18. (My italics).

of their parents there was "not desirable from an economic and moral standpoint, and that endeavours should be made to settle them on the land"; it noted that a commission of Afrikaners in the days when the Boers were masters in the Transvaal had reached the same conclusion.[51]

For years this attitude persisted. In 1916, a member of the Relief and Grant-In-Aid Commission decided that the "remedy" for the problem lay in keeping as many Poor Whites on the land as possible.[52] On the occasion of the 1923 Poor White Congress, the Bloemfontein English-language newspaper, *The Friend*, according to Dr. Malan, called for a stepping-up of British immigration as a protective measure for city dwellers against the lowering effect of the Afrikaner influx.[53] Two years later, a "witness of standing" advised the Economic and Wage Commission that the Poor Whites should all be exported "to other countries."[54] The mood of the migrants was perhaps captured by a Afrikaner poet, who later spoke of them as

om stief op stasies uit te klim,
klein stippels teen 'n blinde kim. . . .[55]
(step-children geeting off at stations,
small specks against a blind horizon. . . .)

In the General Election of 1924, the economically conservative and mainly English-supported South African Party of General Smuts was defeated. A Nationalist-Labour coalition took office and immediately inaugurated a systematic policy for dealing with the problems of Poor White unemployment and unemployability.

---

51 *Ibid.*, para. 54.

52 Province of the Transvaal, *Report of the Relief and Grants-In-Aid Commission*, Transvaal Province [hereafter, T.P.], No. 5, 1916, First Minority Report, para. 27.

53 Dr. D. F. Malan, *Die Groot Vlug: 'n Nabetragting van die Arm-Blanke-Kongres, 1923, en van die Offisiele Sensusopgawe* (pamphlet containing articles appearing between 10 and 24 July, 1923, in *Die Burger*), 6.

54 *Report of the Economic and Wage Commission* 1925, 1926 (*U.G.* 14-'26), Andrews-Lucas-Rood Report, para. 171.

55 G. A. Watermeyer, "Die Tweede Trek," in *Die Republiek van Duisend Jaar* (Johannesburg, 1957). I am indebted to Mr. Watermeyer for permission to quote this extract and the poem at the end of this article. I owe the English renderings to the work of Mrs. Marcelle Varney.

"Civilised labour" (i.e., white) was ordered to be substituted for "uncivilised labour" wherever feasible in the public service. The substitution was given effect on the largest scale by the State-owned Railways where, between 1924 and 1933, the proportion of unskilled white laborers employed rose from 9.5 to 39.3 per cent (representing an absolute increase of 13,023), while that of Africans fell from 75 to 48.9 per cent (an absolute decrease of 15,556).[56] By 1953-54, over 100,000 mainly unskilled and semi-skilled whites were working for the Railways, then the greatest single employer of white labor in the country.[57]

The "civilised labour policy" was also implemented in the Post Office and other Government agencies and departments. It was introduced on the local governmental level by Central Government grants reimbursing municipalities for most of the extra expense incurred through the substitution of equally productive but more highly-paid white for black laborers.[58] By means of subsidies, as well as by threats to lower tariff protection for, and withhold Government contracts from firms not employing a "reasonable proportion of civilised workers,"[59] the policy was also extended to private industry where it was similarly effective: in six industrial categories affected by the threat or promise of tariff adjustments, white employment rose 111.9 per cent from 1924 to 1933, against a 37.25 per cent increase in non-white employment.[60]

Although this policy opened a protected route for landless Afri-

---

[56] *Report of the Commission of Inquiry Regarding the Cape Coloured Population of the Union*, 1937 (U.G. 54-'37), para. 217.

[57] C. S. Richards, "The Growth of Government in South Africa since Union,"*South African Journal of Economics*, XXV (Dec. 1957), 248 ff.

[58] J. H. Botha, "Maatreëls tot Werkverruiming in Stedelike Werkkringe," *Verslag van die Volkskongres oor die Armblanke Vraagstuk Gehou te Kimberley, 1934.*

[59] Social and Economic Planning Council, *Report No. 13: The Economic and Social Conditions of the Racial Groups in South Africa*, 1948 (*U.G.* 53-'48), para. 54.

[60] *Report of the Customs Tariff Commission 1934–1935*, 1936, (*U.G.* 5-'36), paras. 37, 39. The proportion of white employees to all employees in the secondary industries of South Africa's major industrial areas rose from 34.99 per cent in 1924-1925 to 41.86 per cent in 1933, *Report of the Industrial Legislation Commission,* 1935 (*U.G.* 37-'35), para. 230.

kaners into the industrial economy, it acted as a drag on that economy, and poverty among whites was not seen greatly relieved. The "civilised labourers" were paid about double the wages received by those whom they had replaced, so that little separated them from the lowest living standards. In 1939, fifteen years after the policy came into force, 58,000 white families, comprising 289,000 persons, were reported to be still living in "terrible" poverty, all with monthly incomes below £12—an amount considered to be the minimum necessary for the preservation of health.[61] Dire poverty disappeared as a general phenomenon among Afrikaners during the industrial boom years of the Second World War, though "porridge and pumpkins, pumpkins and porridge, porridge and pumpkins" remained, no doubt, the menu of some.

Thus, although a solution was achieved to the problem of Afrikaner unemployability, it was not of such a nature as to close the economic gap between the two white language groups. Most Afrikaners entered the urban occupational pyramid at the bottom, as far as whites are concerned; theirs and the Bantu tongues remained the languages chiefly heard in mine shafts, factories and railway yards, and more rarely in offices and banks.

It will be seen below that as recently as 1948, Afrikaners were heavily over-represented, in relation to the proportion they comprised of the big city white population, in physically hazardous, low status occupations, and under-represented in high prestige, high salary occupations. The nature of the general income differentials obtaining between the two groups was brought out by the 1951 census. At that time, the annual per capita income of Afrikaners in Johannesburg and nine other cities along the Witwatersrand (where Afrikaners comprised 43 per cent of the total white population) was £182, compared with £349 for English-speaking whites. A similar disparity prevailed in the other leading urban areas—Pretoria, Cape Town, Durban, Port Elizabeth; even where Afrikaners predominated among whites numerically, as in Bloemfontein (73.3 per cent), the corresponding figures are £180 and £318.[62]

---

61 *Die Transvaler,* May 31, 1941.

62 Lukas Johannes Potgieter, "Die Ekonomie van die Afrikaner en sy Aandeel in die Sakelewe" (Unpublished Master of Commerce Dissertation, Pot-

TABLE II

Percentage of Afrikaners Among White Men in Various Occupational Groups in the Cities of South Africa, Based on Census Data and Voters' Lists[63]

Occupational Group	Percentage 1926	1939	1948
1. Unskilled Laborers	60	82	86
2. Mineworkers	53	69	79
3. Railway Workers	42	57	74
4. Factory Workers	—	50	63
5. Carpenters	18	31	46
6. Bricklayers	32	53	65
7. Fitters	10	8	21
8. Clerks	13	19	32
9. Civil Servants	32	43	54
10. Teachers	28	49	61
11. Business Managers (Commerce)	6	8	15
12. Merchants	—	4	10
13. Professional People	11	9	15
14. Company Directors, Manufacturers (Industry), etc.	—	3	5
Percentage of Afrikaners Among All Whites Surveyed	23	30	40[64]

chefstroom University, 1954), 40 f; G. T. Visser, "Stedelike Koopkrag van Afrikaans- en Engelssprekendes," *Volkshandel,* XV (Mar., 1954), 56, Table III.

[63] The figures for 1926 are taken from Pauw, *Beroepsarbeid,* Table XXIII, 222-25, and those for 1939 and 1948 from S. Pauw, "Die Afrikaanse Ondernemer, die Verbruiker en die Werker," in *Verslag van die Tweede Ekonomiese Volkskongres (1950), 4, 5, en 6 Oktober 1950, Bloemfontein* (Johannesburg, n.d.), Table II, p. 113. Omissions and the composite figure in the 1926 column are due to the lack of comparable statistics. A discussion of the methods employed in the collection of the data appears in the sources cited.

[64] Approximate estimate based on the 1951 Census. At that time, the Afrikaans-speaking (home language) white population of the nine urban areas represented in the table was 40.2 per cent of their total white population (excluding 26,826 persons with both English and Afrikaans listed as home language). *Union Statistics for Fifty Years 1910–1960* (Compiled by the Bureau of Census and Statistics, Pretoria, 1960), A-18.

There is no evidence that establishes a causal relationship between Afrikaner economic inferiority and the revival and spread of Afrikaner nationalist sentiment after the formation of the United Party. However, there are several connections between the two phenomena. One is that the relative economic positions of the two white groups (as distinct from the Poor White problem) became a public issue in the period after 1934. It was made so by Afrikaner Nationalists, and it is to them that we owe most of our information about it. "*The Economic Position of the Afrikaner,*" "*The Occupations of the Afrikaner in the City,*" "*Capitalism, Party Politics and Poverty,*" "*The Economy of the Afrikaner and His Share in Business Life,*" "*The Afrikaner's Present Position and Struggle on the Economic Terrain,*"—these are the titles of some Afrikaans publications that had not been written when the United Party was born.

Much, though not all, of this literature attributes the Afrikaner's relative economic backwardness "to political circumstances forced on the Afrikaner at a former stage of his economic development"[65]—forced on him by "British Imperialism" and "Anglo-Jewish Capitalism"—the terms often used. In a chapter entitled, "Direct Economic Losses as a Consequence of [British] Domination," in a work published under Nationalist auspices in 1942 as part of the "Second Trek Series" (i.e., the trek to capture the cities), the author gives a tally of economic setbacks suffered by the Afrikaner as a result, allegedly, of British policy. The listing includes the human and material losses inflicted on the Afrikaner during the Anglo-Boer War, and goes back to the number of houses burned, horses, cattle and sheep stolen, in an 1834 frontier war with Africans that broke out under British colonial administration.[66]

It is hard to doubt that such interpretations seemed valid to those who advanced them. On the other hand, it has been seen that the Afrikaner's economic backwardness vis-à-vis other whites originated in conditions established before English-speaking people set foot in the country, and was subsequently affected by natural disasters as well as by human intervention. The reasons why the Afrikaner's economic standing was explained by such a selective reading of

---

[65] Dr. P. J. Meyer, "Die Afrikaner se huidige Posisie en Stryd op Ekonomiese Gebied," *Volkshandel,* XV (Aug., 1954), 37.

[66] Coetzee, *Verarming.*

history—why, indeed, the Nationalist outlook survived—must therefore be sought in the contemporary situation. To say that an anti-British viewpoint was useful to the National Party does not explain why it was so widely shared. There must have already existed widespread animosity towards the English-speaking section, due in part to the latter's tendency to regard Afrikaners as social inferiors. It was probably circumstances of this nature, which are bound up with the economic disparities between the two groups, that helped make a disinterested view of the past impossible.

The Afrikaner's economic circumstances became after 1934 the subject not only of studies and polemics, but of an organized movement aimed at completely altering them. Launched at Bloemfontein in October 1939, the Afrikaner Economic Movement set out to "penetrate the existing economic structure and gain [for Afrikaners] a controlling share in the economic life of the country."[67] At the time, Afrikaner-controlled businesses accounted for only 5 per cent of the total volume of business turnover.[68] As Afrikaners comprised almost 60 per cent of the country's white population, at least half the businesses in every town ought to belong to them, Dr. N. Diederichs, a leader of the Movement and presently Minister of Economic Affairs, declared shortly after its inception.[69] A number of agencies were established with functions co-ordinated towards the attainment of this goal. One of these agencies, the *Reddingsdaadbond* (Deed of Rescue Union), was designed for mass membership. Within two years of its founding, it claimed 63,000 members organized in 343 branches throughout the country.[70]

The methods and course of the Afrikaner Economic Movement belong to the foreground of Afrikaner nationalism and do not concern us here. It may be noted, however, that even after 1948, by which time the Movement had made headway, the National

---

67 *Volkshandel,* Aug., 1943.

68 Dr. A. J. Visser, "Die Ekonomiese Posisie van die Afrikaner," *Volkshandel,* XVI (May, 1955), 25.

69 *Die Volksblad,* Nov. 21, 1940, in *Press Digest,* 215/1940.

70 *Verslag van die Reddingsdaadbond van sy Werksaamhede Gedurende die 10 Jaar van sy Bestaan,* in *Verslag van die Tweede Ekonomiese Volkskongres (1950),* 161.

Party had come to power, and Black-White relations had become the major national problem, Afrikaner socio-economic inequality vis-à-vis English-speaking whites remained an obstacle to white unity[71] and continued to evoke a sense of injustice among Afrikaners:

Ons het die poorte wyd gebloei
waardeur die handel vrugbaar vloei,

ons het die vlaktes oopgeslaan
waar mynstellasies rifdiep staan;

met Trekkerswee en Driejaar-leed
het ons die erwe uitgemeet

waar winkelsentrums volkhoog reik;
maar weining van ons name pryk

op uithangborde, staan gegrif
in swaarvergulde bodeurskrif;

en word daar dividend verklaar
oor voorbladruimte in die "STAR"

blaai ons verby—soek volgens loon
na huurvertrekke om te woon.[72]

(We opened up the gates with blood
to let trade flow prosperously,

we hewed open the wide plains
where mine headgears grow from reefs;

with doleful Trek and Three-year woe[73]
we measured out the plots of land

where shopping centers reach the clouds;
but few names of our people stand

---

[71] At the second Afrikaner Economic Congress held at Bloemfontein in 1950, by which time the Afrikaner's overall share of business turnover had increased to 11 per cent, requests by two English-speaking businessmen for more co-operation between the two white groups were rejected by a leading Afrikaner manufacturer with the statement that the Afrikaner's economic share was "far too small for us now to pull out all the props from beneath this little *volk's* edifice ("Volksgebou") in order to go building bridges to others." This view was formally endorsed by the Congress which declared the "recommendation in connection with further co-operation with other race groups" to be unacceptable "at this stage," and referred the matter to a committee. See *Verslag van die Tweede Ekonomiese Volkskongres (1950)*, 96, 134.

[72] G. A. Watermeyer, "Volkshandel III" in *Die Republiek van Duisend Jaar* (Johannesburg, 1957).

[73] I.e., the Anglo-Boer War.

> on nameboards, or are etched
> in heavy gilt upon the doors
>
> and when the dividends are declared
> for front-page space in "THE STAR"[74]
>
> we page on—and seek furnished apartments
> according to wages.)

Aside from continued resentment over inferior status, there is probably another principal reason for the revival of Afrikaner Nationalism. The Afrikaner has had to enter and remain in the urban-industrial structure mainly as a worker. He has had to contend for job opportunities and job security not only against the competition of the non-white, but simultaneously against the efforts of the English-speaking employer to hire his often equally capable but lower paid rival. He has sought this opportunity and security through the passage of laws designed to reserve certain jobs for his own color group. The fact that laws have been necessary to restrain white employers from giving preference to non-white workers indicates the existence of limits to voluntary co-operation among the whites, and implies one of the bases for their continued division.

The struggle to secure legal job reservation was initiated by English-speaking immigrant workers, but with the steady influx of landless Afrikaners into the cities and the gradual transformation of the white working class into one of predominantly Afrikaans composition (*cf.* tables I and II), the maintenance and extension of such protection has become primarily an Afrikaner effort. Thus the National Party enacted a new labor law in 1956, empowering the Minister of Labour on the recommendation of a Government-appointed Industrial Tribunal to reserve any job for white workers that was previously not subject to legal reservation. The relevant section of this law (section 77 of the Industrial Conciliation Act of 1956) was carried over the objection of the South African Federated Chamber of Industries, other English-speaking employers' organizations, and the United Party. The Opposition in and outside Parliament argued that the measure would limit opportunities for non-whites; would enable the Government to reserve

---

[74] The Johannesburg afternoon English-language daily.

unemployment for non-whites during recessions and depressions and thus "light flames in the country which would be difficult to put out"; and, in limiting management's right to select its labor, would block optimum productivity and lead to increased costs of production. The Minister of Labour saw the measure as a "warning to employers not to replace employees under some pretext or other when the true reason is cheaper labour. . . ."[75]

Although some trade union organizations, particularly those accepting affiliation from mixed or African unions, objected to the measure, predominantly Afrikaner employee organizations have taken the initiative in requesting its implementation where the jobs of their members have been threatened by non-white competition. Thus at the request of *Die Yster en Staalbedryfsvereniging* (The Iron and Steel Industry Union) specified types of jobs were legally reserved for white workers to prevent employers, who were finding it difficult to compete successfully in the open market, from replacing the Union's members by non-white workers.[76] In some sectors of private industry, such as the domestic appliance industry, application of the law involves the removal of non-white workers from positions that they have hitherto held.[77]

Job opportunity and security for white workers has been a recurring issue since the advent of a white working class in the country after 1870. It was this issue that led to the last violent clash between organized groups of white people in South African history in 1922, when the Chamber of Mines, to meet a decline in gold prices, sought to replace 2,000 whites by non-white workers. The result was a general strike which turned into an unsuccessful revolution when the Smuts Government sent in troops to curb the strikers' violence. Within two years of the strike's suppression the Smuts Government was overthrown at the polls and the first Nationalist Government took office in coalition with an English-speaking Labour Party. Since that time, the rapid Afrikanerization of the white working class has resulted in a pronounced ethnic as well as class alignment on this issue, and it has seen the National Party

---

[75] See *A Survey of Race Relations in South Africa, 1955–1956,* 178-84.

[76] *A Survey of Race Relations in South Africa, 1959–1960,* 177.

[77] *Ibid.*, 179.

capture most of the white working class vote.[78] As English employer-Afrikaner employee discord over the racial organization of employment opportunities is likely to remain chronic, political quarrels between the two sections of the ruling population are unlikely to cease. Only a common, imminent threat to their positions, arising out of foreign intervention or an African uprising, seems capable of causing them to close ranks. In normal circumstances, that is while the border of African authority approaches South Africa's frontier and the problem of managing the indigenous African population becomes simultaneously more acute, threats to their respective positions will probably continue to be partly mutually posed.

That the Afrikaner's economic position brings him into simultaneous conflict with White as well as Black may yet have far reaching consequences. Should the country experience a serious economic set back leading to an attempted large scale substitution of white for non-white labor, one wonders whether the resulting political crisis would not then be more complex than a confrontation of only Black and White.

---

[78] It was this vote which brought the present Nationalist Government to power in 1948, according to B. J. Schoeman, a member of that Goverment, *Die Vaderland,* June 12, 1957. In the 1948 General Election, the Nationalists took 19 working class constituencies from the United and Labour Parties, E. S. Sachs, *The Choice Before South Africa* (London, 1952), 208.

X.

Sir Alfred Milner on British Policy in South Africa in 1897

by

JEFFREY BUTLER

Research Associate, African Studies Program, Boston University

On 18 November, 1897, Sir Alfred Milner, High Commissioner for South Africa and Governor of Cape Colony, wrote a letter to H. H. Asquith, a member of the front bench of the Liberal party, then out of office. Until now our knowledge of this letter has been based on a lengthy extract published by Cecil Headlam[1] and it has rightly been regarded as an excellent statement of the conflict of obligations facing a British High Commissioner.[2] The full text of the letter, however, raises some interesting questions, particularly if it is placed in political context. Furthermore, the letter was sent by Asquith to John Morley, Liberal Secretary for Ireland, 1892-95, to Lord Ripon, Liberal Secretary for the Colonies, 1892-95, and to Sir Arthur Lyall, a member of the Council of the Secretary of State for India. Their comments, and those of Asquith, will be examined here.[3]

The conflict of obligations arose from the fact that in South Africa white minorities were in power over native[4] majorities and all British governments felt that they had some obligations to the native population. However, the definition of obligations was com-

---

1 C. Headlam. (Ed.), *The Milner Papers,* (2 vols., London, 1931), I, 177-81.

2 For example, G. B. Pyrah, *Imperial Policy and South Africa 1902–1910* (Oxford, 1955), 87; *Cambridge History of the British Empire* (8 vols., Cambridge, 1929-1941), III (1959), 355. (C.H.B.E.)

3 This paper is an expanded version of one given at the Institute of Commonwealth Studies, London University, in January 1961. I would like to thank C. F. Goodfellow of Rhodes University, South Africa, R. Davenport and Mrs. Z. Katzen of University of Cape Town, and John Livingston of Newton High School, Newton, Mass., for critical comment. I thank also the following for giving me access to material: Mr. Mark Bonham Carter (the Asquith Papers); Viscount Harcourt (the Sir William Harcourt Papers); the Warden and Fellows of New College, Oxford (the Milner Papers); and the Trustees of the British Museum (the Ripon Papers).

4 The contemporary terms "native" and "Dutch," as well as the modern "African" and "Afrikaner" respectively, will be used throughout this paper.

plicated by questions of interest. Cape Colony contained a major strategic point in the naval base at Simonstown. Since the discovery of diamonds and gold, South Africa had become an important market for British goods, a field for British capital and the home of a large number of British subjects. Dutch, British and native populations were widely dispersed in two self-governing colonies, two Dutch republics, the territory of the British South Africa Company, and directly administered "protectorates" like Basutoland and the Bechuanaland Protectorate. Could British obligations to South African white men be met, and British interests in South Africa be secured, without prejudicing the rights of South African natives? It was characteristic of Milner to attempt a definite answer to a difficult question which most of his contemporaries evaded.

I

The full text of Milner's letter is as follows; omissions by Headlam have been placed in squared brackets:

Confidential

Government House
Cape Town
18 November, 1897

Dear Asquith,

I have just been reading with great interest, [though alas! in a bad Reuter abstract,] the substance of a speech [at Wormit] in which you dealt largely with our South African difficulties. With your two great principles that (1) we should seek "to restore the good relations between the Dutch and English" and (2) we should "secure for the Natives, particularly in that part of S. Africa called Rhodesia, adequate and sufficient protection against oppression and wrong," I most cordially agree with this reservation, that I don't quite see the ground for your "particularly." It seems to me, we are equally bound to secure the good treatment of the natives in the Transvaal, where we specially and most solemnly promised them protection when we gave back the country to the Boers, and inserted the provision in the Convention giving us the fullest right to intervene in their behalf.

This, however, though an important point, is not the particular point, which I want to make in this letter. What I am so anxious that you and other English Statesmen—especially Liberal Statesmen—should understand is that object No. 2 is the principal obstacle to the attainment of object No. 1,—is, and always has been.

I should feel quite confiident of being able to get over the Dutch-English difficulty, if it were not so horribly complicated by the Native question.

[In spite of Majuba, in spite of Jameson, I remain firmly of the opinion that, if it were not for my having some conscience about the treatment of blacks, I *personally* could win over the Dutch in the Colony and indeed in all the S.A. dominions in my term of office, and that I could do so without offending the English. You have only to sacrifice "the nigger" absolutely and the game is easy. But any attempt to secure fair play for him makes the Dutch fractious and almost unmanageable. Deep down in the heart of every Dutchman in S. Africa is the ideal of a white landowning aristocracy resting on slave labour. (Of course the word "slave" is carefully eschewed nor do they exactly want slaves but simply cheap labour of a black proletariat *without rights of any sort or kind.*)]

Rhodesia is a case in point. The blacks have been scandalously used. Even now, *though there is great amendment*, and though the position of the black man in Rhodesia is now probably more hopeful than in any part of South Africa not under direct imperial control, except Natal, I am not at all confident that many [very] bad things will not happen. I am doing my best, in fact there is nothing out here which I consider either so important or so difficult—but I have to walk with extreme caution, for nothing is more certain than that if the Imperial Government *were to be seen taking a strong line* against the Company for the protection of the blacks, the whole of Dutch opinion in South Africa would swing round to the side of the Company and the bulk—not the whole—of British Colonial opinion would go with it, [for the British Colonist though far better than the Dutchman in his attitude to the black is still essentially selfish with regard to him and regards the views, not only of the professional negro-philist, but of the average healthy-minded Englishmen on this subject as "*cant*" or "*fad.*"] You have therefore this singular situation, that you might unite Dutch and English by protecting the blackman, but you would unite them against yourself and your policy of protection.

There is the whole *crux* of the South African position. [You say and say truly that self-government is the basis of our colonial policy and the key stone of colonial loyalty. That principle fearlessly and unflinchingly applied would make S. Africa as loyal as Canada—but what would be the [?]? The abandonment of the black races, whom you have promised protection, and the tolerance of a state of things in a self governed state under the British flag which we should never tolerate for a moment in India, in Egypt, or in any of our Crown Colonies.

The following is the order of the S. African States and Colonies as regards their treatment of the black man—bear in mind that in the best of them his *status* is worse than it would be in any country under the Imperial control:

The best is Natal, for here the black population is so enormous, compared with the white, that though they are kept in subjection, prudence, apart from all other consideration, would necessitate their not being treated too harshly. Besides, the white men are mainly of British race.

The next best is Rhodesia, I mean the *somewhat purified* Rhodesia of to-day, not the Rhodesia entirely run by fortune hunters, as it was in the first years of the occupation. Here, too, it is the fact that the settlers are mostly British, and to a great extent *nowadays*, a good type of British, who helps. A good step lower down is the O.F.S. This is run on the pure Dutch principle—white aristocracy—black proletariat—: But the Dutchmen of the Free State are of a comparatively refined type and there being *no longer any struggle* the complete subjugation of the black being a *fait accompli* and he is a useful animal, the kindly natured master is not needlessly brutal to the servant.

Next worse is the Cape Colony. The laws here are better, but their administration is bad, because all Cape governments are forever angling for the Dutch vote, and there is no panacea for obtaining it like disregard of native rights.]

By far the worst is the Transvaal. Here the black has no rights whatever and there is neither kindliness nor wisdom to restrain the brutality of the ruling oligarchy.

In contrast with all these more or less sharp contrasts according to the particular rung of the ladder which you look at, is the position of the black man in Basutoland and the Bechuanaland Protectorate. Here there is absolute "protection" of the black man "against oppression and wrong." In fact, they are the preserves of the black man, in which our authority, a very light one, is simply exercised to keep the peace. But look at the result. The Imperial position in Basutoland and the Bechuanaland Protectorate is a source of constant friction with the Colonists. The Cape Colony is constantly trying to get hold of the former, the Chartered Company of the latter—it had just got it in 1895, as you remember, when the Raid occurred and the whole arrangement was knocked on the head. Personally, I am dead against all these efforts. I want to preserve the Basuto and the Bechuana, for the present at least, from the tender mercies of the Bond and our friend Cecil J. Rhodes. But observe, that by doing so I am weakening my hand in the game of conciliating the Colonists, Dutch and English, and in uniting Dutch and English. Dutch and English in the Colony are united in wanting to take over Basutoland. Even the Dutch would like to see Rhodes pocket Bechuanaland, I mean the Bechuanaland Protectorate. The Colony of British Bechuanaland is already incorporated with the Colony and has consequently been the scene of a needless rebellion, *[brutally put down.]* They hate Rhodes for the moment—but they hate an independent Native State more—and at all times.

I tell you all this, not to magnify my difficulties but to help you to understand them. I feel that, if I fail out here, it will be over the Native Question. Nothing else is of the same seriousness. At the same time my course is clear. I have a strong conviction of what policy I ought to pursue, having regard at once to Colonial rights of self-government and to the plighted faith of Great Britain to the natives. Within the Colony of which I am Governor, I can only use personal influence, doing all I can to encourage the minority, which is for fair treatment of the Natives, and to restrain the majority without overstepping the limits of my power as a strictly constitutional ruler. In Rhodesia, I still have, and if the Imperial Government retains, as I hope it will retain, a certain control over the administration, I shall continue to have greater power, and I shall exercise it, through the agents of the Company, to introduce not an ideal system, but one which I hope will be at least as humane and progressive as that of Natal. The great thing here is to secure the appointment of honourable and capable men as Magistrates and Native Commissioners. If that can be done, I think the lot of the natives may be a very tolerable one, and that even a system of compulsory labour, indeed under fair conditions and proper safeguards, may be turned to their advantage. As regards Basutoland and the Protectorate, I am *dead opposed* to any change in the *status quo.* I know that some day or other these districts must become a part of some self-governed white community. But I want to defer the change as long as ever I can and to make it dependent upon a great improvement, in the interval, in the treatment of the Natives already subject to the Colonial rule. "Do you want to govern more Natives?" in effect I say to them, "then show yourself worthy of the trust by governing better those whom you already have." Lastly, as regards the Transvaal, I think very likely the question will solve itself, because the Transvaal oligarchy is bound sooner or later to topple over. But if it does not, then *some years hence,* I may see my way to giving some effect to our promises and the Boer pledges to treat the Natives fairly. But *it is much too soon* to attempt anything of the kind. The Transvaal Boers are still so sore with us, that it is useless for us to make any remonstrance which we are not prepared to support by war.

Forgive this long lecture—*liberavi animum.* It is a great comfort to me to think that if these questions ever become the subject

> of discussion in England *where the intemperate or ill-informed discussion of them may do infinite harm,* there will be at least one outside critic, who knows what my difficulties are and what I am driving at, and who, whether he approves or disapproves my methods, will, at least, understand and, I believe, sympathise with, my objects.
>
> P. S. If you like at any time to show this letter to Morley, or to any other good man and true on your side, do so. I know that you would only do so with all discretion. Remember, the Colonials are intensely sensitive about English criticism, and any criticism which does not recognize their difficulties—(and the difficulties of governing a vast black population are very great)—does more harm than good.[5]

When one considers how committed Headlam was to Milner's views of empire, the two published volumes of Milner's papers are remarkable for the degree to which Headlam allowed Milner to speak for himself. The omissions in this case, however, alter seriously the sense of the letter. First, Headlam omitted Milner's very large claim that by sacrificing the "nigger" the game of white conciliation would be easily won. Secondly, with a fine impartiality he omitted that very strong criticism which Milner made of both Englishmen and Dutchmen in South Africa. When taken with the excision of Milner's emphatic phrase "*brutally put down*" when writing of the "needless rebellion," these omissions suggest that Headlam wished to tone down the criticisms of South African white men.[6] Thirdly, the analogy of South Africa with Canada, as a region to which a policy of "self-government" could be applied, was left out. Fourthly, the fascinating—and revealing—ordering of the South African states and colonies was omitted: by going straight from "the crux of the South African question" to "by far the worst is the Transvaal," Headlam once more toned down the criticism of South African white men generally, and he effectively concealed the strongly "racial"—i.e., anti-Dutch—basis of Milner's analysis. Finally, for the record, Headlam understandably failed to notice that the letter was written from Rhodesia, not from Cape Town.[7]

---

[5] Asquith Papers, Bodleian Library, Oxford.

[6] It is just possible, though rather far-fetched, that Headlam wished to do nothing to spoil the harmony of the year of the Statute of Westminster.

[7] Milner did not tell Asquith that he was writing from Rhodesia; there seems to be no reason for thinking that the omission was a calculated one.

Milner was on an extended tour of Rhodesia and on 18 November, he was still in Salisbury.[8]

II

Milner was writing with an object, as he stated candidly enough: he wanted, so he said, to point out to Opposition statesmen that ill-informed discussion of the native question could make his problems more serious. An examination of Asquith's speech, and the context in which it was made will show, however, that Milner probably had another aim as well, viz., to stop the Liberals from attacking Rhodes and the Chartered Company, and to show that the real villains were elsewhere.

On 29 December, 1895, Dr. Jameson had invaded the South African Republic—the Transvaal—with a force employed by the British South Africa Company. This unsuccessful Raid was an event of the first importance in British, European and South African history. In 1897 a Select Committee of the House of Commons held an inquiry and its report was debated on 25 July, in the House of Commons, with much reluctance on the part of both front benches. Joseph Chamberlain, the Colonial Secretary, made his celebrated "man of honour" speech, by which he was widely held to have wiped out the emphatic censure passed by the Committee on Cecil Rhodes for preparing a rising in, and an invasion of, the Transvaal. Moreover, a motion calling on the Company's solicitor, Bourchier Hawksley, to produce a set of telegrams withheld from the Committee, was rejected by the House.[9] The Leader of the Opposition in the Commons, Sir William Harcourt, and Sir Henry Campbell-Bannerman, the next Liberal Prime Minister, had both been members. They were seriously embarrassed within their own party by the failure of the Committee to prove complicity on the part of the Imperial government, and by the apparent willingness of both Government and Committee to allow themselves to be defied by the widely hated Company.[10]

---

8 *Milner Papers,* I, 85, 134.

9 For a short account of the genesis and course of the debate, see J. Van der Poel, *The Jameson Raid* (London, 1951), 235-41.

10 A. G. Gardiner, *The Life of Sir William Harcourt* (2 vols., London, 1923), II, 432-37.

Asquith spoke at Wormit on 12 October, 1897. He devoted nearly the whole of his speech to South Africa, applauding the censure passed by the Committee on that "sordid and criminal enterprise." He tried to move the responsibility for the failure to extract the telegrams from the Committee on to the House of Commons, to which the Committee was responsible.[11] For twelve months before the Committee first met, said Asquith,

> the apologists and champions of Mr. Rhodes . . . were bruiting it about that these telegrams . . . would prove conclusively that the Imperial Government of Great Britain was in connivance and complicity with these criminal transactions.

The failure to force production of the telegrams had been made worse by Mr. Chamberlain's speech, he continued.

> He did not think [Asquith said] that these proceedings would facilitate the heavy task of administration in South Africa. . . . The problem . . . was, on the one hand, to restore the relations, broken for the time being, between the English and the Dutch populations, and on the other hand, to secure for natives, particularly in that part of South Africa called Rhodesia, adequate protection against oppression and wrong.[12]

The speech by a future Liberal Imperialist was an attempt to help the Liberal leaders in a politically embarrassing position and to attack the Government at the same time. Secondly, Asquith resented what he regarded as attempts by Rhodes and his friends to pin the major share of responsibility for the Raid on to the Imperial government. The Raid was, it should be noted, an event in the struggle between white men, and Asquith was aware of its South African significance, i.e., as affecting relations throughout colonies and republics. Thirdly, however, Asquith apparently regarded the native question as "particularly" a Rhodesian one, a point Milner commented on. It was the Company, Asquith clearly implied, that was the major sinner in relation to both the native question and conciliation of white men. Moreover, the Committee and the "pro-

---

[11] Asquith was being kind to the Committee and to his leader. The problem had arisen because the Committee had failed to report a recalcitrant witness *at once* to the House. For a ruling by the Speaker see *Parliamentary Debates* (*P. Deb.*), LI, 1093, July 25, 1897.

[12] *The Times*, Oct. 13, 1897.

ceedings" which preceded and followed its report, had made the task no easier.

There were probably two reasons for Asquith's saying this. First, the Committee had lamentably failed to follow its own terms of reference, which were:

> . . . To inquire into the origin and circumstances of the incursion into the South African Republic by an armed force, and into the administration of the British South Africa Company, and to report thereon, and further to report what alterations are desirable in the government of the territories under the control of the Company.[13]

The second half of the inquiry—into the administration of the Company—was never undertaken, and no "alterations" were suggested. Indeed, the Committee made no proposals of any kind. For anyone who was interested in good government generally, and of natives in particular, the Committee had been of no use at all, and it had even failed to convince many people in both British parties that it had investigated the "incursion" properly.[14] Secondly, Asquith may have been afraid that Chamberlain's defence of Rhodes, and the failure of the Committee to assert itself, indicated an unwillingness—even an inability—to control the Company in Rhodesia.

III

Asquith and Milner had been contemporaries at Balliol College, Oxford. When Milner was given an impressive public dinner before leaving to take up his duties in South Africa, Asquith had taken the chair.[15] They were not regular correspondents, however, as Milner makes clear; this letter was written with the clearly stated purpose of keeping in touch with the leaders of the Opposition in England and, if possible, of influencing their course of action. Asquith was a rising star in the Liberal Party and he was, for Milner, an obvious point of contact.

Milner was not concerned with the success or failure of the South African Committee. He had disliked the Committee virtually from its appointment in August, 1896, praying for an Act of God

13 *P. Deb.*, XLV, 762, Jan. 28, 1897.

14 See note 9 above.

15 *The Times*, Mar. 29, 1897.

in the form of an earthquake to destroy it at its first sitting.[16] Furthermore, halfway through of the sittings of the Committee he had seen, with considerable prescience, what effects its proceedings would have on Anglo-Boer relations. He wrote to Sir William Harcourt on 6 April, 1897:

> I feel rather low to-night. What is the use of sending me out, with a penny squirt, to try to extinguish a raging fire in South Africa, if the great and wise at home are going to pour gallons of oil upon it all the time? First we have Rhodes to madden the Dutch, then Schreiner to madden the English; now we have to have all the gossip of the Raiders' camp to remadden the Dutch. Surely I would be as much use in Piccadilly?[17]

Secondly, Milner was not as hostile to Rhodes and his friends as Asquith had been. Asquith's complaint had been based on the Committee and on the Company's administrative record. Milner clearly wanted to ignore the Committee. It was in any case becoming an historical issue, the discussion of which embittered, rather than allayed, white conflict. He was optimistic about Rhodesia and he wished to give Rhodes every encouragement there. Furthermore, he regarded the revival of an alliance between Rhodes and the Afrikander Bond as perfectly possible, perhaps probable, if the Imperial Government acted unwisely. He implied that he did not want to see the alliance renewed: Rhodes was not an obstacle to the Anglo-Dutch conciliation for which he was working. It was probably going to be protection of native rights, not the failure of the Committee, which would delay an acceptable union of South African whites.

Thirdly, Milner emphasised the South African, not merely the

---

16 F. Whyte, *The Life of W. T. Stead* (2 vols., London, 1925), I, 98; Milner to Stead, Nov. 16, 1896: ". . . An earthquake which should engulf the Committee at its first sitting would clearly be the best thing."

17 Harcourt Papers, Stanton Harcourt, Oxon. Rhodes and W. Schreiner, a former colleague of Rhodes' who broke with him on the issue of the Raid, had both given evidence. On Apr. 5, 1897, Sir John Willoughby, the commander of Jameson's troops, had declined "on public grounds" to tell the Committee why he had believed that the Imperial government had known and approved of the invasion of the Transvaal. House of Commons, *Sessional Paper* No. 311 (1897): Report of the Select Committee on British South Africa, Question 5646.

Rhodesian, character of the problem of the protection of African rights. Asquith appeared to him to be ignoring British rights of intervention in the Transvaal, "the brutality" of the Transvaal "oligarchy," and the poor record of Cape Colony.

Milner's analysis was a "racial" one, i.e., his problems increased almost in direct proportion to the percentage of Dutchmen in the population. The two areas which had homogeneous English speaking white populations, Natal and Rhodesia, were the "best" in South Africa, outside the areas governed as Crown colonies or protectorates. The Orange Free State was better than the Cape or the Transvaal because its Dutchmen had been "refined" in some way. The Transvaal was "by far the worst." Furthermore, Milner implied that one of the reasons why it was "by far the worst" in its administration of native races was that Englishmen had no part in its government. There was no need to intervene, he said, because the oligarchy was sure to "topple." When that happened, the question would "solve itself" and the need for "remonstrance" would either disappear, or be less. It was also a "racial" analysis in another sense, and characteristic of the time: it was unthinkable for Milner to antagonize South African white men by an active trusteeship on behalf of native races. Retaining the friendship of whites was a crucial limiting condition.

Milner claimed that protection of natives by the British government "is and always has been" the "principal obstacle" to the acceptable conciliation of South African white men to each other. This was neither an imprecise nor a modest claim and both the historical and the contemporary versions of it require considerable qualification. There had, it is true, been many conflicts between the British government and Dutchmen which had their origin, partly or entirely, in the willingness of the British government to protect native rights. But the protection extended by British governments had neither created an unacceptable union of South African whites, nor stimulated conflict between them. Hostility to Britain was not a result of this protection which had been an additional, not a sole, basis of conflict. To take an important example: between 1872 and 1881 Liberal and Conservative governments made the first major attempts to create a loyal and stable union of the South African states and colonies. The attempts failed, not because the

British government had been too solicitous of African rights, but largely through poor political management, particularly in failing to extend self-government to the newly annexed Transvaal in 1877.[18] Moreover, it could also be argued that the annexation of Basutoland to the Crown in 1868, bringing the expansion of the Orange Free State to a halt, had not prevented a considerable degree of conciliation by 1890. Within the Orange Free State, between the Orange Free State and Cape Colony, and between the Orange Free State and Great Britain, serious Anglo-Dutch conflict was subsiding.[19]

What then of the period of which Milner was writing? Conflict between South African whites became serious in the nineties. First, the rulers of the Transvaal failed to come to a political accomodation with their largely British immigrant population; secondly, that conflict was exacerbated in the Transvaal, and exported to Cape Colony, by the Jameson Raid and its aftermath. It is important to emphasise that that conflict was new: British settlers had sympathised with Trekkers in the eastern Cape Colony in 1836.[20] Indeed, in the nineties Milner's proposition could be reversed: the need to conciliate whites and to mitigate conflict on issues concerning white men only, had become the major obstacle to the protection of Africans.

Milner's use of the analogy with Canada was especially misleading. He implied that the crucial difference between Canada and South Africa was that South Africa had a native population and Canada did not. But there was a profound constitutional, and an equally profound political difference. The devising of the policy of self-government after the Canadian rebellion of 1838 had come after seventy years of British rule. A colonial constitution was amended and colonial responsible government developed. The reconciliation of a non-British people to imperial rule was achieved. But in South Africa sovereignty was itself an issue. Milner, like many, even most, British statesmen of his day, spoke of "South Africa"

---

18 C. W. de Kiewiet, *The Imperial Factor in South Africa* (Cambridge, 1937), 238-40; E. A. Walker, *A History of Southern Africa* (London, 1957), 363-65, 376-77.

19 Walker, *Southern Africa*, 405-09.

20 Walker, *The Great Trek* (London, 1960), 99-105.

as a region for which Britain had some overall responsibility.[21] "South Africa"—not only Cape Colony, Natal, or Rhodesia—would be made "as loyal as Canada" by "self-government." Moreover, Milner claimed a right of intervention in the Transvaal on behalf of the natives there.[22] But it was precisely this claim to an overall supremacy, with a consequent right of intervention, that clashed with the vigorous republicanism of the Transvaal, and it was the resistance to the British claim that brought on the South African War in 1899.[23]

It might well be asked which "nigger" rights could be used in 1897 as a means of gaining the loyalty of all South African whites. As Milner acknowledged, the only important bargaining counter remaining to him was the territory still under imperial control, which could be used as a sort of bribe to raise the quality of South African native administration. Three points can be made here: first, he thought only of retaining these territories for a few years.[24] Secondly, he thought of transferring them to colonial governments. They could not be used to solve the problems created by the rival ambitions of Kruger and of Rhodes, to mitigate the conflict over the Raid, or to bring about an agreement on bitterly fought issues of tariff and railway policy. Thirdly, the bribe of the ultimate transfer to the South African Union of the High Commission Territories, Basutoland, the Bechuanaland Protectorate and Swaziland, was written into the South Africa Act of 1909.[25] The bribe has clearly proved to be of limited effectiveness and Milner's opposition to territorial transfer in 1897 seems to have been a part of a long term change in British policy.

---

21 R. E. Robinson and J. Gallagher, *Africa and the Victorians* (London, 1961), 410, 420, 427, 437-38.

22 See p. below.

23 J. S. Marais, *The Fall of Kruger's Republic* (London, 1961), 327-32.

24 *Milner Papers*, I, 106: Milner to Lord Selborne (Under-Secretary of State for the Colonies), June 2, 1897: "No doubt the [Bechuanaland] Protectorate is costly in itself, but if the expenditure of £60,000 or thereabout for just a year or two longer makes a really great improvement in your whole position, it is folly to consider it," i.e., folly to consider transfer to the British South Africa Company.

25 L. M. Thompson, *The Unification of South Africa 1902–1910* (Oxford, 1960), 269-79. Swaziland was separated from the Transvaal in 1902.

To sum up: Milner's political analysis was defective. His "racial" approach in this letter foreshadows that shown in his diplomacy and in his public conduct in South Africa from 1898 on.[26] He was to work for the mobilisation of British sentiment across republican and colonial boundaries, rather than to recognize the deep divisions within the Dutch community, and perhaps to take advantage of them until an acceptable union of South African white men could be achieved. Writing from Rhodesia, in close touch with Englishmen on the frontier, he wanted to give the Company every opportunity to develop its domain.[27] He tried, therefore, to persuade Liberals to abandon an attack on Rhodes and the Company. It was, apparently, the first time that he attempted to influence his friends on the Liberal front bench on questions of South African policy. It was not to be the last.[28]

IV

Asquith sent the letter to John Morley (as Milner had suggested), who replied:

> Many thanks for sending me the enclosed. It is a wonderfully clear and concise statement of the well known difficulty of the situation. That difficulty will be enormously aggravated for Milner and J[oseph] C[hamberlain] if or when it suits Rhodes to play for the Dutch vote by anti-native proposals in which he has gone pretty far before now.
>
> I have great confidence in Chamberlain's humanity. He has real feeling about ill treatment of natives and will do as much as anybody to keep the brutes of colonists in order in those matters. . . . When you write to Milner be sure to convey to him all good wishes from me.[29]

---

[26] In particular his celebrated Graaff Reinet speech on Mar. 3, 1898, in which he called on the Cape Dutch to urge reform on the rulers of the Transvaal. *Milner Papers,* I, 244-47. For the effect on South African politics see Marais, *Fall,* 208: "From this time he [Milner] was regarded as the commander-in-chief of the 'British party'. . . ."

[27] *Milner Papers,* I, 139-46: Milner to Chamberlain, Dec. 1, 1897.

[28] Milner was in close touch with the Liberal Imperialists, and particularly with Haldane, throughout the South African War. See *Milner Papers,* II, 263-64: a letter from Milner to Haldane July 1, 1901 and reply, July 6, 1901, a characteristic exchange at the time of the crisis brought in the Liberal party by Sir Henry Campbell-Bannerman's speech on "methods of barbarism" in South Africa.

[29] Asquith Papers, Dec. 21, 1897.

Morley had accepted Milner's "statement of the well known difficulty." He then underlined Milner's fear of handing over native people, in Milner's words, "to the tender mercies of the Bond and our friend Cecil J. Rhodes." In doing this, Morley was probably taking a line which Milner would have disliked. Within a month of arriving in South Africa Milner had pressed for the support of Rhodes in South Africa, though with strict control over the methods used by Rhodes, a clear reference to the proven danger of trusting Rhodes with military force.[30] A month later Lord Selborne, Under-secretary at the Colonial Office, replied:

> . . . Mr. Chamberlain was a good deal disturbed by your last letter. He evidently had not expected that you would be so impressed that Rhodes is still a great factor to reckon with in South Africa.[31]

Chamberlain was closer in opinion to Morley than he was to Milner. He had long disliked Rhodes on several grounds: for wanting to "eliminate the Imperial factor in South Africa,"[32] for this treatment of natives,[33] and he clearly hoped that Rhodes' political position in South Africa had been destroyed by the Raid.[34] Moreover, throughout 1896 and in January, 1897, there had been a fierce conflict, behind the scenes, in which Rhodes had tried to blackmail Chamberlain into suppressing the Select Committee.[35] On the crucial issue of support of Rhodes, Milner, the "Man on the Spot," was differing both from his chief and from an important figure in the Opposition.

V

After Christmas Asquith sent the letter to Lord Ripon, adding "I have never seen the crucial problem of South African administration more clearly or forcibly stated."[36] Ripon replied:

> . . . I have no doubt that his general view of the situation in South Africa is right. The native question is our abiding difficulty there.

---

30 *Milner Papers,* I, 105: Milner to Selborne, June 2, 1897.

31 *Ibid.,* 112: Selborne to Milner, July 6, 1897.

32 J. L. Garvin, *Life of Joseph Chamberlain* (3 vols., London, 1934), III, 32-33.

33 *Ibid.*

34 See note 30.

35 Van der Poel, *Raid,* 156-57, 182-83.

36 Ripon Papers, British Museum, Add. Mss., 43518 f 194, Dec. 28, 1897.

> In the self-governing colonies the more fully we can accept their self government in its fullest sense and leave them to deal with the natives in their own way on their own responsibility the better for our relations with them and for the maintenance of their loyalty. But I doubt whether people in this country would accept the whole consequences of this doctrine—though anything short of this must lead to constant friction.
>
> I agree with Milner as to native policy in British dominions outside Cape Colony and Natal and like him I would let no more natives come under the management of those Colonists until we have greater security than now exists as to how they would be treated. I cannot help being somewhat doubtful whether Milner or anyone else could if the native difficulty were out of the way, restore trust and good feeling between the British and the Dutch as soon and as easily as he seems to expect. I would have thought that the mischief done by the conspiracy and the raid was too deep and bitter for such early removal. But he is more likely to be right than I.
>
> I do not quite concur with what he says about the Transvaal. We are not *equally* bound to secure the good treatment of the natives there as in our own dominions. The Treaty obligations of the South African Republic in regard to the natives give us a right of remonstrance but as we have no other means of enforcing such remonstrances than war our duty to the Transvaal natives is surely of a different character from that which we owe to natives in British territory. The point however is not of much practical importance, as Milner says towards the end of his letter that he does not think of raising the questions with the S.A. Republic *till some years hence.*[37]

Ripon, as a former Colonial Secretary, was better informed about South Africa than was Morley; his reply was more critical though he agreed that protection of Africans produced an "abiding difficulty." Between 1892 and 1895 Ripon had controlled the negotiations which had resulted in the transfer of Swaziland to the Transvaal[38] and British Bechuanaland (not the Protectorate) to Cape Colony.[39] In the latter case there had recently been, in Milner's

---

[37] Asquith Papers, Dec. 29, 1897.

[38] N. G. Garson, "The Swaziland Question and a Road to the Sea, 1887-1895," *Archives Year Book for South African History,* II (Pretoria, 1957), 407-15.

[39] *C.H.B.E.*, VIII, 559. The transfer of British Bechuanaland was done under Ripon's successor, in August, 1895, but the negotiations had been begun under the Liberal government.

words, "a needless rebellion *brutally put down*."[40] Ripon's conversion to a doctrine of retaining land under imperial control was a recent one.

It is, perhaps, surprising that it should have been Ripon, rather than Morley, though both men showed a common hostility to Milner in the South African war, who saw the flaws in Milner's political argument. Ripon emphasized the blow to Afrikaner confidence by the Raid *and* the conspiracy which had preceded it, and he questioned, surely correctly, the ability of Milner to reconcile the conflicting aims of British and Transvaal policy even if no native difficulty existed.

Less surprising, but equally fundamental, was Ripon's objection to Milner's doctrine of a legal right to intervene on behalf of the natives in the Transvaal. It should be noted that Milner was making a very large claim, indeed, he seemed to be suggesting that Britain's rights stemmed from the Convention of 1881 "when we handed the country back," rather than from that of 1884.[41] The status of the 1881 Convention became a major diplomatic issue later.[42] Ripon denied that Britain had an equal responsibility for natives in Rhodesia and the Transvaal respectively. But he appeared also to confuse the issue by basing the nature of the obligation on the type of sanction which would have to be applied to enforce it. The Convention imposed a duty on the Transvaal but apparently it gave to Britain a right of remonstrance only.

Ultimately, the enforcement of remonstrances within and between political systems rests on force. Within a political system, however, the status of rules, if questioned, can be determined by a recognized judicial procedure and if necessary, force under the law can be used. Britain had the legal right, if it chose, to force responsibly governed colonies and chartered companies to live up to their obligations. If force were used it would be regarded as a "police operation" unless it became so serious as to change its character into a "war of independence." Ripon's argument that a remonstrance could only be enforced by "war" was to imply that

---

40 See p. 249 above.

41 G. Eybers, *Select Constitutional Documents Illustrating South African History* (London, 1918), 455, 469.

42 Marais, *Fall*, 195-202.

the Transvaal was outside the British political system and to recognize that there was no accepted way of deciding a conflict of interpretation of the obligations which the Transvaal had to Britain. Milner claimed a right and a duty; Ripon admitted the right but denied the duty. Both, however, were unwilling to take immediate action. The difference between them shows an important difference of emphasis: Milner was prepared to expand rights of intervention; he claimed rights as great as Britain possessed the case of the Company; Ripon was far nearer to regarding the Transvaal as an independent state.[43] This was to be a major issue between Britain and the Transvaal, particularly in 1898-99.[44]

VI

Asquith replied to Milner on January 12, 1898.

> I was very glad to get your letter of Nov. 18th, and I need not say that it interested me greatly. The ἀκορια [translated by Headlam as "impasse" or "difficulty"] is a very formidable one, and the more so as one does not see any natural force at work in the direction of a better treatment of the natives. There is, morever, I should imagine a real danger that Rhodes or his successors might play for the Dutch vote in the Cape Colony by anti-native proposals such e.g. as an agitation for the incorporation of Basutoland. I am aure that you are right in setting your face strongly, in the circumstances, against the extension of the area in which the white aristocracy is able to lay down its own laws for the government of the blacks. I am glad that you are able to perceive a real change for the better in Rhodesia: the difficulty there of keeping any real supervision and still more any effective control over the administration must be enormous. I showed your letter to J. Morley and to Ripon, who were both much struck by it, and you may be sure that, in carrying out the general scheme of policy which you indicate, we shall all watch you with great sympathy, with a full disposition to appreciate and make allowance for the fetters upon free action and the checks to rapid progress which the local conditions impose.[45]

---

[43] Ripon was shifting his ground from a stand he had taken at the beginning of 1895, when he refused to allow the drafting of a Foreign Office despatch which would have conceded that independence had virtually been granted in 1884. L. Wolf: *Life of the Marquess of Ripon* (London, 1932), II, 228: Ripon to Kimberley (Foreign Secretary), Feb. 15, 1895.

[44] Marais, *Fall,* 195-200, 325-27.

[45] *Milner Papers*, I, 180, Jan. 12, 1898.

It is interesting to note that Asquith virtually lifted a phrase from Morley's letter in referring to Rhodes' "anti-native proposals" and that a transfer of territory was regarded as anti-native in itself. Asquith, Morley, and Chamberlain all thought that a reunion of the Bond and Rhodes was possible. Indeed, when Chamberlain was taken to task for his "man of honour speech," he wrote to John Ellis, a Liberal fellow member of the South African Committee:

> Have you and others thought of what would be the consequences of driving Rhodes to the wall? If in his despair or desperation he joined forces with the extreme Dutch element and took advantage of the prejudices so easily roused against the "unctious rectitude" of a British government, we could hardly keep the Cape Colony without a war.[46]

The fear of such a reunion appears far-fetched today, but only because today we have evidence denied to contemporaries. One historian has vehemently rejected the idea that Chamberlain could have thought that an effective political combination was possible between Rhodes and the Bond.[47] But there is evidence that Chamberlain was concerned, and like many other imperialists, he feared the founding of an Uitlander republic in the Transvaal. He was not one to take the loyalty of the South African British for granted.[48] Moreover, he regretted that the British party in South Africa "has no leader except Rhodes."[49]

Chamberlain, of all people, was not one to believe in eternal friendships or animosities in politics. Ripon, however, appeared to put a far higher value on the political consequences of the Raid: he pointed to the bitterness which the Raid, not protection of natives, had created. It was on Ripon's part, it is argued, a typical Gladstonian reaction: moral outrage at the Raid would not, and perhaps should not, soon be forgotten. It showed a better awareness of the length of Dutch historical memory.

---

46 A. T. Bassett, *The Life of John Edward Ellis* (London, 1914), 157-58: Chamberlain to Ellis, Oct. 14, 1897.

47 Van der Poel, *Raid*, 243.

48 Memo by Chamberlain, June 12, 1896, stating his fears of "an entirely independent Republic governed by or for the capitalists of the Rand." See E. Drus: "A Report on the Chamberlain Papers Relating to the Jameson Raid and the Inquiry," *Bulletin of the Institute of Historical Research*, XXV (1952), 49.

49 *Milner Papers*, I, 71: Chamberlain to Milner, July 5, 1897.

VII

One other comment on Milner's letter was found in the Asquith Papers, made by Sir Alfred Lyall, member of the Council of the Secretary of State for India.

14 January, 1898
India Office

My dear Asquith,

I return with many thanks Milner's very interesting letter. I have no doubt that his estimate of the "black" difficulty is so far right that it is one of the most important with which an English governor has to deal in South Africa. Any one who knows the outlying [?] countries [?] under British rule is aware of the strong indomitable race feeling which Europeans carry with them into dependencies inhabited by a mixed population, whether African or Asian and of the great difficulty in which this places the government that has to keep conscientiously on just terms with all races. The native question has troubled us at the Cape from the earliest times and was at the bottom of our earlier wars. I tried, very cautiously, to sound H. M. Stanley on the subject yesterday; but he was, naturally, on the European side, and declared that in Rhodesia the native is decently treated. He went on to say, however, that the opposition to English authoritative interference in the matter is only part of the rooted antipathy, which he tells me is universal in South Africa, from Cape Town to Bulawayo, against any interference by the Colonial Office, as represented by the Governor, in the domestic affairs of the Colony. The colonists, Dutch or English, Cape or Company, he says, are all for entire independent self-government, and will unite against any attempt of the Governor, or High Commissioner, to exercise any real authority over their internal administration. So long as he remains King Log, he is popular; when he begins to govern then his popularity decreases in proportion to his interference. Stanley assures me that he found, to his great surprise, precisely the same feeling among the English residents in the Transvaal—though of course the case is here different. They like to have the support of the Colonial Office in pressing their grievances upon Kruger; but they are quite against any possible interference with the Boer government; and Chamberlain's military menaces only alarmed the English. One leading Englishman related to Stanley how Chamberlain, at an interview in London, mentioned to him the possibility of 30,000 British troops being sent to enforce the claims of the injured Britisher in the Transvaal; and how he, the colonist, replied that in that event he would himself take up a rifle against them. I give this for what

> it may be worth—but Stanley was clear that a British army landing at Cape Town will find English and Dutch combined to invite them to go away. One instance of Colonial jealousy, Stanley noted, in their saying that Milner had been "making too many speeches"—they did not, apparently, like his coming forward so much. All this surprised Stanley quite as much as it might surprise us in England; and he says he talked to everybody everywhere—he is not a bad observer. My conclusion, if Stanley's observations are sound, is that Milner's situation is delicate and difficult; yet if any one can manage it, he is the man.
>
> A. C. Lyall[50]

Lyall's letter is interesting for its account of the conversation with Stanley, who had recently returned from South Africa and was at the time Liberal Unionist member for Lambeth North. He was not likely to exaggerate South African antipathy to *any* intervention. In public he pointed out the necessity of continued British "protection" if South Africa were not to become a "Dutch republic." He assumed victory "after a short campaign," if a war were to come, but he emphasized that there would be great political costs.[51] There is, moreover, other evidence of resistance on the part of South African colonials, British as well as Dutch, in Cape Colony and in what became ultra-Loyalist Natal, to forcible intervention in the affairs of the Transvaal.[52]

British colonists have almost always combined an extravagant loyalty with a touchy sense of their ability to govern themselves without assistance from London. In 1897 there were many expressions of loyal devotion to the Queen and not only from people of British stock. The Diamond Jubilee was widely celebrated, in the Transvaal as well as in the colonies.[53] Milner made glowing and public reference to the loyalty of the Cape Dutch and the warmth

---

50 Asquith Papers.

51 *The Times*, Feb. 24, 1898.

52 R. H. Wilde, "Joseph Chamberlain and the South Africa Republic," *Archives Year Book of South African History* (Pretoria, 1957), I, 37, for evidence of pressure from the governments of Cape Colony and Natal in April, 1896 for a peaceful policy in South Africa. By the middle of 1897 racial divisions in Cape Colony had deepened but Sir John Sprigg's government in Cape Colony was too weak to adopt an aggressive "Imperial" policy. Marais, *Fall*, 164-70.

53 *Milner Papers*, I, 49, 51-52.

of the celebrations.[54] The highly mobilized British loyalist sentiment that was to be such a phenomenon in mid-1899[55] had not appeared in 1897. Stanley's observations, if accurate, made Milner's problem even more difficult than he (Milner) had stated it; i.e., there was not only British South African opposition to interference with native policy, there was also opposition to taking a high hand with the Transvaal on white questions. South African Englishmen had not yet despaired of a political settlement among whites without the help of the imperial government.

VIII

Milner's letter is one of the early statements of the dilemmas facing the Imperial Government and, in spite of its shortcomings it is a remarkably detached and able analysis. Furthermore, whatever its motives, it is an excellent statement of the long-term problems of South African society. Milner's suggestions as to policy and the comments of his English contemporaries show both impotence in the present and pessimism about the future.

The impotence arose from the facts of self-government. These men were well aware that self-government in South Africa, far from solving the long-term problem, had, in fact, destroyed much of the Imperial government's ability to deal with it. Even the loyalty of the South African British was fragile, and on more than one issue. In Cape Colony, important English-speaking leaders like W.P. Schreiner had moved to a position of political, not personal, hostility to Rhodes.[56] If the retention of the loyalty of South African white men was essential, then there was little freedom of manoeuvre over native policy. Support of Rhodes, in Rhodesia or in Cape Colony but particularly in the latter, might be hazardous. Milner recognized the limits clearly enough and in talking of native policy the only policy which he suggested, besides delay of transfer to remaining territory,[57] was to improve the quality of adminis-

---

[54] *Ibid.* A despatch from Milner to Chamberlain, June 23, 1897 commenting on the loyalty of all races was published in *The Times,* Sept. 9, 1897.

[55] Robinson et al., *Africa,* 453-54.

[56] E. A. Walker, *W. P. Schreiner, A South African* (1937), 73, 81-82, 95.

[57] See p. 249 above.

tration by better recruitment. Yet even in this limited field he could do nothing in either the self-governing colonies or the republics.

It was characteristic of Milner to think in such administrative terms. He was appalled at the low standards of administration in South Africa when compared with "India, Egypt, or any of our Crown Colonies." Though he claimed that the "native question" was ultimately the most serious, he did not act on that claim nor did he regard the 'question' as a political one. He gave the Cape no credit for its more liberal franchise, indeed, he denied its effectiveness in protecting the rights of non-whites by asserting poor administration of "better" laws, through appeals to the "Dutch vote." During the war he made his position clear. In abortive peace negotiations with General Botha in February and March, 1901, it was Chamberlain who had pressed for better terms in future for the Coloured population.[58] In 1902, presumably in their desperation to end the wasteful war, British negotiators dropped all reference to Coloureds in the peace terms.[59] Furthermore, it was Milner who persuaded Chamberlain to allow the ex-republics to deal with the franchise after "self-government," not "representative government," as had been the case in the suggested terms in 1901.[60] Milner's views were characteristic, consistent with the line in his letter to Asquith, and had been formed long before any peace negotiations began. He wrote to Chamberlain on 5 March, 1900:

> It will be very unfortunate to raise the question of native voters. There would be practically none in the Transvaal, and for the sake of a theory it would be unwise to start with a conflict with the whites. The Cape experience is not encouraging. If necessary the thing could possibly be brought in *sub silentio*.[61]

And in 1903, at an Inter-Colonial Conference at Bloemfontein, Milner had strongly supported F.R. Moor, Secretary of Native Affairs in Natal, when he asked for acceptance of the principle

---

58 *Milner Papers,* II, 212: Chamberlain to Milner, Mar. 3, 1901. "Coloureds" here refers to non-whites of mixed racial origin, not to "natives."

59 *Ibid.*, 350-60.

60 Thompson, *Unification,* 11-12.

61 Milner Papers, New College, Oxford: XXV, f. 16. I would like to thank Professor G. H. Le May of the University of Witwatersrand for drawing my attention to this document.

that "the political status of the Native should conform to conditions which will ensure the constant dominance of the white race."[62]

Milner was later to regret, according to Headlam, "that he had yielded to the Boers over the Native franchise," regarding this as the greatest mistake he had ever made.[63] But it is clear that Milner had yielded before any negotiations began, and in fact persuaded his Chief to do so as well. In 1905 he protested that "if I had known as well as I know now the extravagance of the prejudice on the part of almost all whites . . . against any concession to any coloured man, however civilized, I should never have agreed to so absolute an exclusion . . . of the whole coloured population from any rights of citizenship."[64] Yet he had long been aware of the extravagance, at least since 1897, and this regret in 1905 was probably an afterthought. The Cape Liberal tradition was not one worthy of extension: a civilisation franchise was a "theory," not a practice to be recommended. Obligations existed to the natives but he thought of them in administrative, not political, terms. In 1905, Milner may have been more aware of the limitations of the administrative approach than he had been in 1897, or even 1902.

The detached pessimism is equally noteworthy. Milner, Asquith, Ripon and Lyall were aware of the difficulties raised by South African British as well as by the Dutch. Asquith could see no "natural force" in favour of natives; Morley referred to "brutes of colonists." No one would suggest the lines of an active trusteeship, such as had been followed by United Kingdom governments in the 1820's and have been followed in the radically changed conditions of the nineteen fifties. Sir Michael Hicks Beach in 1899 expressed both the impotence and the pessimism. "We can never govern from

---

62 Thompson, *Unification*, 117.

63 *Milner Papers*, II, 353. See W. K. Hancock, *Smuts, I: The Sanguine Years 1870–1919*, I (1962), 159, for an account of an amendment of a clause in the draft terms of peace in 1902 from: "The Franchise will not be given to Natives until after the Introduction of Self-Government" to "the question of granting the Franchise to Natives will not be decided until after the introduction of self-government." According to Hancock, Smuts was responsible for the new draft which was accepted. Milner could hardly describe this change as "yielding" to the Boers if this is meant to imply serious reluctance on his part. See note 59 above.

64 Milner to Selborne, May 10, 1905, in *Milner Papers,* II, 353.

Downing Street any part of South Africa in which the whites are strong enough to defend themselves against the natives."[65] History has proved Sir Michael only partly right, for with the end of acquiescence on the part of the African majority, Downing Street has begun to govern once more in Kenya and Central Africa, with the object of soon ending its government altogether, and placing the lion's share of power in the hands of the natives.

Milner was clear enough in his letter in arguing that the immediate problem was that of conciliation, to which trusteeship was an obstacle. He was equally clear that he preferred Englishmen and hoped they would gain power in the Transvaal. His major failing has been held by historians to have been a lack of political understanding, particularly of Afrikaners, and therefore, a serious weakness as a diplomat.[66] All that can be acknowledged. But the failing may have been even more fundamental. He did not act on his own logic. Having argued correctly that self-government would not have the same effects in South Africa as it had had in Canada, he did not argue, as he could have done as an interventionist, that societies like South Africa needed close ties to a larger political unit until a stable political system had been developed. He was, in fact, unable to answer a question which he posed in 1899. "It is clear that the white man must rule, but how?"[67] On his own showing the creation of a united, loyal, white oligarchy would not necessarily produce a justly governed South Africa.

In his letter to Asquith, Milner was writing only six months after arriving in South Africa. Though he was not yet writing in the strident interventionist tone which he was to use later, he showed clearly enough that he regarded the South African problem as one to be solved by changes in the composition of the governing oligarchy. The first question to be answered was not "How to rule?", but "Which white men to rule?" In the latter half of 1898, he set about mobilising British opinion in South Africa to support an intervention in the Transvaal[68] and the war which broke out in 1899

---

[65] Robinson, *Africa,* 456.

[66] See, e.g., Marais, *Fall,* 329-31; *C.H.B.E.,* III, 362.

[67] *Milner Papers,* II, 35: Milner to Fitzpatrick, Nov. 28, 1899.

[68] Robinson *et al., Africa,* 453-54. See also N. G. Garson, "British Imperialism and the Coming of the Anglo-Boer War," *South African Journal of Economics,* XXX (June, 1962), 150-53.

was regarded by some of his contemporaries as essentially "Milner's" war.[69] The Union of South Africa, which came into being in 1910, was one of the results of that war, but it failed to achieve three of Milner's objects. First, Dutch and English have drifted into separate political camps; secondly, the Dutch (i.e., Afrikaners) —not yet anglicised and still republican in sentiment—are in control of the country; thirdly, the question of "how to rule" the African majority is as unanswered as when he posed it.

As a "British Race Patriot,"[70] Milner believed that British obligations to natives need not necessarily be sacrificed in the attempt to create a British-dominated oligarchy. He was prepared to use his power to encourage British immigration, to promote the anglicisation of the Dutch, and thereby, he hoped, to create the basis of a stable, loyal and united South Africa. When he wrote this letter, he was still feeling his way in a situation which was new to him. But he did not explore systematically the question of "how to rule" or deal with the probability that a united white South Africa would be even more difficult to influence as to the manner of its ruling. It is perhaps ironic that since World War II the question of "who to rule" has become important once more. Milner, like Dr. Nkrumah later, but with very different objects in view, sought a political kingdom. It was, however, a political kingdom for an oligarchy already entrenched and one which required, in Milner's view, an internal reconstruction. Milner hoped that this would guarantee its loyalty to the imperial power of which he was such a devoted and distinguished servant. Like most of his contemporaries, he believed that a united, loyal, white oligarchy would be better able to answer the question "How to rule?" than a divided one.

---

69 Richard Haldane, a Liberal Imperialist, used the term "Milner's . . . war" with approval on the outbreak of war. *The Times,* Oct. 11, 1899. See E. Stokes: "Milnerism," *The Historical Journal,* V (1962), 53 for another, less approving, contemporary view, that of Henry Sidgwick, brother-in-law of Arthur Balfour.

70 A statement of Milner's "Credo" was found in his papers and published after his death in *The Times,* July 26, 1925. For an extract, see Hancock, *Smuts,* I, 74. There is no reason to think that this "Credo" was not the basis of his thinking in the nineties.